Register Your Book

at ibmpressbooks.com/ibmregister

Upon registration, we will send you electronic sample chapters from two of our popular IBM Press books. In addition, you will be automatically entered into a monthly drawing for a free IBM Press book.

Registration also entitles you to:

- Notices and reminders about author appearances, conferences, and online chats with special guests

- Access to supplemental material that may be available

- Advance notice of forthcoming editions

- Related book recommendations

- Information about special contests and promotions throughout the year

- Chapter excerpts and supplements of forthcoming books

Contact us

If you are interested in writing a book or reviewing manuscripts prior to publication, please write to us at:

Editorial Director, IBM Press
c/o Pearson Education
800 East 96th Street
Indianapolis, IN 46240

e-mail: IBMPress@pearsoned.com

Visit us on the Web: ibmpressbooks.com

Requirements Management Using IBM® Rational® RequisitePro®

Requirements Management Using IBM® Rational® RequisitePro®

Peter Zielczynski, Ph.D.

IBM Press
Pearson plc
Upper Saddle River, NJ • Boston • Indianapolis • San Francisco
New York • Toronto • Montreal • London • Munich • Paris • Madrid
Cape Town • Sydney • Tokyo • Singapore • Mexico City

Ibmpressbooks.com

IBM Press Program Managers: Tara Woodman, Ellice Uffer

Cover design: IBM Corporation

Associate Publisher: Greg Wiegand
Marketing Manager: Kourtnaye Sturgeon
Publicist: Heather Fox
Executive Editor: Chris Guzikowski
Senior Development Editor: Chris Zahn
Managing Editor: Gina Kanouse
Designer: Alan Clements
Project Editor/Proofreader: Jovana San Nicolas-Shirley
Copy Editor: Gayle Johnson
Indexer: Brad Herriman
Compositor: Nonie Ratcliff
Manufacturing Buyer: Dan Uhrig

Published by Pearson plc

Publishing as IBM Press

IBM Press offers excellent discounts on this book when ordered in quantity for bulk purchases or special sales, which may include electronic versions and/or custom covers and content particular to your business, training goals, marketing focus, and branding interests. For more information, please contact:

U. S. Corporate and Government Sales
1-800-382-3419
corpsales@pearsontechgroup.com

For sales outside the U.S., please contact:

International Sales
international@pearsoned.com

This Book Is Safari Enabled

The Safari® Enabled icon on the cover of your favorite technology book means the book is available through Safari Bookshelf. When you buy this book, you get free access to the online edition for 45 days. Safari Bookshelf is an electronic reference library that lets you easily search thousands of technical books, find code samples, download chapters, and access technical information whenever and wherever you need it.

To gain 45-day Safari Enabled access to this book:

- Go to www.awprofessional.com/safarienabled.
- Complete the brief registration form.
- Enter the coupon code QIN3-2YRP-1CA9-C7PE-R4MC.

If you have difficulty registering on Safari Bookshelf or accessing the online edition, please e-mail customer-service@safaribooksonline.com.

Library of Congress Cataloging-in-Publication Data

Zielczynski, Peter.

  Requirements management using IBM Rational RequisitePro / Peter Zielczynski.

    p. cm.

  Includes index.

  ISBN 0-321-38300-1 (pbk. : alk. paper) 1. Computer software—Development. 2. IBM software. I. Title.

  QA76.76.D47Z54 2007

  005.3—dc22

2007037390

ISBN-13: 978-03-2138300-6

ISBN-10: 0-32-138300-1

Text printed in the United States on recycled paper at R.R. Donnelley in Crawfordsville, Indiana.
First printing: December 2007

To my parents, Helena and Mietek, who taught me how to achieve goals,
and to my lovely wife, Dorota,
and our daughter, Julia—the sunshine for all of us.

Contents

Part IV: Review   311

Foreword

For many years I have taught courses on the best practices of Requirements Management with Use Cases, as well as how to apply these techniques using the industry-leading tool—namely, IBM® Rational® RequisitePro®. For each course I teach, I like to recommend a book to my students that they can reference for supplemental material to support the theory. Fortunately, there are several excellent texts on the theory that I highly recommend.

When learning requirements management best practices, such as change management, scoping, prioritization, and traceability, it becomes obvious that the benefits are difficult to achieve without the use of a tool.

So when I teach the RequisitePro course, it has been discouraging that there has not been a text that actually shows how to properly use this great tool. Thankfully, Peter has finally shown us in this book how to combine best practices with a great tool to bring order to your requirements process.

Peter also goes the extra mile, showing us how well-articulated and managed requirements feed naturally into well-designed software with object-oriented analysis and design and the use of complementary IBM Rational tools.

I have been waiting for a long time for a book like this that I can recommend to my RequisitePro students. If you are currently using IBM Rational RequisitePro, or are considering the benefits of this great tool, this book is a must-have.

—*Mark Lines*
Co-founder, UPMentors.com

Preface

One of the most important elements of a software development project is requirements management (RM)—a systematic approach to eliciting, organizing, documenting, and tracking a system's requirements. Proper RM helps validate and verify the system, manage change, and analyze the project's status. It's much less expensive to fix a problem during requirements analysis than during design, testing, or production. Regardless of this fact, RM is often neglected in projects, and time spent on it is proportionally too small.

A research study called CHAOS, done by the Standish Group in 1995, indicated that three main factors cause projects to fail to come in on time, adhere to budget, and deliver required functionality:

- Lack of user input
- Incomplete requirements and specifications
- Changing requirements and specifications

Proper RM can improve all three factors.

What This Book Is About

Using an RM tool can organize the process and facilitate the creation and maintenance of requirements. One of the most popular tools is IBM® Rational® RequisitePro®. (For simplicity, it is called RequisitePro throughout the book.) This book provides hands-on instruction in using this tool. At the end of each chapter describing an RM step is a description of how RequisitePro can be used to facilitate this step. This is the first book to combine descriptions of RequisitePro features with their practical applications. Usage of this tool is shown based on a sample project.

Examples include creating the most important documents (Use Cases, Vision, and Supplementary Specification), creating and maintaining actual project requirements, traceability between requirement types, and the most important steps in requirements handling. To promote better understanding, the documents and other artifacts are created in the order that they would appear in an actual project.

The Online Travel Agency is a sample project that illustrates how to apply RequisitePro to maintain requirements and documents. This project is a web application similar to the ones that can be found at www.travel.yahoo.com, www.expedia.com, and www.travelocity.com.

How This Book Is Organized

This book presents an organized approach to RM. Each main step is described in a separate chapter. The chapters correspond to activities related to RM, including creating an RM Plan, eliciting stakeholder needs, creating a Vision document, and creating use cases. These activities are presented in a sequence that is close to chronological order. However, because a software project represents a complicated process with many iterations and complex relationships between activities, the steps described may be performed in a slightly different sequence. The actions performed by different people often overlap, and many actions performed by the same person are repeated during the process. This book also teaches techniques of modern requirements management, such as traceability.

Part I, "Overview," contains a couple of chapters that do just that: provide an overview of requirements and RequisitePro. Chapter 1, "Requirements Management," presents an overview of the RM process. Various types of requirements are introduced. The relationship between these types is shown in the form of a requirements pyramid. Chapter 2, "Overview of RequisitePro," presents an overview of RequisitePro.

The RM process is split into the following steps:

1. Establishing an RM Plan
2. Project setup
3. Requirements elicitation
4. Developing the Vision document
5. Creating use cases
6. Supplementary specification
7. Creating test cases from use cases
8. Creating test cases from supplementary specification
9. System design
10. Creation of other documents

These steps are described in this order in Chapters 3 through 12. Examples included at the end of most of these chapters show how the described RM activities may be implemented in practice using RequisitePro. Steps 3 through 9 are related to creating elements in the requirements pyramid (refer to Chapter 1, Figure 1.1).

In Part II, "Requirements Management Activities," Chapter 3, "Establishing a Requirements Management Plan," and Chapter 4, "Setting up the Project," describe how to structure the whole process.

The rest of the chapters corresponding to the steps in the RM process are as follows:

- Chapter 5, "Requirements Elicitation"
- Chapter 6, "Developing a Vision Document"
- Chapter 7, "Creating Use Cases"
- Chapter 8, "Supplementary Specification"
- Chapter 9, "Creating Test Cases from Use Cases"
- Chapter 10, "Creating Test Cases from Supplementary Requirements"
- Chapter 11, "Object-Oriented Design"
- Chapter 12, "Documentation"

In Part III, "Other Topics," Chapter 13, "Managing Projects," describes some additional RequisitePro features related to project management. Chapter 14, "Requirements Management in the Rational Unified Process," shows relationships between the requirements pyramid and the Rational Unified Process. In the final part, Part IV, "Review," Chapter 15, "Summary," summarizes the approach presented in this book.

Appendix A, "Sample Requirements Management Plan," presents a finished requirement plan for your reference.

The Audience for This Book

The book is primarily for those who are responsible for RM on a project. As evidence that this position is often neglected, this function does not even have a name. This book can help many people involved in software development:

- Business analysts
- Use case designers
- Project managers
- System architects
- Testers
- System designers
- Developers

The book is aimed at current RequisitePro users as well as people new to this tool. There are no prerequisites for being able to read and understand this book. Some knowledge of the software development lifecycle and familiarity with use cases may be helpful but is not necessary.

This book offers the following benefits:

- An overview of the RM process with emphasis on the most important documents
- A quick start to using RequisitePro
- An opportunity to learn RequisitePro before purchasing it
- A reference for the most important tool features
- Examples of applying RequisitePro in a sample project
- Guidelines related to specific steps in RM

Acknowledgments

I would like to thank the entire Addison-Wesley/IBM Press team for their great support. Although it is impossible to mention everyone who has been involved, I would like to acknowledge Senior Development Editor Chris Zahn for top-class editing and Executive Editors Chris Guzikowski, William Zobrist, and Mary O'Brien.

I would also like to thank Mark Lines and Celso Gonzalez for reviewing the book and providing exceptionally valuable comments. In addition, I'd like to thank Karen Hyland for reviewing the initial chapters.

I am grateful to the people whose publications inspired my research related to requirements management: Dean Leffingwell and Don Widrig for introducing the concept of the requirements pyramid, and Jim Heumann for his works on deriving test cases from use cases.

Special words of appreciation go to David Grady for his support.

I am also thankful to all my clients, coworkers, and employees. Dealing with them has increased my experience.

Most of all, I would like to thank all the readers who are interested in requirements management and who have chosen this book.

About the Author

Peter Zielczynski has 25 years of experience in information technology. He holds a Ph.D. degree in computer science from the Technical University of Warsaw. He has published more than ten articles in technical journals and has made several presentations at international conferences, including the Rational Users Conference. Peter worked at Cyfronet developing expert systems, and then as a consultant for such clients as IBM, Merrill Lynch, Ernst & Young, and AIG. He was cofounder and CEO of a consulting company, International Object Technology, which was eventually acquired by a publicly traded company, The A Consulting Team (currently Helios & Matheson North America). Peter specializes in Requirements Management, Object-Oriented Analysis and Design, and Project Management and has been using Rational tools since 1994.

PART I

Overview

1

Requirements Management

This chapter starts by defining the concepts of requirements and stakeholders. Then we describe what types of requirements can exist in a project. The relationships between these requirements are presented in the form of a pyramid. The concept of traceability is introduced (which requirement is derived from which). Characteristics of a good requirement are presented. Examples of problematic requirements are given, together with some guidelines on how to fix them. General steps in requirements management (RM) during the project lifecycle are shown. The main steps navigate through the requirements pyramid from top to bottom.

1.1 Definition of a Requirement and a Stakeholder

A requirement is defined as "a condition or capability to which a system must conform." It can be any of the following:

- A capability needed by a customer or user to solve a problem or achieve an objective

- A capability that must be met or possessed by a system to satisfy a contract, standard, specification, regulation, or other formally imposed document

- A restriction imposed by a stakeholder

Let's define a concept of a stakeholder because this word occurs many times in this book. Usually the stakeholder is defined as someone who is affected by the system that is being developed. The two main types of stakeholders are users and customers. Users are people who will be using the system. Customers are the people who request the system and are responsible for approving it. Usually customers pay for the development of the system. It is important to distinguish between these two groups of stakeholders because sometimes requirements provided by both groups conflict. In most of these types of conflicts, customer requests take precedence over user requests. In the travel agency website example used in this book, a customer is a travel agency owner, and the users are all the people who will be using this website through the Internet. Besides customers and users, many other types of stakeholders cannot be neglected.

For the purposes of this book, we will call the stakeholder anybody involved in the system (either during development or after it is completed) and anybody who may have any requirement for the system.

Here are some of the people who may be considered stakeholders:

- Anyone participating in the development of the system (business analysts, designers, coders, testers, project managers, deployment managers, use case designers, graphic designers)
- Anyone contributing knowledge to the system (domain experts, authors of documents that were used for requirements elicitation, owners of the websites to which a link is provided)
- Executives (the president of the company that is represented by customers, the director of the IT department of the company that designs and develops the system)
- People involved in maintenance and support (website hosting company, help desk)
- Providers of rules and regulations (rules imposed by search engines regarding content of the website, government rules, state taxation rules)

1.2   Requirements Pyramid

Depending on the format, source, and common characteristics, the requirements can be split into different requirement types. Here are some requirement types that are often used in projects:

- Stakeholder need: a requirement from a stakeholder
- Feature: a service provided by the system, usually formulated by a business analyst; a purpose of a feature is to fulfill a stakeholder need
- Use case: a description of system behavior in terms of sequences of actions
- Supplementary requirement: another requirement (usually nonfunctional) that cannot be captured in use cases
- Test case: a specification of test inputs, execution conditions, and expected results
- Scenario: a specific sequence of actions; a specific path through a use case

These requirement types can be presented in the form of a pyramid, as shown in Figure 1.1.

At the top level are stakeholder needs. On the lower levels are features, use cases, and supplementary requirements. Quite often, at different levels of these requirements, different levels of detail are captured. The lower the level, the more detailed the requirement. For example, a need might be "Data should be persistent." The feature can refine this requirement to be "System should use a relational database." On the supplementary specification level, the requirement is even more specific: "System should use Oracle 9i database." The further down, the more detailed the requirement. One of the best practices of requirements management is to have at least two different levels of requirement abstraction. For example, the Vision contains high-level requirements (features), and the lower levels in the pyramid express the requirements at a detailed level. Senior stakeholders (such as vice presidents) do not have time to read 200 pages of detailed requirements but should be expected to read a 12-page Vision document.

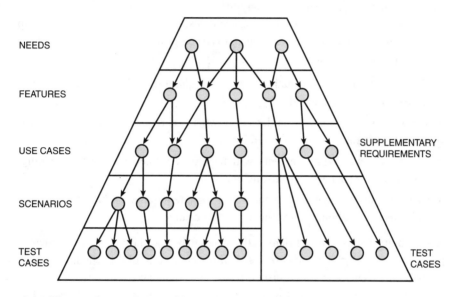

Figure 1.1 The requirements pyramid.

However, it is up to business analysts to decide on the granularity of requirements at each level. Nothing is wrong with placing quite detailed requirements from stakeholders on the stakeholder needs level.

The main difference between needs and features is in the source of the requirement. Needs come from stakeholders, and features are formulated by business analysts.

The role of test cases is to check if use cases and supplementary requirements are implemented correctly. Scenarios help derive use cases from test cases and facilitate the design and implementation of specific paths through use cases. In RequisitePro we can define many other requirement types, such as glossary terms and actors. They are not pure requirements conforming to the definition provided at the beginning of this chapter, but if we represent them in RequisitePro as requirements, we gain flexibility to track their attributes and traceability using same mechanisms that are provided for other requirement types.

1.3   Traceability between Requirements

Traceability is a technique that provides a relationship between different levels of requirements in the system. This technique helps you determine the origin of any requirement. Figure 1.1 illustrates how requirements are traced from the top level down. Every need usually maps to some features. Generally, it is a many-to-many relationship because one need can trace to many features, but one feature may be derived from many needs. One need mapping to one feature is also a common case. The features map to use cases in a many-to-many relationship. The features also map to supplementary requirements in a many-to-many relationship.

Every use case maps to one or more scenarios, so a one-to-many relationship exists between use cases and scenarios. Scenarios map to test cases in a one-to-many relationship.

Traceability plays several important roles:

- Verifying that an implementation fulfills all requirements: Everything that the customer requested was implemented.

- Verifying that the application does only what was requested: Don't implement something that the customer never asked for.

- Impact analysis: What elements will be affected when we consider adding a new requirement or changing an existing one?

- Helping with change management: When some requirements change, we want to know which test cases should be redone to test this change.

A traceability item is a project element that needs to be traced from another element. In terms of RequisitePro, it's everything that is represented by an instance of the requirement type. Some examples of requirement types in RequisitePro are stakeholder needs, features, use cases, actors, and glossary terms. RequisitePro has a convenient way of showing traceability in special views.

1.4   Characteristics of a Good Requirement

A requirement needs to meet several criteria to be considered a "good requirement" [HUL05] [LEF03] [LUD05][YOU01]. Good requirements should have the following characteristics:

- Unambiguous
- Testable (verifiable)
- Clear (concise, terse, simple, precise)
- Correct
- Understandable

- Feasible (realistic, possible)
- Independent
- Atomic
- Necessary
- Implementation-free (abstract)

Besides these criteria for individual requirements, three criteria apply to the set of requirements. The set should be

- Consistent
- Nonredundant

- Complete

The sample project used in this book is an online travel agency, as shown in Figure 1.2. You're probably familiar with this type of application because variations of it can be found on several websites. The project is complex enough to show possible relationships between various requirements types, but it is small enough to be easily understood. Most of the examples in this chapter (and the other chapters) are related to this project.

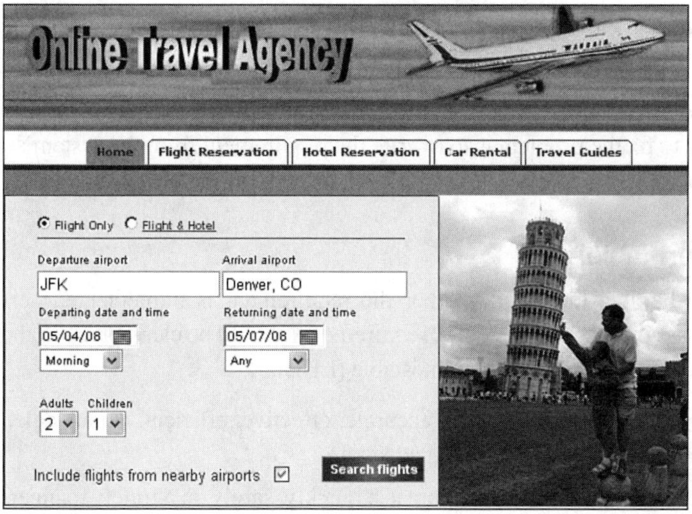

Figure 1.2   The home page of an online travel agency.

Let's discuss each of the criteria of a good requirement and show some examples.

Unambiguous

There should be only one way to interpret the requirement. Sometimes ambiguity is introduced by undefined acronyms:

> *REQ1   The system shall be implemented using ASP.*

Does ASP mean Active Server Pages or Application Service Provider? To fix this, we can mention a full name and provide an acronym in parentheses:

> *REQ1   The system shall be implemented using Active Server Pages (ASP).*

Here's another example:

> *REQ1   The system shall not accept passwords longer than 15 characters.*

It is not clear what the system is supposed to do:

- The system shall not let the user enter more than 15 characters.
- The system shall truncate the entered string to 15 characters.
- The system shall display an error message if the user enters more than 15 characters.

The corrected requirement reflects the clarification:

> *REQ1   The system shall not accept passwords longer than 15 characters. If the user enters more than 15 characters while choosing the password, an error message shall ask the user to correct it.*

Some ambiguity may be introduced through the placement of a certain word:

> *REQ1   On the "Stored Flight" screen, the user can only view one record.*

Does this mean that the user can "only view," not delete or update, or does it mean that the user can view *only one* record, not two or three?

One way to fix the problem is to rewrite the requirement from the system's point of view:

> *REQ1   On the "Stored Flight" screen, the system shall display only one flight.*

Testable (Verifiable)

Testers should be able to verify whether the requirement is implemented correctly. The test should either pass or fail. To be testable, requirements should be clear, precise, and unambiguous. Some words can make a requirement untestable [LUD05]:

- Some adjectives: robust, safe, accurate, effective, efficient, expandable, flexible, maintainable, reliable, user-friendly, adequate
- Some adverbs and adverbial phrases: quickly, safely, in a timely manner
- Nonspecific words or acronyms: etc., and/or, TBD

Such a requirement might look something like this:

> *REQ1   The search facility should allow the user to find a reservation based on Last Name, Date, etc.*

In this requirement, all search criteria should be explicitly listed. The designer and developer cannot guess what the user means by "etc."

Other problems can be introduced by ambiguous words or phrasing:

- Modifying phrases: as appropriate, as required, if necessary, shall be considered
- Vague words: manage, handle
- Passive voice: the subject of the sentence receives the action of the verb rather than performing it

> *REQ1   The airport code shall be entered by the user.*

> *REQ2   The airport code shall be entered.*

The first example shows a classic example of passive voice. In active voice it would read "The user shall enter the airport code." As the second example shows, another result of the use of passive voice is that the agent performing the action is sometimes omitted. Who should enter this code—the system or the user?

- Indefinite pronouns: few, many, most, much, several, any, anybody, anything, some, somebody, someone, etc.

  REQ1   The system shall resist concurrent usage by many users.

What number should be considered "many"—10, 100, 1,000?

Clear (Concise, Terse, Simple, Precise)

Requirements should not contain unnecessary verbiage or information. They should be stated clearly and simply:

REQ1   Sometimes the user will enter Airport Code, which the system will understand, but sometimes the closest city may replace it, so the user does not need to know what the airport code is, and it will still be understood by the system.

This sentence may be replaced by a simpler one:

REQ1   The system shall identify the airport based on either an Airport Code or a City Name.

Correct

If a requirement contains facts, these facts should be true:

REQ1   Car rental prices shall show all applicable taxes (including 6% state tax).

The tax depends on the state, so the provided 6% figure is incorrect.

Understandable

Requirements should be grammatically correct and written in a consistent style. Standard conventions should be used. The word "shall" should be used instead of "will," "must," or "may."

Feasible (Realistic, Possible)

The requirement should be doable within existing constraints such as time, money, and available resources:

REQ1   The system shall have a natural language interface that will understand commands given in English language.

This requirement may be not feasible within a short span of development time.

Independent

To understand the requirement, there should not be a need to know any other requirement:

> *REQ1   The list of available flights shall include flight numbers, departure time, and arrival time for every leg of a flight.*
>
> *REQ2   It should be sorted by price.*

The word "It" in the second sentence refers to the previous requirement. However, if the order of the requirements changes, this requirement will not be understandable.

Atomic

The requirement should contain a single traceable element:

> *REQ1   The system shall provide the opportunity to book the flight, purchase a ticket, reserve a hotel room, reserve a car, and provide information about attractions.*

This requirement combines five atomic requirements, which makes traceability very difficult. Sentences including the words "and" or "but" should be reviewed to see if they can be broken into atomic requirements.

Necessary

A requirement is unnecessary if

- None of the stakeholders needs the requirement.

or

- Removing the requirement will not affect the system.

An example of a requirement that is not needed by a stakeholder is a requirement that is added by developers and designers because they assume that users or customers want it. For example, the fact that a developer thinks that users would like a feature that displays a map of the airport and he knows how to implement it is not a valid reason to add this requirement. An example of a requirement that can be removed because it does not provide any new information might look like the following:

> *REQ1   All requirements specified in the Vision document shall be implemented and tested.*

Implementation-free (Abstract)

Requirements should not contain unnecessary design and implementation information:

> *REQ1   Content information shall be stored in a text file.*

How the information is stored is transparent to the user and should be the designer's or architect's decision.

Consistent

There should not be any conflicts between the requirements. Conflicts may be direct or indirect. Direct conflicts occur when, in the same situation, different behavior is expected:

> *REQ1   Dates shall be displayed in the mm/dd/yyyy format.*
>
> *REQ2   Dates shall be displayed in the dd/mm/yyyy format.*

Sometimes it is possible to resolve the conflict by analyzing the conditions under which the requirement takes place. For example, if REQ1 was submitted by an American user and REQ2 by a French user, the preceding requirements may be rewritten as follows:

> *REQ1   For users in the U.S., dates shall be displayed in the mm/dd/yyyy format.*
>
> *REQ2   For users in France, dates shall be displayed in the dd/mm/yyyy format.*

This can eventually lead to the following requirement:

> *REQ3   Dates shall be displayed based on the format defined in the user's web browser.*

Another example of a direct conflict can be seen in these two requirements:

> *REQ1   Payment by PayPal shall be available.*
>
> *REQ2   Only credit card payments shall be accepted.*

In this case the conflict cannot be resolved by adding conditions, so one of the requirements should be changed or removed.

Indirect conflict occurs when requirements do not describe the same functionality, but it is not possible to fulfill both requirements at the same time:

> *REQ1   System should have a natural language interface.*
>
> *REQ2   System shall be developed in three months.*

Some requirements do not conflict, but they use inconsistent terminology:

> *REQ1   For outbound and inbound flights, the user shall be able to compare flight prices from other, nearby airports.*
>
> *REQ2   The outbound and return flights shall be sorted by the smallest number of stops.*

To describe the same concept, in the first requirement the term "inbound flights" is used, and in the second requirement the term "return flights" is used. The usage should be consistent.

Nonredundant

Each requirement should be expressed only once and should not overlap with another requirement:

> *REQ1   A calendar shall be available to help with entering the flight date.*
>
> *REQ2   The system shall display a pop-up calendar when entering any date.*

The first requirement (related to only the flight date) is a subset of the second one (related to any date entered by the user).

Complete

A requirement should be specified for all conditions that can occur:

> *REQ1   A destination country does not need to be displayed for flights within the U.S.*
>
> *REQ2   For overseas flights, the system shall display a destination country.*

What about flights to Canada and Mexico? They are neither "within the U.S." nor "overseas."

All applicable requirements should be specified. This is the toughest condition to be checked. There is really no way to be sure that all the requirements are captured and that one week before the production date one of the stakeholders won't say, "I forgot to mention that I need one more feature in the application."

A good requirement should have more criteria. However, they usually can be expressed as a combination of the criteria we have just discussed:

- Modifiable: If it is atomic and nonredundant, it is usually modifiable.
- Traceable: If it is atomic and has a unique ID, it is usually traceable.

1.5   An Overview of the Requirements Management Process

A simplified description of the requirements management process contains the following major steps:

- Establishing a requirements management plan
- Requirements elicitation
- Developing the Vision document
- Creating use cases
- Supplementary specification
- Creating test cases from use cases
- Creating test cases from the supplementary specification
- System design

The first step (requirements management plan) defines the requirements pyramid. In each of the next seven steps, one of the elements of the pyramid is built. Table 1.1 describes which requirement types and what documents are created in each step. As you can see, the process navigates through the pyramid from the top down and from left to right.

Table 1.1   Requirements and Documents Created in Each Phase

Step	Requirement Types	Documents
Requirements elicitation	Stakeholder needs	Stakeholder requests
Developing the Vision document	Features	Vision
Creating use cases	Use cases, scenarios	Use case specifications
Supplementary specification	Supplementary requirements	Supplementary specification
Creating test cases from use cases	Test cases	Test cases
Creating test cases from the supplementary specification	Test cases	Test cases
System design	Class diagrams, interaction diagrams	UML diagrams

Requirements management is an interactive process. In a typical iteration, a full pass through the pyramid is performed. Even in the same iteration, we can go back a few steps and repeat the activity. For example, during the creation of a test case, we can discover that some information is missing, and we need more input from a stakeholder, so we go back a step to "gathering requirements." To maintain the model's integrity, it is important to update all affected requirements. In initial iterations the emphasis is placed on the first few steps (the top of the pyramid), and in later iterations more time is spent on the lower part of the pyramid.

This description is simplified because only major steps are described. For example, some activities defined by the Rational Unified Process (RUP) are more granular. (For example, our step of creating use cases contains the following RUP activities: find actors and use cases, structure the use case model, prioritize use cases, and detail use cases.)

Let's briefly look through all the steps.

Establishing a Requirements Management Plan

One of the first tasks in the project is developing a Requirements Management Plan (RMP). The RMP describes the overall approach to managing requirements in the project. The document details how requirements are created, organized, modified, and traced during the project lifecycle. It also describes all requirement types and their attributes used in the project.

Here are some questions that can be answered in the RMP:

- Will any RM tool be used?
- What requirement types will be tracked in the project?
- What are the attributes of these requirements?

- Where will the requirements be created—in the database only or in the documents?
- Between which requirements do we need to implement traceability?
- What documents are required?
- Which requirements and documents will be used as a contract with customers?
- If part of the project is outsourced, what requirements and documents will be used as a contract with a vendor?
- Will we follow the RUP or some other methodology?
- Does the customer need any specific documents to comply with his development process?
- How will change management be implemented?
- Assuming that RequisitePro is used, will the whole system be stored in one RequisitePro project or spread among many projects?
- What process will guarantee that all requirements were implemented and tested?
- Which requirements or views do we need to generate reports?

Chapter 3, "Establishing a Requirements Management Plan," describes all these decisions in detail.

Requirements Elicitation

At the top level of the pyramid are stakeholder needs, as shown in Figure 1.3.

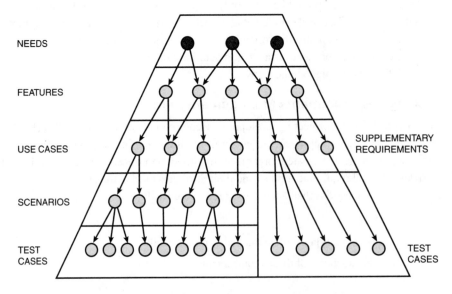

Figure 1.3   Needs (stakeholder requests) are at the top of the pyramid.

This book uses the terms "stakeholder needs" and "stakeholder requests" as synonyms. However, if project specifics require, it is possible to define them as two separate requirement types. In that case, needs would be very high-level requirements, such as "The system shall have the capability to book a flight." Usually there are no more than five high-level needs per stakeholder and no more than 15 needs per project. All detailed requirements would be captured as stakeholder requests. However, in many projects it is easier to capture all input from the stakeholders in the same type of requirement, so in the example used in this book, stakeholder needs represent all input from the stakeholders, regardless of granularity. In some projects there may be a need to distinguish between "stakeholder needs" describing initial requirements and "stakeholder requests" that may include subsequent change requests.

Requirements elicitation, also called requirements gathering, is a very important step. Missing or misinterpreting a requirement at this stage will propagate the problem through the development lifecycle.

Here are some of the techniques used to elicit requirements from stakeholders:

- Interviews
- Questionnaires
- Workshops
- Storyboards
- Role-playing
- Brainstorming sessions

- Affinity diagrams
- Prototyping
- Analysis of existing documents
- Use cases
- Analysis of existing systems

These techniques are described in Chapter 5, "Requirements Elicitation."

Developing the Vision Document

Section 1.3 discussed attributes of a good requirement. However, information that comes from stakeholders does not necessarily have these attributes. It is especially the case that requirements coming from different sources may be conflicting or redundant.

During development of the Vision document, one of the main goals of business analysts is deriving features from stakeholder needs (see Figure 1.4). Features should have all the attributes of a good requirement. They should be testable, nonredundant, clear, and so on.

The Vision document should contain essential information about the system being developed. Besides listing all the features, it should contain a product overview, a user description, a summary of the system's capabilities, and other information that may be required to understand the system's purpose. It may also list all stakeholder needs in case they were not captured in separate documents.

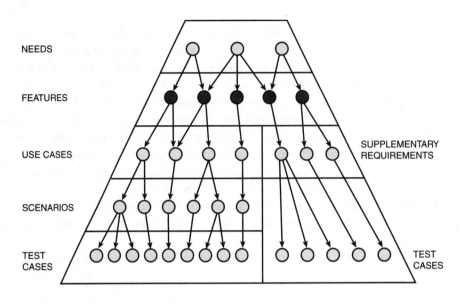

Figure 1.4   Features are derived from needs.

Some parts of the Vision are created at the very beginning, before we even start eliciting requirements from stakeholders. Examples of these sections are

- A description of the problem being solved.
- Identification of users/customers/stakeholders.

Creating Use Cases

Functional requirements are best described in the form of use cases. They are derived from features, as shown in Figure 1.5.

A use case is a description of a system in terms of a sequence of actions. It should yield an observable result or value for the actor (an actor is someone or something that interacts with the system). The use cases

- Are initiated by an actor.
- Model an interaction between an actor and the system.
- Describe a sequence of actions.
- Capture functional requirements.
- Should provide some value to an actor.
- Represent a complete and meaningful flow of events.

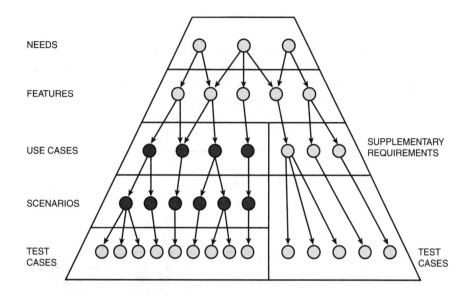

NEEDS

FEATURES

USE CASES   SUPPLEMENTARY
                                                       REQUIREMENTS

SCENARIOS

TEST   TEST
CASES   CASES

Figure 1.5   Use cases are derived from features that describe the system's functionality.
Scenarios are derived from use cases.

Here is a fragment of a use case:

1. The user enters required flight information: departure airport and date, arrival airport
   and date.

2. The system displays all outbound flights matching the search criteria.

3. The user selects an outbound flight.

4. The system displays a list of available return flights.

The purpose of a use case is to facilitate agreement between developers, customers, and
users about what the system should do. A use case becomes sort of a contract between developers
and customers. It's also a basis for use case realizations, which play a major role in design. In
addition, you can produce sequence diagrams, communication diagrams, and class diagrams
from use cases. Furthermore, you can derive user documentation from use cases. Use cases may
also be useful in planning the technical content of iterations and give system developers a better
understanding of the system's purpose. Finally, you can use them as an input for test cases.

While designing use cases we will also define scenarios—specific paths through the use
case. We usually implement systems scenario by scenario, not the whole use case at once.
Scenarios are required when we derive test cases from use cases. On the requirements pyramid,
scenarios are one level below use cases (see Figure 1.5).

Supplementary Specification

Supplementary specification captures nonfunctional requirements (usability, reliability, performance, supportability) and some functional requirements that are spread across the system, so it is tough to capture them in the use cases. These requirements are called supplementary requirements and are derived from features, as shown in Figure 1.6.

Chapter 8, "Supplementary Specification," discusses this type of requirement in detail.

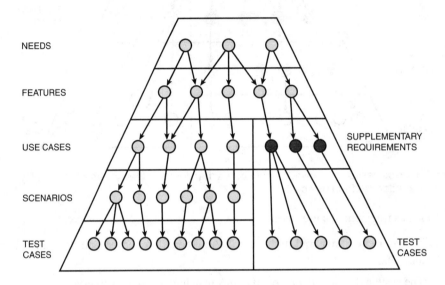

Figure 1.6   Supplementary requirements are derived from features that cannot be captured in the use cases.

Creating Test Cases from Use Cases

As soon as all the requirements are captured, we should design a way to check whether they are properly implemented in the final product. Test cases will show the testers what steps should be performed to test all requirements. In this step we will concentrate on creating test cases from use cases. If we did not create scenarios while generating use cases, we need to define them now. Test cases are at the lowest level of the pyramid, as shown in Figure 1.7.

This process is described in detail in Chapter 9, "Creating Test Cases from Use Cases."

Creating Test Cases from the Supplementary Specification

The approach used in the preceding step does not apply to testing supplementary requirements. Because these requirements are not expressed as a sequence of actions, the concept of scenarios does not apply to them. An individual approach should be applied to each of the supplementary requirements because techniques used to test performance requirements are different from techniques used to test usability requirements. In this step we also design testing infrastructure and platform-related issues.

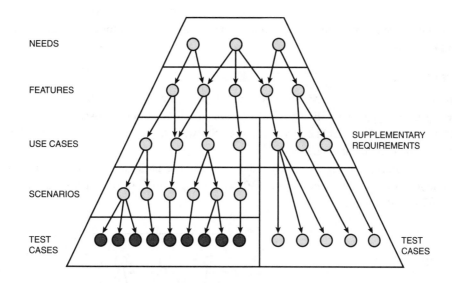

Figure 1.7 Test cases for testing use cases.

Sometimes we need to "borrow" one scenario that was created to test use cases (see Figure 1.8). For example, to test the requirement "The system should run using the Internet Explorer (IE) browser and using the Netscape browser," we should select one scenario (preferably basic flow of the most popular use case) and test the full scenario in the IE browser. Then we should test the same scenario again in the Netscape browser. There is no need to test all test cases created in the preceding step in both browsers. Just select those that contain some functionality that may be browser-specific.

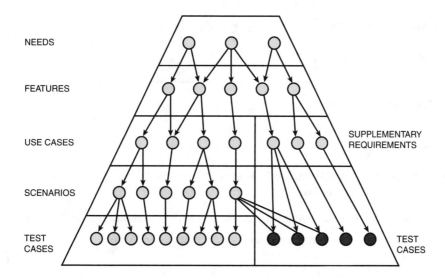

Figure 1.8 Test cases for testing supplementary requirements.

Some of the supplementary requirements can be tested using automated testing tools such as Rational Robot.

System Design

Requirements are the basis for system design, which is often facilitated by use of the Unified Modeling Language (UML) [BOO98]. Many tools, such as Rational Rose, Rational Software Architect, Rational Data Architect, and Rational Software Modeler, can significantly facilitate the creation of all required diagrams.

One approach is to create interaction diagrams from scenarios and, at the same time, assign functionality to the classes (see Figure 1.9). This topic is discussed in detail in Chapter 11, "Object-Oriented Design."

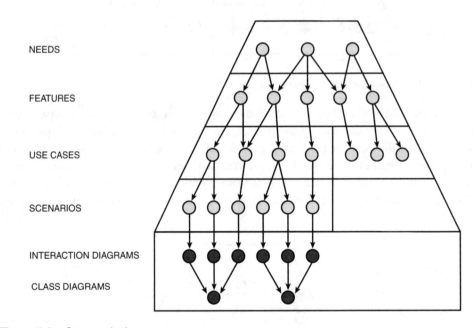

Figure 1.9   System design.

1.6   Summary

This chapter presented the RM process from the point of view of created requirements and documents. In short, this is the approach:

1. Stakeholder needs are gathered and documented in stakeholder requests documents.
2. Features are derived from needs and are documented in Vision.

3. Use cases and supplementary requirements are derived from features.

4. Test cases are derived from use cases and supplementary requirements.

These steps should be applied iteratively during the project lifecycle.

References

[BOO98] Booch, Grady, James Rumbaugh, and Ivar Jacobson. *UML User Guide*, Boston, MA: Addison-Wesley, 1998.

[HUL05] Hull, Elizabeth, Kenneth Jackson, and Jeremy Dick. *Requirements Engineering*, London: Springer, 2005.

[LEF03] Leffingwell, Dean, and Don Widrig. *Managing Software Requirements: A Use Case Approach,* Second Edition, Boston, MA: Addison-Wesley, 2003.

[LUD05] Ludwig Consulting Services, LLC, www.jiludwig.com.

[YOU01] Young, Ralph R. *Effective Requirements Practices*, Boston, MA: Addison-Wesley, 2001.

CHAPTER 2

Overview of RequisitePro

IBM Rational RequisitePro is a tool that facilitates requirements management. It allows input, updates, tracking, and review of requirements during the project lifecycle.

RequisitePro integrates Microsoft Word (a familiar environment for document processing) and a powerful database infrastructure. By combining document-centric and database-centric approaches, RequisitePro provides a powerful yet easy-to-use framework for managing requirements. Navigation between documents and the database is easy and intuitive. You can create, organize, prioritize, and trace the requirements. The tool allows detailed customization of documents, requirement types, and attributes. Change management is facilitated by tracking traceability between the requirements. RequisitePro also has provisions for collaboration with the whole team.

RequisitePro was developed by Requisite, Inc. in 1996. Requisite was acquired by Rational Software Corp. in 1997 and subsequently by IBM in 2003.

Recently, version 7 of RequisitePro was released. However, because the majority of companies are still using version 2003, it was used for the figures in this book. The differences between versions 2003 and 2007 regarding the topics discussed in this book are insignificant.

2.1   Interface

The RequisitePro interface contains the following main areas, as shown in Figure 2.1:

- Explorer window on the left
- Views on the right
- Menus and toolbar at the top

When you work with documents, the Word workplace opens in a separate window.

View

Explorer Window   Toolbar

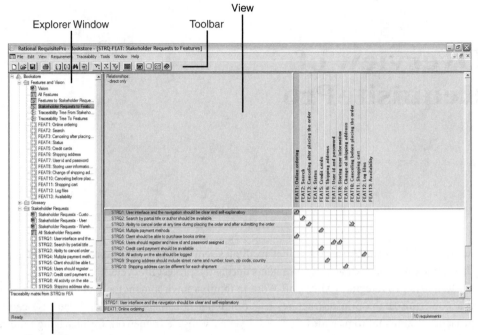

Description

Figure 2.1   The main parts of the RequisitePro interface.

Explorer

Explorer is the main navigation window, which displays components of the project in a tree structure (see Figure 2.2). The word Explorer in this book refers to RequisitePro Explorer, not Windows Explorer or Internet Explorer.

Documents, requirements, and views are organized into packages. The default packages in the Use Case template are

- Features and Vision
- Glossary
- Stakeholder Requests
- Supplementary Requirements
- Use Cases

You can add any number of project-specific packages. The packages appear in the Explorer as folders. Packages may contain documents, views, requirements, and other packages.

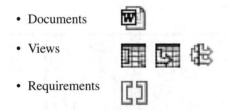

Figure 2.2   RequisitePro Explorer.

Project elements are identified in Explorer with specific icons indicating element type:

- Documents

- Views

- Requirements

In the Explorer you can perform basic operations (create, view, update, delete) on views, requirements, and documents. You can change the organization of elements just by dragging and dropping them between the packages.

Explorer provides easy access to project elements. Double-clicking a document opens it in the Word workplace. Double-clicking a requirement navigates to the requirement in the document where it is specified. Double-clicking a view opens it in the View window. Instead of double-clicking a view or document, you can also right-click and select Open. When you highlight an element, its description appears in the window below the Explorer (see the lower-left corner of Figure 2.1).

Views

A view is an area in which to analyze requirement information. A view displays requirement attributes or relationships between requirements. It can be displayed in a matrix or tree form. In a view you can also create and update requirements, set relationships between them (such as hierarchy and traceability), sort or filter requirements, and query project status.

The three types of views are as follows:

- The Attribute Matrix displays requirements of the specific type and their attributes, as shown in Figure 2.3.

Requirements:	Priority	Status	Difficulty	Stability	Unique ID	Location
FEAT1: Online ordering	High	Proposed	Medium	Medium	36	Vision
FEAT2: Search	High	Proposed	Medium	Medium	37	Vision
FEAT3: Canceling after placing the...	Medium	Proposed	Medium	Medium	38	Vision
FEAT4: Status	Medium	Proposed	Medium	Medium	39	Vision
FEAT5: Credit cards	High	Proposed	Medium	Medium	40	Vision
FEAT6: Shipping address	Low	Proposed	Medium	Medium	41	Vision
FEAT7: User id and password	Medium	Proposed	Medium	Medium	42	Vision
FEAT8: Storing user information	Low	Proposed	Medium	Medium	43	Vision
FEAT9: Change of shipping address	Medium	Proposed	Medium	Medium	44	Vision
FEAT10: Canceling before placing the..	Low	Proposed	Medium	Medium	45	Vision
FEAT11: Shopping cart	Medium	Proposed	Medium	Medium	46	Vision
FEAT12: Log files	Medium	Proposed	Medium	Medium	47	Vision
FEAT13: Availability	Low	Proposed	Medium	Medium	48	Vision

Figure 2.3   Attribute Matrix.

- The Traceability Matrix displays relationships between two types of requirements in the form of a matrix, as shown in Figure 2.4.

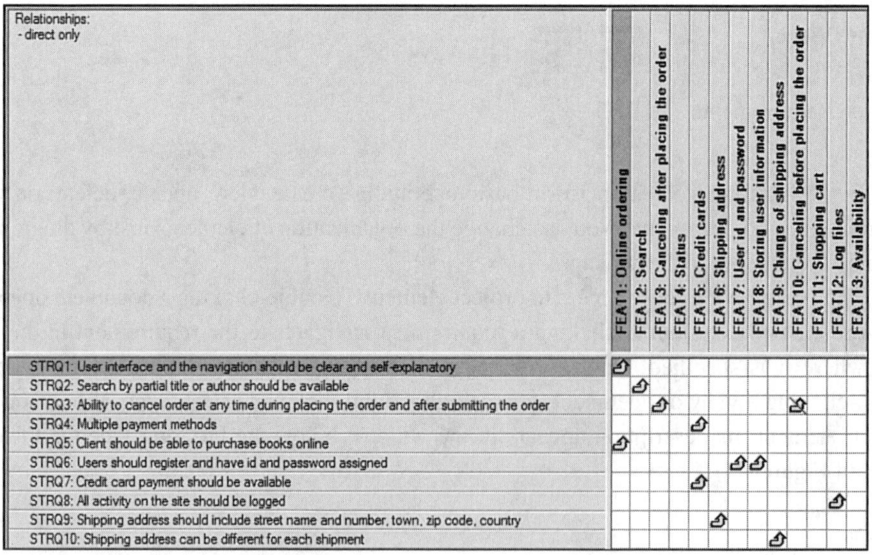

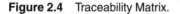

Figure 2.4   Traceability Matrix.

- The Traceability Tree displays the whole chain of traceability in a tree form, as shown in Figure 2.5.

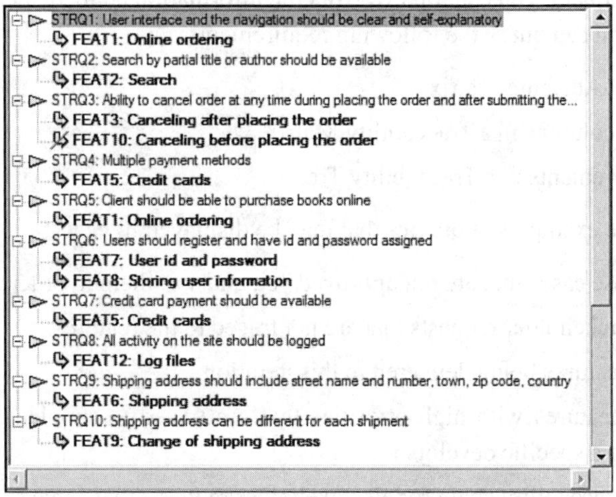

Figure 2.5   Traceability Tree.

Views are discussed in detail in Chapter 5, "Requirements Elicitation."
The Attribute Matrix can be used to perform the following tasks:

- Browsing through requirements of a specific type
- Adding, updating, and deleting requirements
- Setting requirements attributes
- Querying requirements that fulfill certain criteria (filtering and sorting requirements based on their attributes)
- Finding requirements in the documents

In addition to these tasks, the Traceability Matrix can be used for the following:

- Setting and analyzing traceability
- Managing change using suspect traceability
- Impact analysis

The Traceability Tree view is mostly used to show and analyze the chain of traceability.
In every view you can do the following:

- Sort and filter requirements
- Save a query that produced a view

- Export view information to other formats
- Print a view

By defining a query, you can filter (restrict the information being displayed) and sort (order the information). You can query the following requirements:

- Rows in an Attribute Matrix
- Rows and columns in a Traceability Matrix
- Root requirements in a Traceability Tree

Here are some examples of queries that may be displayed in views:

- Show all use cases that are not approved yet, and sort them in order of priority.
- Show all stakeholder requests that are not traced to the features.
- Show all features being delivered in this iteration.
- Show all features with high priorities that are traced to supplementary requirements assigned to a specific developer.
- Show the traceability chain for all stakeholder requests that came from end users.

Toolbar

The RequisitePro toolbar, shown in Figure 2.6, provides quick access to project information and main operations. The full toolbar functionality and options available from the menus are discussed in later chapters.

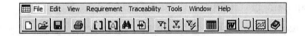

Figure 2.6   RequisitePro toolbar.

2.2   Word Workplace

Word workplace is the environment in which you create, display, and modify documents. It opens as a Microsoft Word window within RequisitePro and provides the same functionality as Microsoft Word. An additional RequisitePro toolbar enables specific operations on RequisitePro documents and requirements. The toolbar can float, as shown in Figure 2.7, or it can be docked with other toolbars at the top of the screen. Figure 2.8 describes the icons in this toolbar. You can import existing Word documents into RequisitePro or create documents in the RequisitePro environment based on existing templates. Each document is identified with the Word icon in RequisitePro Explorer. Double-clicking the icon opens the document.

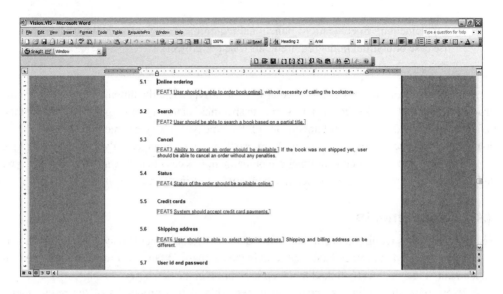

Figure 2.7 Word workplace.

Figure 2.8 RequisitePro-specific toolbar in the Word workplace.

2.3 Documents

Many standard document types can be created in RequisitePro. You can also create your own project-specific or company-specific document types (and associate them with templates). Here are some examples of widely used documents:

- Vision: Contains the overall system description and specific features (one per project).
- Use Case: Describes system behavior in terms of sequences of actions (many per project).

- Supplementary Specification: Functional requirements not associated with any specific use case or nonfunctional requirements (one per project).

- Glossary: Explains all project-related terms (one per project).

Each document belongs to a particular document type. The document type defines a template that is applied to a document. This template specifies standard formatting, table of contents, default sections, and headings. All documents of the same type have the same file extension. They do not have extensions used by Microsoft Word, so they can be changed only from RequisitePro.

The most common document types are predefined. It is easy to define a new document type and create a new template (as discussed in Chapter 9, "Creating Test Cases from Use Cases").

2.4   Requirements

RequisitePro stores requirements in the project database. Requirements may be stored in a database only, or located in project documents and in the database. When you create a requirement in a document, it is dynamically linked to its representation in the database.

Every requirement has associated attributes. They define properties of the requirement, such as Priority, Status, Difficulty, Risk, and Origin. Attributes provide information for managing the requirement. They may be used to plan, communicate, and monitor project activities. It is easy to customize values of default attributes or define your own attributes.

Each requirement belongs to a particular requirement type. It defines default attributes and a set of values that these attributes can have.

Here's an example of a requirement:

> *FEAT5   The system shall accept credit card payments.*

From the prefix we can recognize that this is a requirement of the type Feature. This type of requirement usually resides in the Vision document.

You can define traceability between related requirements of the same or different types. This functionality enables you to track the origin of each requirement as well as establish and analyze the impact of change. Documents and requirements are discussed in detail in further chapters.

2.5   Summary

This chapter presented the main parts of the RequisitePro interface:

- You use the Explorer window to navigate through packages, documents, views, and requirements.

- You use the Views window to display requirements information in the form of a matrix or tree.

- You use the menus and toolbar to select an operation.

Views are a powerful analysis mechanism. You can issue complicated queries based on values of requirements attributes.

Word workplace, opened in a separate window, is used to edit documents. Creating and updating documents is straightforward because it is done using the Word environment, which is familiar to most users.

A big advantage of RequisitePro is user-friendliness and flexibility. It is easy to customize the document types, requirements types, attributes, and their candidate values. Each of these changes takes no more than a few minutes.

In summary, RequisitePro is an easy-to-use yet powerful solution for requirements management.

PART II

Requirements Management Activities

33

CHAPTER 3

Establishing a Requirements Management Plan

To manage requirements, you must begin with a plan. This chapter addresses the issue of when to create a Requirements Management Plan (RMP) and the questions that must be answered to develop one. It finishes with a look at a sample RMP.

The RMP describes the approach to managing requirements in the project. This document specifies how requirements are created, organized, modified, and traced during the project lifecycle. It also describes all requirement types and their attributes used in the project.

The main part of this chapter describes what decisions should be made and what factors influence these decisions.

3.1   When the RMP Is Created

The RMP can be created from a template included in RequisitePro. However, to create a project in RequisitePro, we need to make the decisions captured in the RMP. We can resolve this chicken-and-egg problem in the following ways:

- Approach 1

    1. All the decisions regarding required document and requirement types are made, but they are not formally documented in an RMP.

    2. A RequisitePro project is created.

    3. An RMP is created from a RequisitePro template.

- Approach 2

    1. An RMP is created in Microsoft Word. It still contains all the paragraphs that the RequisitePro template contains, but it is created outside the tool.

    2. A RequisitePro Project is created based on the RMP.

    3. The Microsoft Word document with the RMP is imported into RequisitePro.

For our sample project, we will use the second approach to illustrate how we can bring existing documents into the RequisitePro environment. Chapter 4, "Setting up the Project," discusses how to import a Microsoft Word document with RMP into RequisitePro.

3.2   Decisions That May Be Documented in an RMP

Chapter 1, "Requirements Management," lists decisions that should be made while developing an RMP. In the following sections, we will discuss each decision and the factors that influence it.

Will an RM Tool Be Used?

Using a requirements management (RM) tool significantly facilitates the creation and maintenance of requirements. Usually tools provide traceability tracking. Various reports can easily be produced. However, most often it costs money to buy a tool, and it takes time to learn it. Usually this expense is worth the benefits.

In some cases it does not cost additional money to have a tool. One option may be to use a free tool (such as Tracer). Some companies may already have a tool because it was included in the package that was bought for another purpose. For example, some companies purchase a Rational Suite Enterprise because of Rational Rose (for design) and Rational Robot (for testing). RequisitePro is already in the suite, so no additional license is required to use it for RM.

Many tools support the RM process. It should be decided early in the project if a tool will be used and which tool is selected. After this decision is made for the first project, the same tool is usually used for subsequent projects. Comparisons of many RM tools can be found on the International Council on Systems Engineering website (www.paper-review.com/tools/rms/read. php). For this book we have chosen RequisitePro, one of the most popular, powerful, user-friendly, and reasonably priced requirements management tools. If because of budget constraints there is no possibility to buy a tool, Microsoft Word and Microsoft Excel can be used to track the requirements. Not having a tool should not be an excuse for neglecting proper formulation of the requirements and implementing traceability.

The remainder of this chapter assumes that RequisitePro was selected.

What Requirement Types Will Be Tracked in the Project?

Simple projects may require only one or two requirement types. A complex software project requires many levels of requirements. The requirements pyramid presented in Figure 1.1 (and shown in Figure 3.1) represents a typical set of requirements for a big corporate project. However, this pyramid may be tailored for the purposes of a specific project. The following list discusses the applicability of each requirement type:

- Needs and stakeholder requests: In our project we treat needs and stakeholder requests as synonyms. However, we may split these two types of requirements in various ways. One approach is to treat needs as very high-level requirements, while having very granular stakeholder requests.

- Features: Usually features are one of the main requirements in the project, but if the user can express all requirements in the form of use cases (UC), features may not be necessary.

- Use cases: If no users are permanently interacting with the system, UCs may not be needed. An example may be some batch programs, where a user only initiates the processing.

- Supplementary requirements: Every project has some nonfunctional requirements that should be placed in the Supplementary Specification. However, since there usually is no big difference between supplementary requirements and nonfunctional features, we may store these requirements on a features level.

- Scenarios: Scenarios are used to identify valid use case paths. This is a very useful requirement type. Scenarios facilitate transition between UCs and test cases. During design, we create sequence diagrams from scenarios, not from the whole UC. They are also critical for the project manager because we implement UCs by scenario. We usually do not build an entire UC in a particular iteration, but rather a set of scenarios from many UCs, gradually fleshing out the fully implemented UCs by the end of Construction. Most often we start with a scenario containing a basic flow and subsequently add scenarios with alternative flows. Because scenarios are not defined in RequisitePro as a standard requirement type, we need to create them ourselves. Unfortunately, quite often, to save maintenance time, they are not explicitly created in RequisitePro.

- Test cases: It is a good practice to keep track of test cases. Unfortunately, many projects do not do this. A simplified approach to testing is directly using UCs and deciding ad hoc what values will be used for testing. This approach saves a lot of time, but it does not guarantee full test coverage.

- Problems: Requirement type "problems" are used to capture main problems with existing solutions, which a new system is supposed to fix. These requirements are at the top of the pyramid, one level above needs. Our sample project does not use this requirement type.

Our sample project has the requirement types shown in Figure 3.1.

What Are the Attributes of These Requirements?

Requirement attributes play an important role in managing the project. Together with views, they provide a powerful analysis tool. Based on the attribute values, you can filter and sort the requirements using queries. The results of queries are displayed in views. Some popular attributes and their values are described in Section 3.4, "Requirements Attributes," of the Appendix, "Sample Requirements Management Plan."

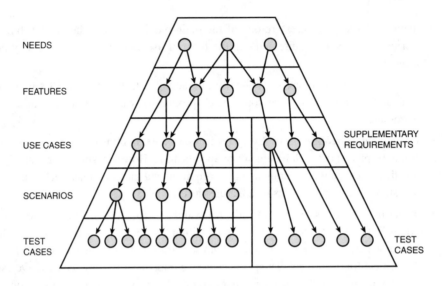

Figure 3.1   The requirements pyramid.

Basic requirements come in RequisitePro with a predefined set of attributes. This set may change depending on which version of the tool you use. Table 3.1 presents the attributes and values included in the UC template in version 2003.6.13 for the following requirement types:

- Features (FEAT)
- Supplementary requirements (SUPL)
- Use cases (UC)
- Stakeholder requests (STRQ)

Table 3.1   Default Attributes and Value Sets for Requirements FEAT, SUPL, UC, and STRQ

Attribute	Values	FEAT	SUPL	1UC	STRQ
Priority	High Medium Low	✓	✓	✓	
Type	Functional Usability Reliability Performance Supportability Design Constraint Implementation Requirement Physical Requirement Interface Requirement	✓			

Attribute	Values	FEAT	SUPL	1UC	STRQ
Status	Proposed Approved Incorporated Validated	✓	✓	✓	
Difficulty	High Medium Low	✓	✓	✓	
Stability	High Medium Low	✓	✓	✓	
Risk	Schedule—High Schedule—Medium Schedule—Low Technology—High Technology—Medium Technology—Low	✓	✓	✓	
Planned Iteration	Integer	✓		✓	
Actual Iteration	Integer	✓		✓	
Origin	Help Desk Partners Competition Large Customers End Users	✓			✓
Contact Name	Text	✓	✓	✓	
Enhancement Request		✓	✓	✓	
Defect		✓	✓	✓	
Obsolete	True False	✓	✓	✓	
Affects Architecture	True False			✓	
Stakeholder Priority	High Medium Low				✓

As you can see, FEAT, SUPL, and UC have many attributes in common. STRQ by default has only two attributes—Origin and Stakeholder Priority.

When you create a project, you may need to tune attributes and their values to better fit your needs.

Because some attribute values are quite vague, it is useful to clarify in RMP what particular values mean. Here are some examples:

- Priority—High: Must be implemented no later than in the first iteration of the Construction phase.

- Priority—Medium: Must be implemented no later than by the end of Construction.

- Priority—Low: May be implemented if time permits.

- Risk—Technology High: Using a new technology with which the team does not have any experience.

- Risk—Technology Low: Using a well-known technology with which the team has a lot of experience.

Where Will the Requirements Be Created—in the Database Only or in the Documents?

For tracking requirements attributes and traceability, it is not necessary to have them in documents. They may just reside in the database. However, also having them in documents offers some advantages:

- Easier access to the requirements by team members who do not have access to RequisitePro

- Opportunity to visually group and organize the requirements

- Presenting them in a more readable form

- Easy to add comments and explanations

An alternative to managing requirements in documents is the use of reports. For example, Use Case Specification SoDA templates can be created so that when use cases need to be communicated, a report can be generated, with an organization scheme similar to that of the corresponding Use Case Specification RequisitePro template.

The following requirement types are usually stored in corresponding documents, not just in the database:

- Because of their descriptive nature, use cases should be associated with the documents—one document per use case.

- Features are included in the Vision document.

- Supplementary requirements are captured in the Supplementary Specification.

Requirements of the type "stakeholder needs" are usually included in Stakeholder Requests documents, but there are three main approaches to handling needs. Requirements of this type may be as follows:

- In the Stakeholder Requests documents

  Pros: All needs are associated with a specific stakeholder.

              There is a place to insert additional comments and to include all stakeholders' answers.

              It is easy to give the whole document to the shareholders for feedback.

  Cons: It increases the number of documents that need to be maintained.

- In the database only

  Pros: It decreases the number of documents.

  Cons: This is a less readable form, especially if we want feedback from a stakeholder.

- In the Vision document

  Pros: It decreases the number of documents.

  Cons: The Vision becomes a document that contains requirements from a problem domain (STRQ) as well as from the solution domain (FEAT).

Between Which Requirements Do We Need to Implement Traceability?

Depending on which requirement types we select, the traceability tree may look different. Figure 3.2 shows the traceability for requirement types selected for the sample project.

What Documents Are Required?

Quite early in the process we need to decide what documents are required in the project. Each document should have a purpose. For example, it may be used for communication between team members or to obtain sign-off from the customers.

The Vision document, Use Cases, and Supplementary Specification are usually main documents that exist in a majority of projects. The main reason for this is that these documents contain important requirement types—FEAT, UC, and SUPL. These documents may also be used as a contract between the development team and the customers.

Stakeholder Requests documents are used in 50% of the projects. A document type called Glossary is provided in almost all project templates. Regardless of that fact, in many projects it is not developed further. The Requirements Management Plan is a very useful document, but it does not change much from project to project. You may decide to have one master RMP for all corporate projects and just document some small changes and exceptions specific to a given project.

Chapter 12, "Documentation," contains a more detailed discussion of possible documents that may need to be created.

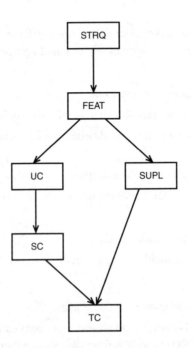

Figure 3.2   Traceability between requirement types used in a sample project.

Which Requirements and Documents Will Be Used as a Contract with Customers?

Usually UCs and Supplementary Specification are used as a contract, but we also may decide to include the Vision document. It does not make sense to sign off on stakeholder requests because these requirements are usually expressed in users' words. In this instance we take responsibility in case the requirement was misinterpreted while STRQ requirements are being translated to FEAT, UC, or SUPL.

If Part of the Project Is Outsourced, What Requirements and Documents Will Be Used as a Contract with a Vendor?

It depends on the level of the vendor's involvement. If design and development are outsourced, we may use supplementary requirements and use cases. If the vendor is also involved in analysis, it may be features. If only the coding part is outsourced, we may use the Rational Rose Model to agree on the scope of the work.

Will We Follow the Rational Unified Process or Some Other Methodology?

The Rational Unified Process (RUP) is an iterative software development process that is becoming more and more popular.

Some of the advantages of using RUP include the following:

- Iterative approach addresses all risks early in the process
- Availability of standard document templates
- Integration with IBM RequisitePro and other Rational tools

RUP can be applied to a one-week project as well as to complex multiyear projects [KRO03]. RUP can be tailored to specific project needs. The requirements management approach presented in this book is in sync with RUP. However, it can also be used in projects where RUP is not used.

Does the Customer Need Any Specific Documents to Comply with His Development Process?

Some companies create a Software Development Lifecycle in-house. They may require some documents specific to that organization. We may need to incorporate these documents into the process.

How Will Change Management Be Implemented?

Some automated tool may be used. It makes sense to use ClearQuest because it is part of the Rational Suite, and it provides some integration with RequisitePro. We also need to detail the process. Do we have a central person through whom change requests are submitted, or do we have a group of authorized testers, business analysts, and users who may submit requests directly to the tool?

Will the Whole System Be Stored in One RequisitePro Project or Spread Among Many Projects?

It is much easier to maintain the requirements model if it is stored in one project. The exception may be for very large systems that are split into almost independent subsystems maintained by different teams.

What Process Will Guarantee That All Requirements Were Implemented and Tested?

Implementing traceability helps achieve this goal. RM may specify when and how we check to see if appropriate requirements are correctly traced from and traced to. One approach is to run reports at the end of each iteration.

Which Requirements or Views Do We Need to Generate Reports?

They are project-specific. However, usually we need the following views:

- Attribute Matrix: Stakeholder Requests
- Attribute Matrix: Features

- Attribute Matrix: Supplementary Requirements
- Attribute Matrix: Test Cases
- Traceability Matrix: Stakeholder Requests to Features
- Traceability Matrix: Features to Use Cases
- Traceability Matrix: Features to Supplementary Requirements
- Traceability Matrix: Supplementary Requirements to Test Cases
- Traceability Tree: Use Cases to Scenarios and Test Cases

3.3 Sample Requirements Management Plan

This book provides a sample RMP that is based on a template included in a previous version of RequisitePro. The sample plan is in the Appendix. Read through it, and use it to make the points described in this chapter more concrete.

3.4 Summary

We have presented examples of topics that may be discussed in the Requirements Management Plan. Depending on the project, some of them are required, and others are not applicable. Here is the most important information that we need to specify in the RMP:

- Which types of documents we store requirements in
- Which types of requirements go in each document
- Which attributes we want to associate with each requirement
- What values are available for each attribute and what they mean

After you create RMP for one project, the document can be used as a template for future projects because many of the decisions will still be valid.

One of the main purposes of RMP is to make all decisions that are necessary to proceed with the creation of the RequisitePro project. This task is described in Chapter 4.

Reference

[KRO03] Kroll, Per, and Philippe Kruchten. *The Rational Unified Process Made Easy*, Boston: Addison-Wesley, 2003.

Setting up the Project

While working with RequisitePro and other Rational tools, we need to set up two kinds of projects:

- A RequisitePro project, in which we specify RM-related settings, such as requirement types, requirement attributes, document types, and traceability rules
- A Rational project that combines information from various Rational tools, such as RequisitePro, Rational Rose, ClearQuest Test Manager, ClearCase, and others

These two setups can be done in either order. We will first set up the RequisitePro project, and then we will attach it while setting up the Rational project.

If you do not intend to use other Rational tools, setting up a Rational project is not necessary. When you set up the Rational Project, the test datastore is created. This is necessary if you want to do testing using Rational Robot and Test Director.

4.1 Setting up a RequisitePro Project

When you create the RequisitePro project, you need to specify what documents are required, what requirement types will be used in the project, and what attributes will be assigned to the requirements. As discussed in Chapter 3, "Establishing a Requirements Management Plan," usually these decisions are already made during the creation of a Requirements Management Plan.

Each project resides in a separate directory. To create a RequisitePro project, Select File > New > Project. A dialog box showing project templates appears, as shown in Figure 4.1.

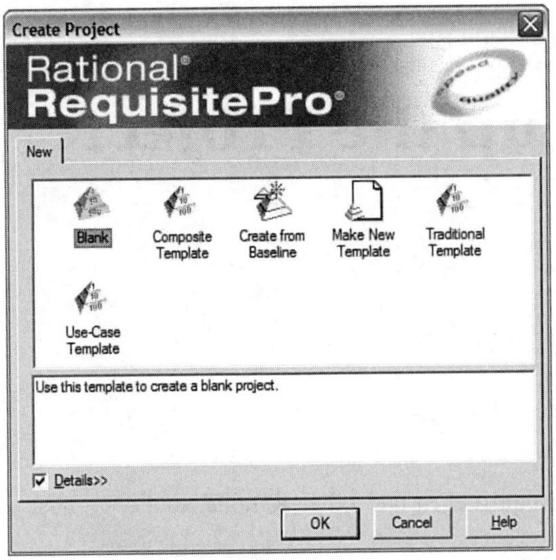

Figure 4.1   Project templates available in RequisitePro.

When you create a new project, you can base it on the following:

- A blank template
- One of the three templates included with RequisitePro: Use Case, Traditional, or Composite
- A template created from an existing project
- Create it from a baseline

When you create a project based on a template, the document types, requirement types, requirement attributes, and security information are copied from the template to the new project.

Additional documents and requirement types can be added later. Using a template can save time and effort if it contains most of the documents you need. The following project templates are available:

- Use Case: Best for projects in which use cases describe functional requirements.
- Traditional: Best for projects in which traditional (declarative) requirements are used instead of use cases.
- Composite: Combines use case and traditional approaches.
- Blank: Best if your project has an unusual set of documents and requirement types.
- Make New: Best if you want to use the same structure in future projects.
- Create from Baseline: Useful if you have ClearQuest baselines integrated with RequisitePro.

Table 4.1 summarizes which document and requirement types are included in the templates.

Table 4.1 Document and Requirement Types Included in the Three Main Templates

Document	Requirement Type	Traditional	Use Case	Composite
Requirements Management Plan	Requirements Management Plan Requirement	✓	✓	✓
Stakeholder Request	Stakeholder Request	✓	✓	✓
Vision	Feature	✓	✓	✓
Glossary	Glossary Item	✓	✓	✓
Software Requirements Specification (SRS)	Software Requirement	✓		✓
Use Case Specification	Use Case		✓	✓
Supplementary Specification	Supplementary Requirement		✓	

In the case of the Composite template, the SRS document is actually called the Modern Software Requirements Specification. In addition to the contents of regular SRS, it contains the Use Case model description.

The difference between templates is mainly in how the software requirements are described. Do we use SRS, Use Cases plus Supplementary Specification, or Modern SRS plus Use Cases?

For our sample project, we will create a project based on a Use Case template.

1. After selecting the template, click OK. The Project Properties dialog box appears, as shown in Figure 4.2.

2. Enter all required fields:

   - Name: Pick a meaningful name for your project (up to 64 characters).

   - Directory: Where the project will reside. (If the directory does not exist, it is created.)

   - Database: The database selected for storing requirements.

     RequisitePro stores requirements in the database, which contains all requirements information (attributes, traceability, previous revisions, discussion, and security information). RequisitePro can use either an internal Microsoft Access database, or it can connect to an enterprise database (Oracle or SQL Server). Connecting to an enterprise database is recommended in only the following cases:

- For very large projects with thousands of requirements
- If you anticipate more than five concurrent users of the project database
- When your team is in several remote locations

    Because we do not have any specific storage requirements for our sample project, we should use a Microsoft Access database, which is offered by default. The last field (Description) is optional, but it is useful to provide a brief description of the project.

3. Click OK.

4. If you see the message "Directory does not exist. Do you want to create one?", click Yes. After some installation time, you should see the message "The RequisitePro Project was successfully created."

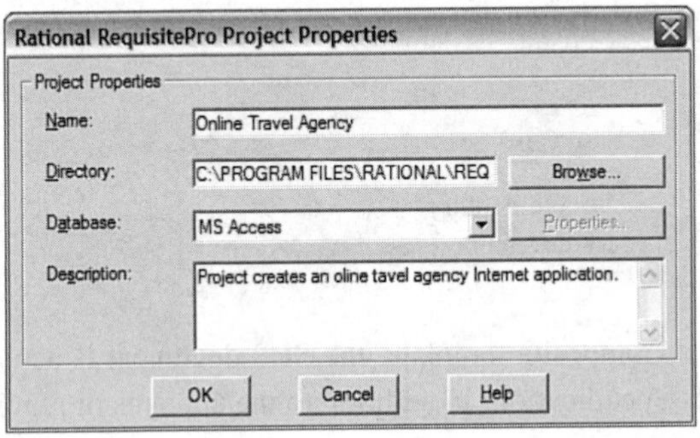

Figure 4.2   Project Properties dialog box.

After the project is created, it appears in the Explorer window, and it is added to the project list in the Open Project dialog box. Because we have used the Use Case template, some documents already appear in Explorer, such as Glossary, Vision, and Requirements Management Plan (see Figure 4.3). Some packages and views also already have been created. When the requirements are created in the project, they automatically appear in the Views.

The following files appear in the project directory:

- Online Travel Agency.rqs: RequisitePro project file
- Online Travel Agency.mdb: Database containing requirements information
- Glossary.gls, Vision.vis, Requirements Management Plan.rmp: Templates for documents
- Online Travel Agency.rql: Contains additional information about the project

To customize the project structure (add, delete, or edit document types, requirement types, and requirement attributes), use the Project Properties dialog box. Most often you will need to add an attribute or change values in existing attributes.

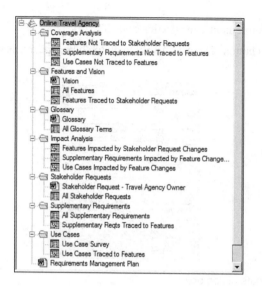

Figure 4.3 Default items in the Use Case template.

Adding Requirement Attributes

Sometimes you may need to add new attributes if the default attributes are inadequate. Let's assume that we want to add an attribute called Status to the requirement type stakeholder requests (STRQ). This attribute will help track the requirement's status.

1. Select File > Properties.
2. Select the Attributes tab, as shown in Figure 4.4.

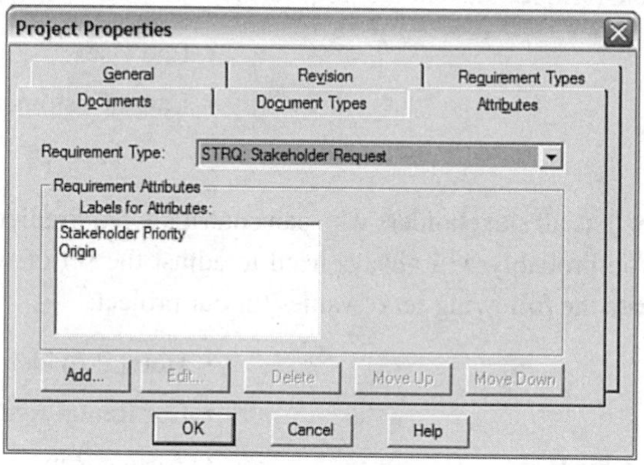

Figure 4.4 Project Properties dialog box: Attributes tab.

3. Select the Requirement Type (in this case, STRQ).

4. Click the Add button. The Add Attribute dialog box appears, as shown in Figure 4.5.

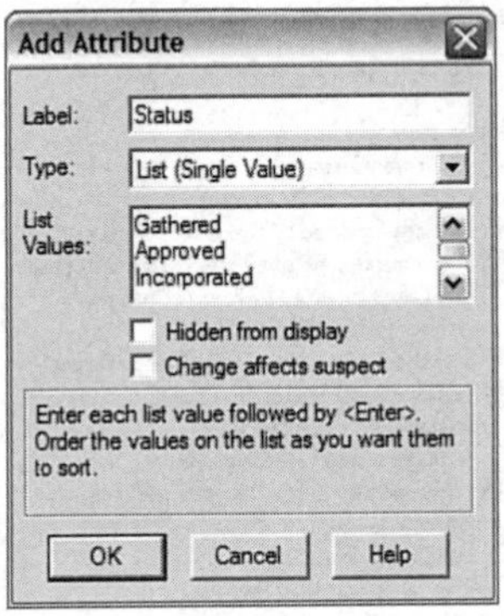

Figure 4.5   Add Attribute dialog box.

5. Fill in the dialog box options:

   - Label: Status
   - Type: List (Single Value)
   - List Values: Gathered, Approved, Incorporated, Cancelled

6. Click OK. The attribute is added to the requirement.

Changing Values of Requirement Attributes

You can change the set of values for existing requirement attributes. For example, a default set of values for the attribute Origin for stakeholder requests is

- Help Desk
- Competition
- Partners
- End Users
- Large Customer

This attribute set lists all stakeholders who can contribute requirements. This set may differ for each project, so you probably will always need to adjust the set of values. Let's delete the default values and create the following set of values for our project:

- User 1
- User 2
- Customer Service Rep
- Administrator
- Content Manager
- Hotel Provider
- Car Rental Agent
- Airline Rep
- Travel Agency Owner
- Developer

1. Select File > Properties.

2. Select the Attributes tab, as shown in Figure 4.6.

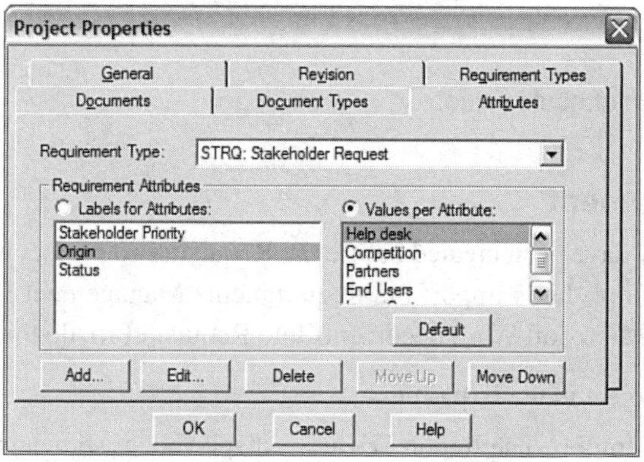

Figure 4.6 Selecting values for an attribute.

3. Select the Requirement Type (in this case, STRQ).

4. Select Attribute Label (in this case, Origin).

5 Select the Values per Attribute radio button.

6. Select the first value (Help desk).

7. Click Delete. You see the following message box: "This function requires that the project be opened exclusively. Do you want to attempt to gain exclusive access to the project now?" Click Yes if you want to open the project exclusively. "Exclusive access" means that a project and its documents are available only to the user who opens the project. Exclusive access is required to change various project characteristics. You can open a project in exclusive mode only if no other users currently have the project and documents open.

8. Click OK on the confirmation dialog that tells you "Successfully gained exclusive access to the project."

9. Keep selecting values from the list box and clicking the Delete button until you have deleted all the values.

10. Click the Add button.

11. Enter value User 1 in the Attribute Value dialog box, as shown in Figure 4.7.

12. Click OK.

13. Keep adding the remaining values (User 2, Customer Service Rep, Administrator, and so on).

14. Click OK.

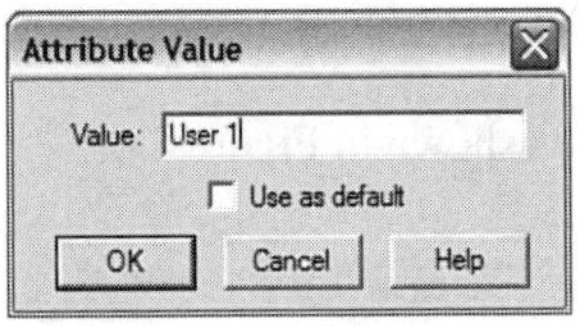

Figure 4.7   Adding an attribute value.

Importing a Document

Some documents may have been created before the RequisitePro project was created. We should import them into the tool. Let's import the Requirements Management Plan that we created in Chapter 3. To import Microsoft Word documents into RequisitePro, do the following:

1. Select the project in the Explorer.

2. Select File > Import. The Import Wizard is displayed, as shown in Figure 4.8.

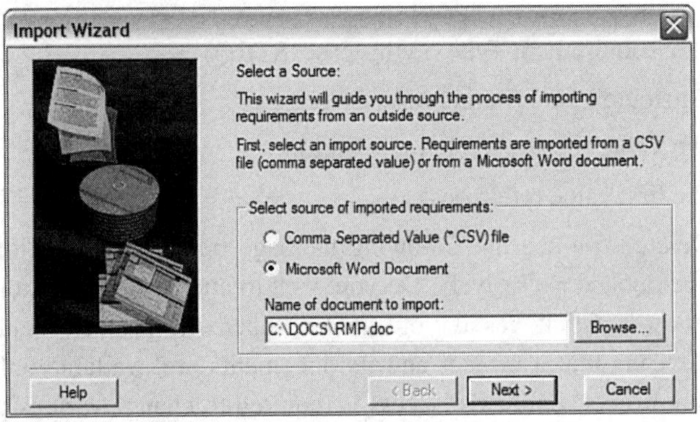

Figure 4.8   Import Wizard.

3. Select the Microsoft Word Document radio button.

4. Browse to the document that you want to import.

5. Click Next.

6. Select Document only because the RMP does not have any requirements (see Figure 4.9).

7. Click Next. The Document Properties dialog box appears, as shown in Figure 4.10.

8. Input the document Name and Description, and select the Document Type.

9. If needed, you can change the default Filename and Directory.

Figure 4.9   Import Wizard: Select content.

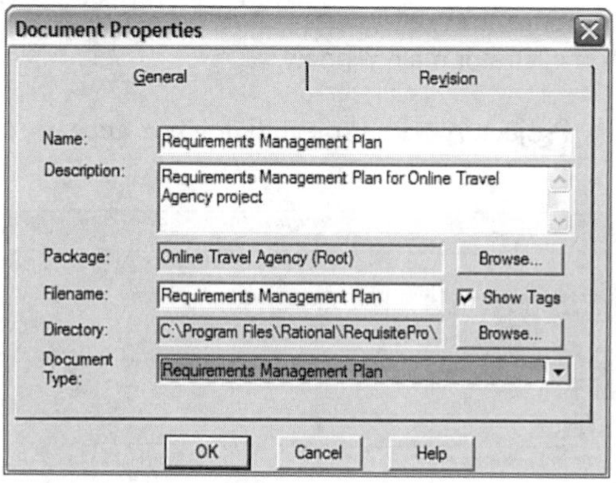

Figure 4.10   Document Properties dialog box.

10. Click Yes on the dialog box that warns you about overwriting the original formatting.

11. Click Commit on the dialog (confirming creation of the file).

4.2   Setting up a Rational Project

If you plan to integrate RequisitePro with other Rational tools, or if you plan to use Rational Robot or ClearQuest Test Manager, besides creating a RequisitePro project, you need to create a Rational project. You do this using Rational Administrator—a separate tool that comes with Rational Suite.

1. Create an empty directory where you want to store project-related files.

2. Start Rational Administrator, as shown in Figure 4.11.

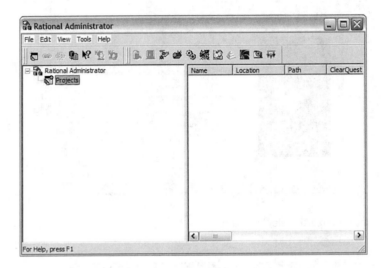

Figure 4.11   Rational Administrator main window.

3. Select File > New Project. A New Project dialog box appears, as shown in Figure 4.12.

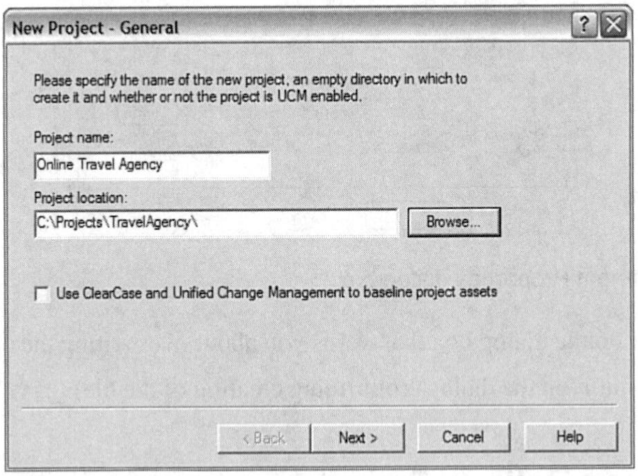

Figure 4.12   New Project - General dialog box.

4. Enter the Project name. It can be the same name you used for the RequisitePro project, or it may be different.

5. Select the project directory in the Project location list box (the directory should already exist). Click the Next button.

6. If you see a message that says "In order for others to access your Rational project in a network environment, you must use a shared directory...," click OK to accept it. Be careful in selecting a directory for the project. If you create it in a nonshared directory, you will be the only one who can access it.

7. Enter a password. If you do not need password protection, leave the Password field blank (see Figure 4.13).

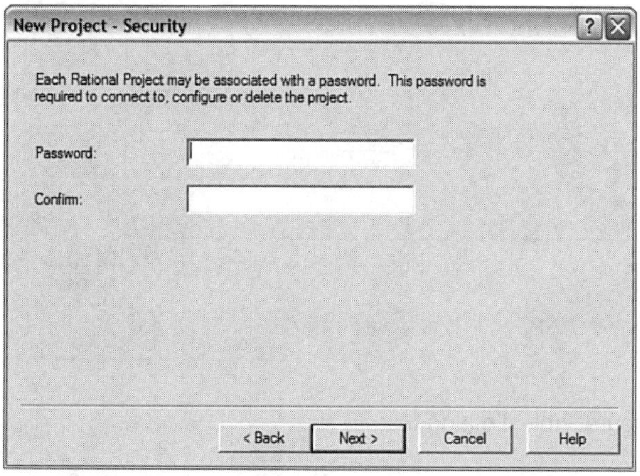

Figure 4.13 New Project - Security dialog box.

8. Click the Next button. The New Project - Summary dialog box appears, as shown in Figure 4.14.

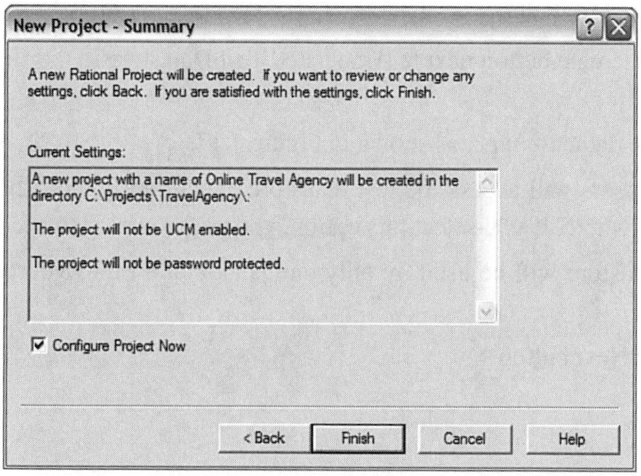

Figure 4.14 New Project - Summary dialog box.

9. Click the Finish button. The Configure Project dialog box appears, as shown in
   Figure 4.15.

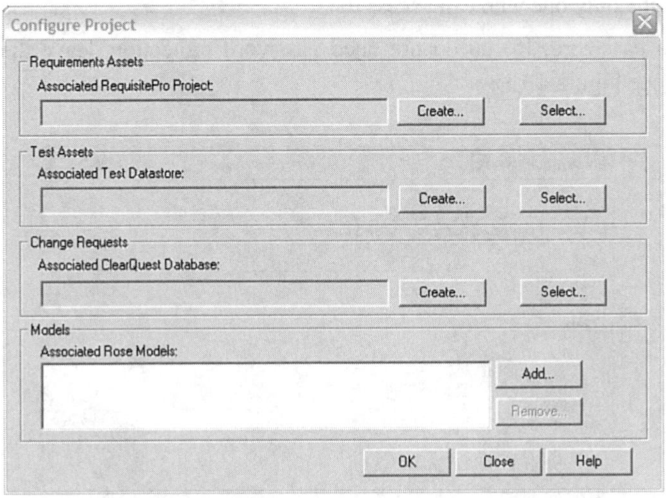

Figure 4.15   Configure Project dialog box.

10. Click the Select button next to Associated RequisitePro Project.

11. As shown in Figure 4.16, select the .rqs file containing the RequisitePro project you
    created earlier, and click Open. Alternatively, you can double-click the project file.
    You see the message "The RequisitePro project was successfully associated with the
    Rational Project: 'Online Travel Agency'" (or whatever the project is called).

12. Click the Close button.

13. Click the Create button next to Associated Test Datastore in the Configure Project dia-
    log box.

14. Select the database type, as shown in Figure 4.17.

    If many users will access the test datastore concurrently, you should choose Sybase
    SQL Anywhere. If you select this option, you are prompted to specify a Sybase server.

    If the datastore will be used by only one person at a time, Microsoft Access is good
    enough.

15. Click the Next button.

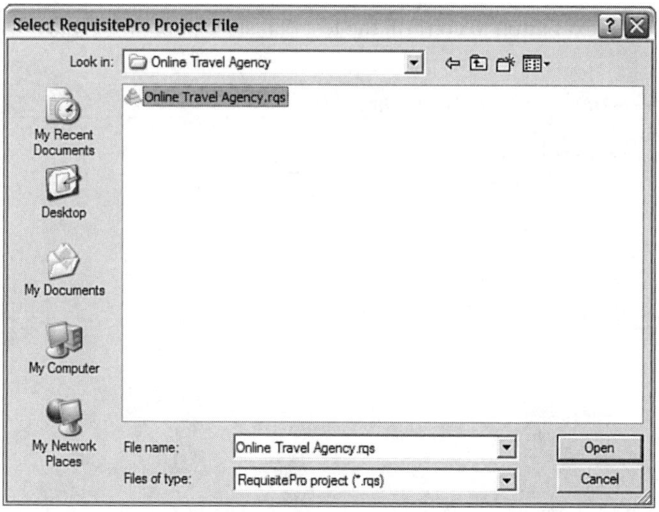

Figure 4.16   Dialog box for RequisitePro project selection.

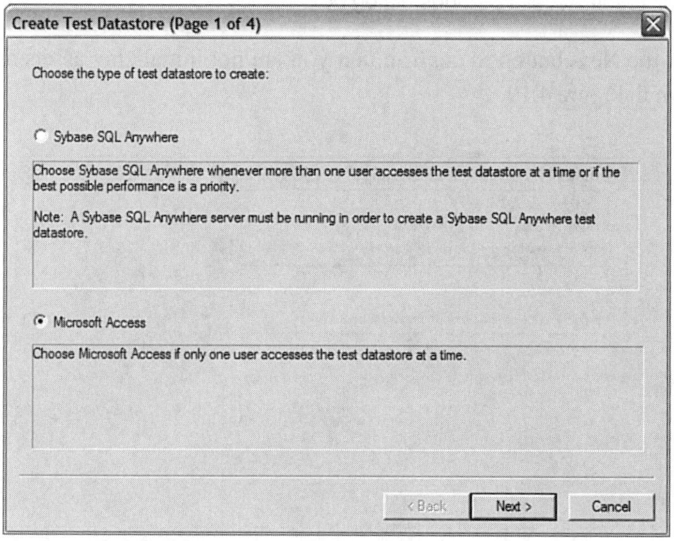

Figure 4.17   Create Test Datastore dialog box.

16. Click the Next button to confirm the test datastore path (see Figure 4.18).

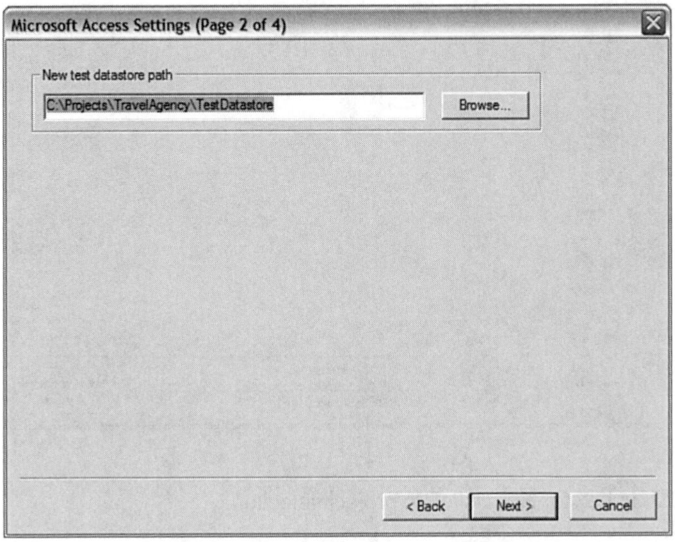

Figure 4.18   Microsoft Access Settings dialog box.

17. Click the Next button to confirm that you are not initializing assets and test users, as shown in Figure 4.19.

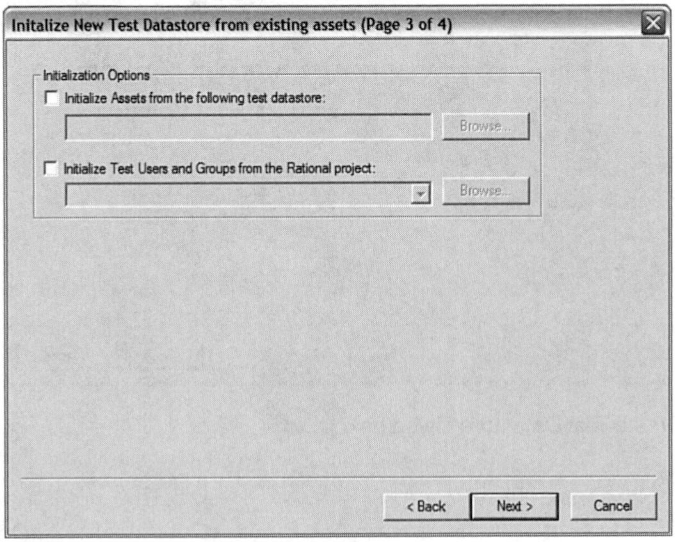

Figure 4.19   Initialization options for the test datastore.

18. Click the Finish button to confirm the summary, as shown in Figure 4.20. You should see the message "The Test Datastore has been successfully created."

19. Click OK to close the message box.

20. If you want to associate a ClearQuest database, click Select and attach the appropriate file.

21. If you want to associate a Rational Rose model, click Add and attach the appropriate .mdl file.

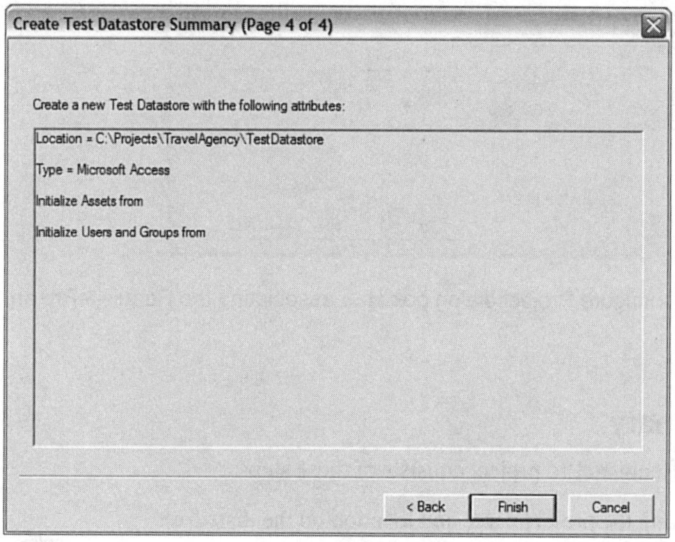

Figure 4.20   Create Test Datastore Summary dialog box.

22. Click OK in the Configure Project dialog box, as shown in Figure 4.21.

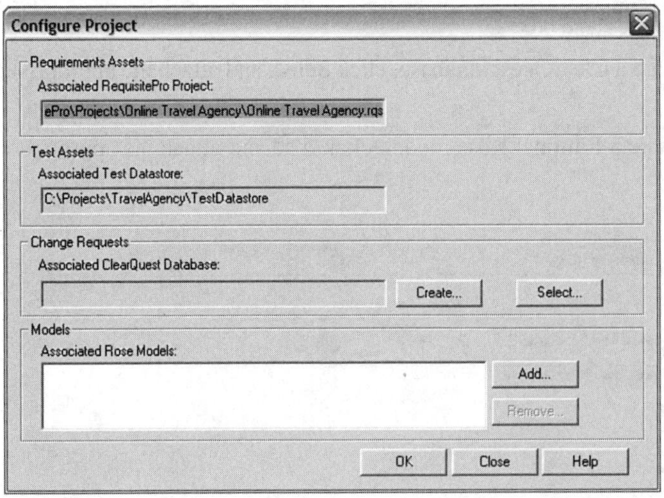

Figure 4.21   Configure Project dialog box after associating the RequisitePro project and test datastore.

4.3   Summary

Setting up the RequisitePro project consists of these steps:

- Selecting the project name and location on the disk drive
- Selecting which template is the closest to the structure you want to create
- Customizing the template
- Importing the documents that were created previously

Customizing may include the following operations:

- Adding new document types
- Removing unnecessary document types
- Adding new requirement types
- Removing unnecessary requirement types
- Adding new requirement attributes
- Deleting unnecessary requirement attributes
- Changing the set of values for a specific attribute

Adding new requirement attributes and changing the set of values for a specific attribute were discussed in this chapter. Other variations will be discussed in future chapters.

Depending on how many customizations are required, setting up a RequisitePro project may take 15 minutes or many hours. Setting up a Rational project usually does not involve any customization and takes less than half an hour.

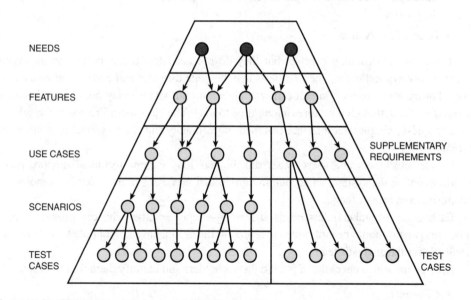

CHAPTER 5

Requirements Elicitation

This chapter starts by describing how you can identify the stakeholders who can supply the requirements. The main part of this chapter presents 11 techniques for gathering requirements. They are used to collect requests from stakeholders on what needs the system should fulfill. These requirements are located at the top level of the requirements pyramid, as shown in Figure 5.1.

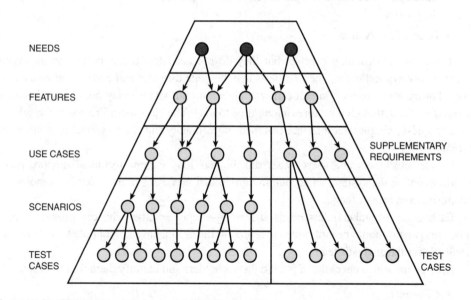

Figure 5.1   Stakeholder requests are at the top of the requirements pyramid.

The second part of this chapter shows you how to document requirements from the stakeholders in Stakeholder Requests documents using RequisitePro. This includes the following tasks:

- Adding a Stakeholder Requests document type to the project (if the project does not contain it already)
- Creating a document from the template
- Filling a document with the information
- Storing requirements in the database
- Using views with requirements

5.1   Identifying Stakeholders

The vast majority of project requirements come from stakeholders. The glossary in the Rational Unified Process (RUP) defines a stakeholder as "An individual who is materially affected by the outcome of the system." The two most important groups of stakeholders are

- Customers who requested the development. They approve the result and usually fund the project.
- Users of the system

These two groups may overlap, but they do not need to. It is important to distinguish between customers and users. Their requests may be quite different and even sometimes contradictory. For example, users of a call center application (call takers) may prefer a sophisticated user interface, even though it requires a long time to load. The customer (director of the call center) may request a simple user interface that loads immediately and allows servicing of more calls per minute.

Besides customers and users, other stakeholders may include technical support, people who will maintain the system, an accounting group that processes transactions, shareholders of the company, and many others.

Each group of stakeholders needs at least one representative who can provide requirements. This person should be authorized to represent the group, have appropriate knowledge, and be available for the analyst's team.

Let's go through a checklist of potential stakeholders and identify them for our project:

- Customers
  Identified stakeholders: travel agency owner.
- Users
  Users who will contribute requirements: User 1 (from the U.S.) and User 2 (from France).

- Anyone participating in developing the system (business analysts, designers, coders, testers, project managers, deployment managers, use case designers, graphics designers)

  Stakeholders who will contribute requirements: developer and content manager.

- Anyone contributing knowledge to the system (domain experts, authors of documents that were used for requirements elicitation, owners of the websites to which a link is provided)

  No contributing stakeholders are identified in this group.

- Executives (president of the company that is represented by customers, director of the IT department of the company that designs and develops the system)

  Travel agency owner was mentioned in the first group.

- People involved in operation, maintenance, and support (website hosting company, help desk)

  Identified stakeholders: customer service representative, administrator.

- Providers of rules and regulations (rules imposed by search engines regarding content of the website, government rules, state taxation rules)

  No contributing stakeholders are identified in this group.

- Third-party companies involved in operations

  Identified stakeholders: hotel provider, car rental agent, airline rep.

5.2   Techniques of Requirements Elicitation

Stakeholders' requests may be gathered using various techniques:

- Interviews (individual dialog with a stakeholder)
- Questionnaires (a set of questions sent to a larger set of stakeholders)
- Workshops (stakeholders gather for an intensive, focused period)
- Storyboarding (using a visual/graphical tool to demonstrate system behavior)
- Role playing (each member of the group is assigned a role, usually one of the users)
- Brainstorming sessions (presenting ideas during a short, intensive session)
- Prototyping (developing a prototype to get feedback)
- Use cases (interaction between a user and a system presented as a sequence of steps)
- Analysis of existing documents (extracting information from Microsoft Word documents, e-mails, and notes)
- Observation and task demonstration (watching users perform a specific task)
- Analysis of existing systems (gathering requirements from a system being replaced or from systems built by the competition)

Table 5.1 describes requirements elicitation methods that were selected in our project to gather requirements from each of the stakeholders identified in Chapter 4, "Setting Up the Project."

Table 5.1   Stakeholders and Requirements Elicitation Methods Used to Gather Requirements from Them

Stakeholder	Elicitation Method	Reason
Travel agency owner	Interview Workshop	This stakeholder is a customer who ordered a system and will pay for it. It makes his or her priority the highest. Usually in this case we apply more than one method of elicitation to ensure the best coverage possible. The interview script included in a template for the Stakeholder Requests document fits quite well, so it may be used as a first step to get some requirements. Next, a workshop may be used to clarify the requirements to minimize the probability that a requirement is missing. Being a customer, the stakeholder should also contribute nonfunctional requirements such as performance and reliability.
User 1	Workshop Storyboarding	A workshop provides more opportunities to get more detailed requirements. Because User 1 is available to meet with the development team, we can invite her to the workshop. Storyboarding is used during the same workshop.
User 2	Document (e-mail)	User 2 is in another country and is unavailable to meet in person. He is doing a favor providing the feedback, so we want to keep his overhead to a minimum. He was asked to send an e-mail summarizing his requirements.
Customer service representative	Role playing	Functionality required by the customer service representative is driven by a dialog with users who call with various problems, so role playing is an adequate tool to re-create possible calls.
Administrator	Workshop	All three stakeholders are members of the IT department and work in the same place. It is easy to gather them at the same time. A workshop usually does not require preparation of formal documents such as a questionnaire or interview script.
Content manager	Workshop	
Developer	Workshop	
Hotel provider	Questionnaire	The same questions apply to all three service providers, so the same questionnaire may be used. All three are from different companies in different locations across the country. They are not available to meet personally.
Car rental agent	Questionnaire	
Airline representative	Questionnaire	

According to the RUP, the person responsible for the activity Elicit Stakeholder Requests is the system analyst. In RUP, system analyst (and all other roles) is a role performed by a member or members of the project team, not necessarily a function in the company. In many projects this task is performed by a business analyst or some other person.

Interviews

One of the most common requirements elicitation methods is interviewing selected groups of stakeholders. The advantage of this approach is its interactive nature, providing the opportunity to add more or follow up on questions depending on the answers received. Interviews are a good way to gather usability, reliability, performance, and supportability requirements. Usually customers do not state these nonfunctional requirements unless explicitly asked. While interviewing, the business analyst should have an initial set of questions prepared in advance. However, during the interview, new questions may be invented. The RequisitePro template for the Stakeholder Requests document contains a sample script that may be used for the interview. This script is generic and probably will need to be tailored for each interview.

Here are some guidelines for conducting the interviews:

- While identifying stakeholders for the interview, be sure to understand which group they represent.
- Prepare a written initial set of questions.
- Repeat the answers in your own words to confirm that you understand.
- You should not suggest an answer in your question. Example: *What response time do you expect? Three seconds?*
- Do not combine more than one question into one. Example: *Will you need to print, e-mail, and fax the report?* The user may need to print and e-mail but not fax.
- At this stage, do not ask about the implementation details. Example: *Do you prefer list box or radio buttons to select the method of payment?*
- Do not use very long and complex questions.
- Do not ask the next question before the preceding one has been answered.
- If an answer is unclear, ask additional questions, even if they are not in the script.
- When users deviate from the answer to ask a question, do not interrupt them. Let them express their thoughts on whatever topic they are discussing. Then, if you do not receive an answer to the initial question, ask it again.
- Capture every requirement that a user articulates, even if it seems irrelevant at the moment.
- Ask users for additional information (such as forms and screenshots).
- When speaking to the customers, do not indicate whether their requirement will be implemented. This will be decided later.

- At the end, ask open-ended questions such as "What else should I know?"
- For each requirement, get its relative importance from the stakeholder.
- Make notes or use a recording device.

As an example, let's use the layout of the Stakeholder Requests document [RUP04] as a framework to interview the travel agency owner:

1. Introduction
2. Establish Stakeholder or User Profile
    - Name: *Mark Murphy*
    - Company/Industry: *Incredible Travel Agency, Inc.*
    - Job Title: *Owner*
    - What are your key responsibilities? *Run the agency, maximize profit from sales.*
    - What deliverables do you produce? For whom? *Number of airplane tickets sold, number of hotel rooms booked, and number of cars rented.*
    - How is success measured? *Profit from sales and from referrals.*
    - Which problems interfere with your success? *Without a website, we are limited to local clients.*
    - Which, if any, trends make your job easier or harder? *The Internet gives us an opportunity to reach many new clients.*
3. Assess the Problem
    - For which problems do you lack good solutions? *Online sales.*
    - What are they?

      For each problem, ask the following:
    - Why does this problem exist?
    - How do you solve it now? *Currently, customers call to make reservations.*
    - How would you like to solve it? *We would like clients to be able to purchase tickets online, without needing to call the travel agent.*
4. Understand the User Environment
    - Who are the users? *Anybody who wants to purchase an airline ticket, rent a car, or reserve a hotel room.*
    - What is their educational background? *Mixed.*
    - What is their computer background? *Computer-literate, capable of using the Internet.*
    - Are the users experienced with this type of application? *Yes.*
    - Which platforms are in use? What are your plans for future platforms? *The application will be platform-independent, and it will be available through the browser.*

- Which additional applications do you use that we need to interface with? *Airline Reservation System.*

- What are your expectations for the product's usability? *The system shall be easy to use.*

- What are your expectations for training time? *Learning time shall be minimal, and navigation shall be easy.*

- What kinds of hard-copy and online documentation do you need? *Online help for users. Hard-copy documentation for customer service rep, content manager, and administrator.*

5. Recap for Understanding

   - You have told me... (list stakeholder-described problems in your own words)

   - Does this represent the problems you are having with your existing solution?

   - What, if any, other problems are you experiencing?

6. Analyst's Inputs on Stakeholder's Problem (validate or invalidate assumptions)

   - What, if any, problems are associated with... (list any needs or additional problems you think should concern the stakeholder or user) *No online sales*

     For each suggested problem, ask the following:

   - Is this a real problem? *Yes.*

   - What are the reasons for this problem? *Not having a website.*

   - How do you currently solve the problem? *Phone calls.*

   - How would you like to solve the problem? *Sales through the website.*

   - How would you rank solving these problems in comparison to others you've mentioned?

7. Assess Your Solution

   - What if you could... (summarize the key capabilities of your proposed solution)

   - How would you rank the importance of these?

8. Assess the Opportunity

   - Who needs this application in your organization? *The main benefit will be to the owners. Administrator, customer service rep, and content manager will use the application.*

   - How many of these types of users would use the application? *One administrator, two customer service reps, and one content manager*

   - How would you value a successful solution? *Measure of success: number of sales through the Internet, number of referrals to car and hotel providers.*

9. Assess Reliability, Performance, and Support Needs

- What are your expectations for reliability? *Comparable with other commercial websites.*

- What are your expectations for performance? *Comparable with other commercial websites.*

- Will you support the product, or will others support it?

- Do you have special needs for support? What about maintenance and service access?

- What are the security requirements? *Hotel providers, car providers, and airline representatives shall have IDs and passwords for the pages where they can submit their offers. Users shall select a userid and password when buying a ticket.*

- What are the installation and configuration requirements? *No installation is required on users' machines.*

- What are the special licensing requirements? *None.*

- How will the software be distributed? *Installed on the server of the web hosting company.*

- What are the labeling and packaging requirements? *None.*

- What, if any, regulatory or environmental requirements or standards must be supported? *None.*

- Can you think of any other requirements we should know about? *The system shall be developed in three months.*

10. Wrap-Up

- Are there any other questions I should ask you? *I would like to add one more piece of functionality. To provide added value for our clients, the website shall provide information about tourist attractions near the destination city.*

- If I need to ask follow-up questions, may I give you a call? *Yes.*

- Would you be willing to participate in a requirements review? *Yes.*

11. Analyst's Summary

- The system shall provide the opportunity to book a flight, purchase a ticket, reserve a hotel, and reserve a car, and it shall provide information about tourist attractions.

- The user shall be able to purchase a ticket online, without needing to call the travel agent.

- The system shall follow implementation guidelines set up in the chain of our travel agencies.

- Hotel providers, car providers, and airline representatives shall have their IDs and passwords to the pages where they can submit their offers.

- The system must be available 24 hours a day, with a level of reliability appropriate to commercial applications.
- The system shall be developed in three months.
- The users shall pick IDs and passwords when buying an airline ticket.

Questionnaires

Questionnaires are most useful if you can ask many stakeholders the same questions and you do not expect to generate ad hoc additional questions. This approach has less overhead, and you can reach a much wider range of stakeholders than if you do direct interviews or invite them to workshops. However, because questionnaires are so structured and noninteractive, you have less control over the results. Questions should be clear and straightforward because there is no opportunity to clarify any issues or misunderstandings, unless you follow up with the stakeholder using some other elicitation technique. The advantage of questionnaires is that they can be e-mailed and self-administered.

In the online travel agency project, we send the following questions to three stakeholders (hotel provider, car provider, airline representative):

1. What information do you need from the client?
2. What information do you want to display to the client?
3. Do you require payment with a reservation?
4. If you require payment, what kinds of payments do you accept?
5. Do you have any other requirements?

Here are the answers received from hotel provider:

1. What information do you need from the client?

   The client shall provide the following information: town, stay dates, number of adults, number of children, room preferences.

2. What information do you want to display to the client?

   When providing the information about a hotel, the following info shall be displayed:

   Address

   Phone

   Fax

   E-mail

   Offered discounts

   Available methods of payment

   and so on

3. Do you require payment with a reservation?

   No.

4. If you require payment, what kinds of payments do you accept?

   No need for payment.

5. Do you have any other requirements?

   The user shall be offered flight and hotel deals.

Workshops

During a requirements workshop, a selected group of stakeholders meets the project team. They gather for an intensive, focused period. A system analyst acts as the facilitator of the meeting.

Here are some of the facilitator's tasks:

1. Before the workshop:
   - Invite attendees.
   - Distribute the agenda and some preliminary material so that participants can prepare for the meeting.
   - Arrange the conference room and required equipment (such as a projector).

2. During the workshop:
   - Assign someone to take notes.
   - Lead the discussion, and keep it on track.
   - Encourage all stakeholders to contribute.
   - Summarize the session.

3. After the workshop:

   - Analyze the findings, and document the information in a presentable format.
   - Distribute results among participants.
   - If needed, schedule follow-up sessions.

The requirements workshop provides an opportunity to apply the other elicitation techniques, such as brainstorming, storyboarding, and role playing. The goal of the workshop can be either to gather new requirements or to review, clarify, and prioritize existing requirements. The results of the requirements workshops should be documented. The best place to do this is in Stakeholder Requests documents.

In our sample project, a workshop was conducted with the business analyst, User 1, project manager, developer, and two people who eventually will maintain the system: the content manager and the system administrator.

Here are sample requirements gathered during the workshop:

User 1:

1. For outbound and inbound flights, the user shall be able to compare flight prices from other, nearby airports.

2. Sometimes the user will enter the airport code, which the system will understand. Other times the user will enter the closest city. Therefore, the user does not need to know the airport code; the system will understand.

3. The system shall be easy to navigate.

4. If the user has purchased a ticket before, the user shall not need to repeat the same information, such as address or credit card number.

5. Payment by PayPal shall be available.

6. Dates shall be displayed in the mm/dd/yyyy format.

7. The list of available flights shall include flight numbers, departure time, and arrival time for every leg of the flight.

8. It shall be sorted by price.

9. Comparison of car rental prices from different companies shall be provided.

10. Car rental prices shall show all applicable taxes (including 6% state tax).

11. A calendar shall be available to help with entering the flight date.

Administrator:

1. The search facility shall allow the user to find a reservation based on the following:
   - Last Name
   - Date

2. All activity on the site shall be logged.

3. Various reports shall be available.

Content manager:

1. While submitting the content information, the content manager shall be able to submit plain text without HTML tags.

2. Content information shall be stored in a text file.

Developer:

1. The system shall be fully tested under specific versions of the most popular browsers only.

2. The system may display a map to the airport.

Storyboarding (described in the next section) was also used during the workshop.

Storyboarding

The idea of storyboarding is to use a visual or graphical tool to illustrate the system's desired behavior. A facilitator shows an initial storyboard to the group. Then, based on comments from participants, the storyboard is changed and presented again. Updating the storyboard is an iterative process. This means that a graphical tool being used should allow quick real-time changes during the workshop. You may use software tools as well as presentation tools from an office supply store.

Here are some sample tools that may be used:

- Paper, pencil, eraser
- Easel, markers
- Dry-erase boards
- Presentation boards
- GUI builders such as Visual Basic or Visual C++
- Microsoft PowerPoint
- Microsoft Visio
- Graphics tools such as Microsoft Paint
- Word processors such as Microsoft Word

In software projects, storyboards often present a sequence of screens that eventually are displayed to the user, as shown in Figure 5.2.

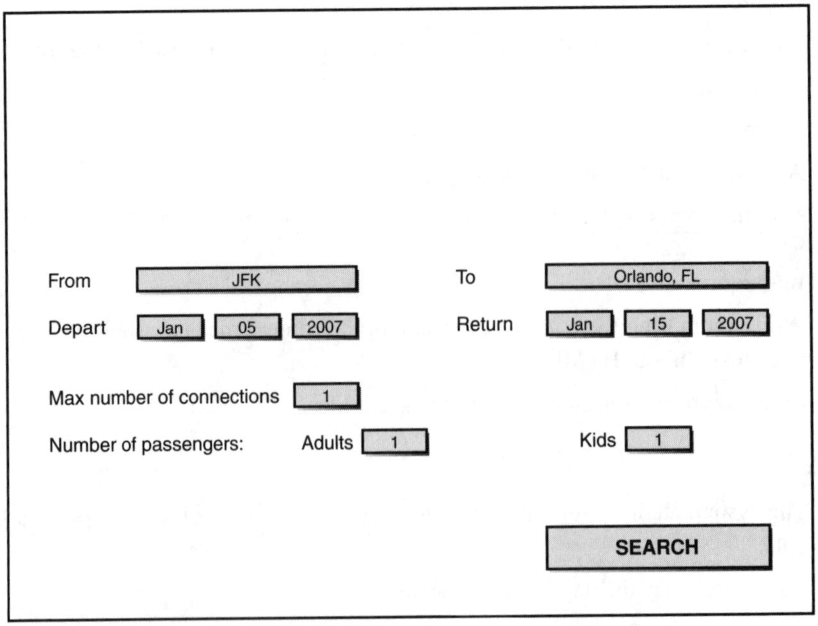

Figure 5.2   A simple storyboard created with Microsoft PowerPoint.

Role Playing

The members of a group are assigned roles related to the system being built. Most often, the roles represent users of the system or other actors interacting with the system. The team walks through various scenarios.

In the online travel agency project, the interaction between a user and customer service representative (CSR) can be modeled using role playing. Let's look at two examples.

Dialog 1

User:	Hi. Yesterday I made a reservation for a hotel. However, I had to cancel my trip, so I would like to cancel my reservation.
CSR:	No problem. What is your last name?
User:	Smith.
CSR:	I have 187 reservations made by people named Smith. What is your first name?
User:	John.
CSR:	Still 47 matches. What is your destination city?
User:	Miami.
CSR:	Date?
User:	September 12th to September 15th.
CSR:	OK. Your reservation is canceled.

Dialog 2

User:	Good afternoon.
CSR:	How can I help you?
User:	I reserved an airline ticket and ordered a seat next to the window. I would like to change it to the aisle.
CSR:	What is your name?
User:	Arctos Postopolis.
CSR:	OK. Your name is unique, so I do not need any other info. The flight to Los Angeles on April 5th?
User:	Yes.
CSR:	OK. The change is made.

The following requirements were formulated from the role-playing session:

- The search facility shall allow the customer service representative to find a reservation based on
  - Last name
  - Destination city
  - Date
- The CSR shall be able to change reservation details or cancel a reservation.

Brainstorming Sessions

During brainstorming sessions, participants gather for short but intensive sessions. At the beginning, the facilitator announces the purpose of the session. It may be generating new requirements related to some part of a system or solving a problem, such as resolving a set of contradictory requirements. Every participant can contribute ideas. The atmosphere should encourage all ideas, even crazy ones. Ideas cannot be criticized. These rules are used to encourage creativity and discourage reticence or conformity. After all ideas have been written down, the mutations and combinations of these ideas can be generated. Only after all the ideas have been documented and the team analyzes every idea, one by one, is criticism allowed.

Brainstorming is especially useful when a problem needs to be solved—either a significant part of the requirement is missing, or requirements are contradictory. Quite often requirements and design are discussed at the same time because some solutions to a problem may be discussed.

Example

During requirements elicitation from users, two contradictory requirements were gathered:
From the user in the U.S.:

> *REQ1   Dates shall be displayed in the mm/dd/yyyy format.*

From the user in France:

> *REQ2   Dates shall be displayed in the dd/mm/yyyy format.*

The following team gathered to resolve this problem using a brainstorming session:

- User 1
- System analyst
- Developer
- Designer

Participants came up with various ideas:

- **Idea 1:** Hardcode the date to mm/dd/yyyy format, and specify the format next to each date entry field.
- **Idea 2:** Ask the user to register on the system. During registration, one of the questions will ask about the user's date format preference.
- **Idea 3:** Create a configuration file that contains the user's preference regarding the date. The program will read the configuration file from the hard drive.
- **Idea 4:** Use the date format that is stored in the web browser settings.

The ideas were gathered and documented. They were not criticized or discussed during the session. After all four ideas were documented, each was analyzed.

Idea 1 was rejected because it is inflexible and does not provide the correct format for non-U.S. users.

Idea 2 was rejected because some users may not want to go through the hassle of registering. Requiring registration may decrease the number of potential customers.

Idea 3 was rejected for technical and security reasons.

Idea 4 was accepted as the best solution.

Using Affinity Diagrams

Affinity diagrams are not a stand-alone technique; they are used in conjunction with brainstorming sessions or requirements workshops. The goal of this method is to group and organize a large number of ideas that come, for example, from a brainstorming session. This method can also be used to group the requirements that were collected during a workshop.

Affinity diagrams were invented by Jiro Kawakita from Japan. They are especially useful when

- There are a large number of ideas.
- Relationships between the items are not obvious.
- The issues are complex.
- Group consensus is necessary.

This technique involves the following steps [TAG04]:

1. Create cards. Each idea is written on a card or sticky note. Use markers so that the text is visible from a greater distance. The cards should be randomly placed on a large working surface such as a board or table.

2. Sort the cards. Each participant looks for items that are related in some way and places these cards next to each other. Participants should not communicate during this step. If one item seems to belong to many groups, it is okay to create copies of the card and place them in many groups. This step may take several days.

3. Discuss the model. After all the cards are sorted, the group can discuss the classification, noticed patterns, and the reasons why the cards were grouped in a specific way.

4. Create headings. A title will be created for each group.

5. Structure the model. If needed, some groups may be combined into supergroups or split into subgroups.

The brainstorming example from the preceding section is not a good candidate for affinity diagrams because it generates only a small number of ideas. However, affinity diagrams may be used to group requirements that result from workshops.

Prototyping

Prototyping is a powerful way to get feedback from users and customers. However, it is one of the most expensive methods because it requires developing the prototype—a simplified version of the system. Much of the functionality is often hardcoded, so the prototype is like a sophisticated storyboard. Sometimes work on the prototypes is abandoned, but in other projects the prototype continues to be enhanced, and eventually it becomes an actual system.

Analyzing Existing Documents

Many requirements can be extracted from existing documents. The following are examples of documents that may be used as a source of requirements:

- Business case
- Statement of work
- Request for proposal
- Business rules

- Notes from meetings
- Corporate guidelines
- Letters
- E-mails

One technique is to read the document and use a highlighter to mark sentences that form a requirement.

For documents that are already in electronic form, you can cut and paste portions of the text into the RequisitePro Stakeholder Requests document—highlight with the mouse any sentence that represents a requirement, and store it in the database. Section 5.4 explains how to do this.

In our sample project, requirements from User 2 came via e-mail:

```
-----Original Message-----
From:       Claude
Sent:       Saturday, August 26, 2006 7:01 PM
To:         Julia
Subject:    Requirements


Dear Julia,

In response to your e-mail, I have compiled some requirements
for your new system:


1. The user shall be able to compare flight prices from other,
nearby airports.
2. Dates shall be displayed in the dd/mm/yyyy format.
3. On data entry screens, the system shall indicate which
fields are mandatory.
4. It should be possible to cancel a ticket purchase.
5. The user shall be able to cancel a car or hotel
reservation.
```

```
6. The outbound and return flights should be sorted by the
smallest number of stops.
7. The user will be able to select a seat.
8. The system shall have a natural-language interface.
9. The system shall display a pop-up calendar when the user
enters a date.
10. The user shall indicate if he or she needs a one-way or
return ticket by checking the checkbox.


Best regards,


Claude
```

Use Cases

Use cases are one of the requirement types in the pyramid from Figure 1.1 in Chapter 1, "Requirements Management." They also are a format in which stakeholders express their needs. The format of a use case created by a stakeholder is the same as that eventually used by an analyst. However, the analyst must review the use case supplied by a user. Before placing use cases on the third level of the pyramid, the analyst should do the following:

1. Check that each step of the use case has all the attributes of a good requirement, as discussed in section 1.4, "Characteristics of a Good Requirement," in Chapter 1.

2. Import the use case to RequisitePro.

3. Create requirements that will be stored in the database.

4. Set traceability from features.

Observation and Task Demonstration

Sometimes users cannot express in words the details about their tasks. It may be easier to show the business analyst how this task is performed [LAU02]. The advantage of this approach is that the user can concentrate on the task, while the analyst takes notes and makes observations. The difference between observation and task demonstration is that in observation the user performs regular tasks without paying attention to the system analyst. In task demonstration the analyst may ask the user to do a specific task, and the user may support the demonstration with explanations.

Analyzing Existing Systems

Analyzing existing systems can be a source of many valuable requirements. Two main types of systems are worthy of analysis:

- A legacy system being replaced
- Systems developed by the competition

Quite often, when a new system replaces an old system, one of the requirements is as follows:

REQ1 The new system shall provide all the functionality of the old system.

This request is vague, so we will encourage customers to give more-specific requirements. However, very often the documentation of the currently used product does not exist, so the best way to get the requirements is to experiment with the existing system and extract its functionality. Because we already have screens that are developed, we can cut and paste them into a use case or storyboard.

If you are developing a system similar to ones that have been developed by other companies, and you have access to the final product, it is worth analyzing their work to learn from their success or their mistakes.

Because many online travel agencies are available on the Internet, for our sample project, system analysts decided to analyze similar websites:

- http://travel.yahoo.com

- www.expedia.com

- www.cheaptickets.com

- www.travelocity.com

5.3 Creating the Stakeholder Requests Document

All information gathered during requirements elicitation should be documented in Stakeholder Requests documents. In your project, you can have one Stakeholder Requests document that combines requests from all stakeholders, you can create one document per stakeholder, or you can combine a few stakeholders per document. If you don't need to describe the stakeholders' requirements in detail, you can create a Stakeholder Needs section in the Vision document. This eliminates the need for a separate Stakeholder Requests document. Let's assume that for the purpose of our project we create six Stakeholder Requests documents, grouping stakeholders by the elicitation method (assigned to them in section 5.2):

- "Stakeholder Requests—Customer" contains requirements from the travel agency owner gathered during the interview.
- "Stakeholder Requests—User 1" contains requirements from User 1.
- "Stakeholder Requests—User 2" contains requirements from User 2 sent in the e-mail.
- "Stakeholder Requests—CSR" contains requirements from the CSR gathered through role playing.
- "Stakeholder Requests—IT Department" contains requirements from the administrator, content manager, and developer gathered during the requirements workshop.
- "Stakeholder Requests—Service Providers" contains requirements from the hotel provider, car rental agent, and airline representative gathered from questionnaires.

Let's create a Stakeholder Requests document. First, you need to open the project created in the preceding chapter.

Opening a Project

When you start RequisitePro, an Open Project dialog box appears, as shown in Figure 5.3.

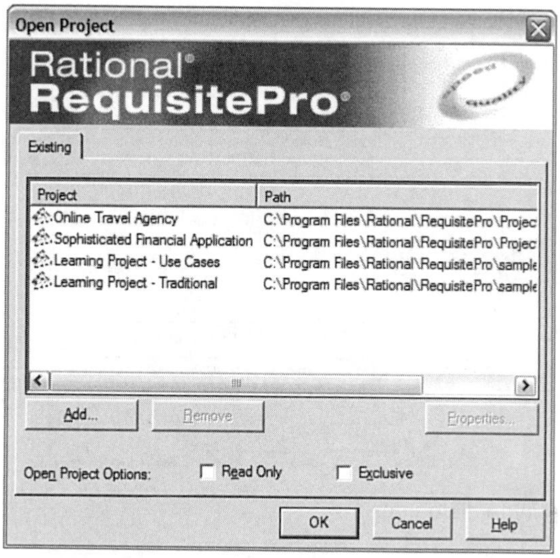

Figure 5.3   Open Project dialog box.

You can select a project from the list (by default it contains all recently used projects) or create a new project. If you want to open an existing project that is not in the list, you must first add the project to the list of existing projects by clicking the Add button. In this case, we select the Online Travel Agency project from the list.

Adding a Document Type to the Project

Each document type is usually associated with an outline—a Microsoft Word template (.dot file). The content of the outline is a starting point for creating new documents. The Outline includes formats, page layouts, and fonts. You can use the predefined RequisitePro templates, or you can create them yourself. If you specify the outline as "None," a blank Microsoft Word document opens when you create a document of this type.

The Stakeholder Requests document type is included in the Use Case template that we used to create our project, so we do not need to add this document type to our project.

If you are not sure whether your project already includes the Stakeholder Request document type, do the following:

1. Select the project in the Explorer.

2. Select File > Properties.

3. Select the Document Types tab.

If the Stakeholder Requests document type is listed, you do not need to add it. However, if this document type is not in the project, the following steps add it:

1. Select File > Properties. The Project Properties dialog box appears.
2. Click the Document Types tab.
3. Click Add. The Document Type dialog box appears, as shown in Figure 5.4.

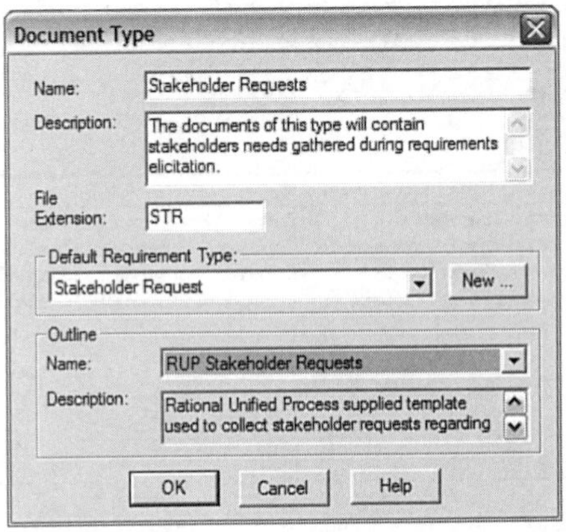

Figure 5.4   Document Type dialog box.

4. Type a document name, description, and file extension.
5. In the Default Requirement Type list, select Stakeholder Request. If it is not in the list, create it by clicking the New button, and fill in the dialog box.
6. In the Outline Name list, select the RUP Stakeholder Requests outline.
7. Click OK to close the Document Type dialog box.
8. Click OK to close the Project Properties dialog box.

Notice that the user provides the file extension. Having an extension different from .doc enforces the usage of RequisitePro to modify the document because people would not be able to open and edit it using Microsoft Word or any other editing tool.

Creating a Stakeholder Requests Document

To create a Stakeholder Requests document, follow these steps:

1. Select the package in which you want to create the document. In the Use Case template, the Stakeholder Requests package is already created.
2. Select File > New > Document (or right-click the package and select New > Document). The Document Properties dialog box appears, as shown in Figure 5.5.

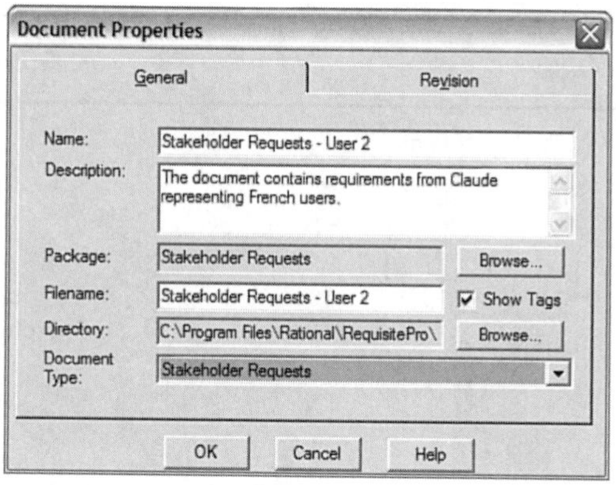

Figure 5.5 Document Properties dialog box.

3. In the Name field, type a name to identify the document. If you have one document per project, it can be called just Stakeholder Requests. If you create one document per stakeholder, include the stakeholder's name or type, such as User, in the title. If it is a combined document for many stakeholders to whom a specific elicitation method was applied, you can include the method in the title, such as Stakeholder Requests-Questionnaires, or you can use a name describing the group of stakeholders such as Stakeholder Requests-Service Providers.

4. In the Description field, type a short description of the document.

5. In the Filename field, type a filename that RequisitePro will use when saving the document. It can be the same as the document name, or some abbreviation of it.

6. Select the Document Type Stakeholder Requests.

7. Click OK.

A newly created document appears in the Microsoft Word window, as shown in Figure 5.6.

RequisitePro manages the documents via a Microsoft Word workplace. You can modify the text in the document the same way that you would update a regular Microsoft Word document. Some fields in the template contain generic names such as <Company Name> or <Project Name>. When selected, these fields have a gray background. They should be replaced by actual values. A convenient way of changing them is to access the Properties dialog box (select File > Properties) and insert the appropriate names, as shown in Figure 5.7.

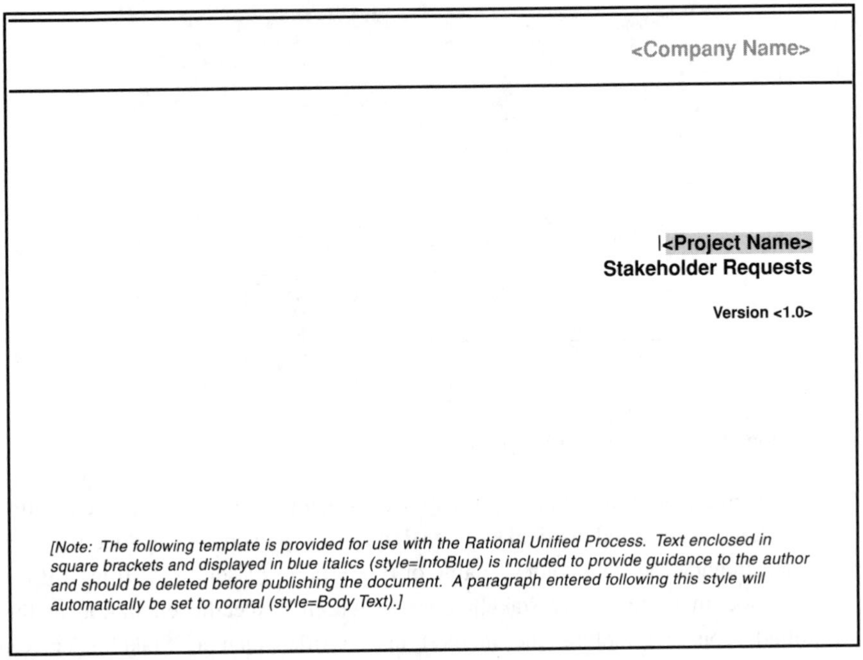

<Company Name>

I<Project Name>
Stakeholder Requests

Version <1.0>

[Note: The following template is provided for use with the Rational Unified Process. Text enclosed in square brackets and displayed in blue italics (style=InfoBlue) is included to provide guidance to the author and should be deleted before publishing the document. A paragraph entered following this style will automatically be set to normal (style=Body Text).]

Figure 5.6   Initial first page of the Stakeholder Requests document.

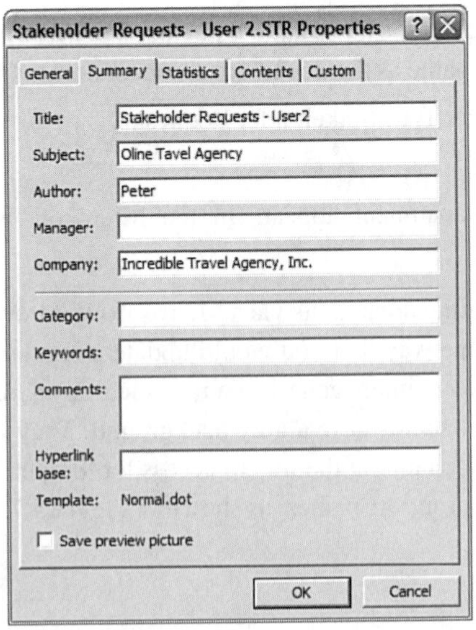

Stakeholder Requests - User 2.STR Properties

General | Summary | Statistics | Contents | Custom

Title: Stakeholder Requests - User2

Subject: Oline Tavel Agency

Author: Peter

Manager:

Company: Incredible Travel Agency, Inc.

Category:

Keywords:

Comments:

Hyperlink
base:

Template: Normal.dot

☐ Save preview picture

[OK]   [Cancel]

Figure 5.7   Document Properties dialog box.

After the document properties are set, you may change a field in the template by position-ing the cursor over the field and pressing F9. The field is filled with the corresponding value from the Properties dialog box, as shown in Figure 5.8.

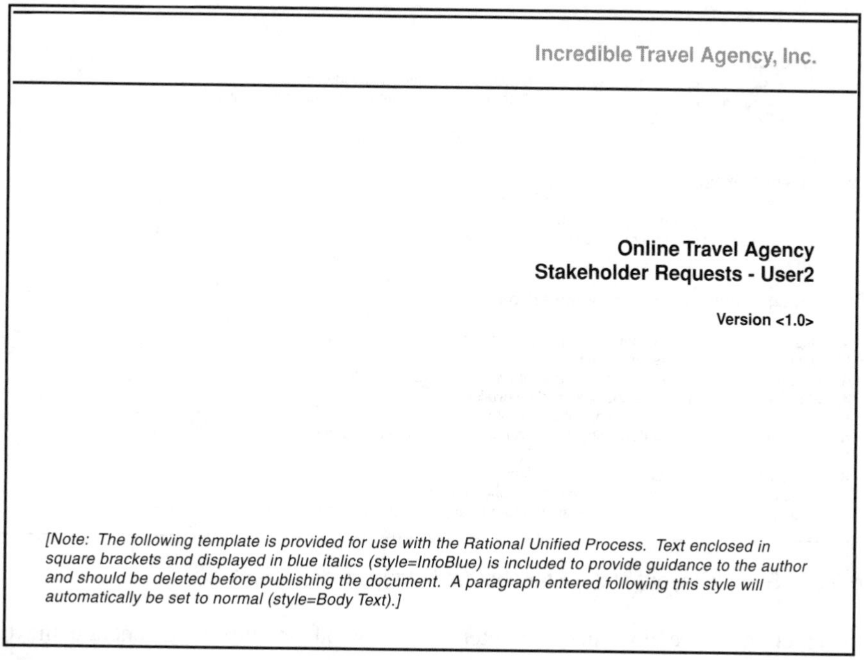

Incredible Travel Agency, Inc.

Online Travel Agency
Stakeholder Requests - User2

Version <1.0>

[Note: The following template is provided for use with the Rational Unified Process. Text enclosed in square brackets and displayed in blue italics (style=InfoBlue) is included to provide guidance to the author and should be deleted before publishing the document. A paragraph entered following this style will automatically be set to normal (style=Body Text).]

Figure 5.8   First page of the document with the appropriate fields inserted from the Properties dialog box.

A default document generated by RequisitePro contains instructional text in blue italic font. It contains explanations of what should be written in a specific section of the document. Replace the default instructional text with project-specific information.

The format of the Stakeholder Requests document depends on which elicitation method was used to gather the requirements. The default version of the document contains an interview script used in the earlier "Interviews" section. However, the whole structure of the document can be modified depending on your needs.

Figure 5.9 shows a simple format that we used to create this document for User 2, who sup-plied requirements via e-mail. The requirements were just cut and pasted from e-mail into para-graph 3 of the document.

Online Travel Agency	Version: <1.0>
Stakeholder Requests - User2	Date: <10/10/2006>
STR-02	

Stakeholder Requests

1. Introduction

The document represents stakeholder's requests submitted by Claude Trudeau via email. Claude represents French users. The requirements are quoted exactly how they appeared in the original email.

2. Stakeholder Profile

- Name: Claude Trudeau
- Represented group: Users
- Represented sub-group: Users from France

3. Requirements submitted by the stakeholder

1. User should be able to compare flight prices from other, nearby airports.
2. Dates should be displayed in the dd/mm/yyyy format.
3. On data entry screens system should indicate which fields are mandatory.
4. Ability of canceling ticket purchase should be available.
5. User shall be able to cancel car or hotel reservation.
6. The outbound and return flights should be sorted by the smallest number of stops.
7. User should be able to select seats.
8. System shall have a natural language interface.
9. System shall display a pop-up calendar when entering any date.
10. User shall indicate if he needs one-way or return ticket by checking the check box.

Figure 5.9   Sample layout of the Stakeholder Requests document.

After creating the document's contents, it is good practice to regenerate the table of contents:

1. Position the cursor on the table of contents.
2. Select Insert > Reference > Index and Tables.
3. Select the Table of Contents tab.
4. Click OK. The message box asks "Do you want to replace the selected table of contents?"
5. Click Yes.

At the end of the session, save the document. Select RequisitePro > Document > Save. (Do not select File > Save, as you would do in a regular Microsoft Word document.)

5.4   Creating Requirements in RequisitePro

After you have entered the free-form information into the document, you should create formal requirements. Defining requirements and storing them in the database is important for controlling traceability from stakeholder requests to features.

The Stakeholder Requests document does not have a clear place defined for where to put the STRQ type requirements. The requirements may be embedded in the text, supplied as answers to the interview questions, or summarized in the last paragraph, called "Analyst Summary."

The main attributes of the requirement are Text (mandatory) and Name (optional). If Text is a short, one-sentence description, you do not need to create a separate Name. If the Text description is long, it is worth creating a concise name for the requirement. If the Name is provided, it is used for requirement identification. If the Name is not provided, the Text is used for identification. For consistency, it is better to either use the name for all requirements of the same type or not to use the name for any of them. In our project we will create names because some stakeholder requests are quite long. Requirement names should be short but meaningful.

Requirements can be created in RequisitePro in five different ways:

- Created in a document (using the Microsoft Word workplace)
- Created in a view
- Created in Explorer
- Imported from a comma-separated file (CSV)
- Imported from a requirements document

This chapter describes creating requirements in the Microsoft Word document, which is the most popular method.

Adding Requirements in Documents

To create requirements in a Microsoft Word document, do the following:

1. Highlight the text describing the requirement, as shown in Figure 5.10.

---

3. Requirements submitted by the stakeholder

1. User should be able to compare flight prices from other, nearby airports.
2. Dates should be displayed in the dd/mm/yyyy format.
3. On data entry screens system should indicate which fields are mandatory.
4. Ability of canceling ticket purchase should be available.
5. User shall be able to cancel car or hotel reservation.
6. The outbound and return flights should be sorted by the smallest number of stops.
7. User should be able to select seats.
8. System shall have a natural language interface.
9. System shall display a pop-up calendar when entering any date.
10. User shall indicate if he needs one-way or return ticket by checking the check box.

Figure 5.10   Highlighting requirement text in a document.

2. Select RequisitePro > Requirement > New, or right-click the text and select Create Requirement, or click the New Requirement icon on the Toolbar:

The Requirement Properties dialog box appears, as shown in Figure 5.11. The Text is already copied from the highlighted area in the document. If necessary, you can add a Name. Type is set to the default requirement type for this document type. You can change it if necessary.

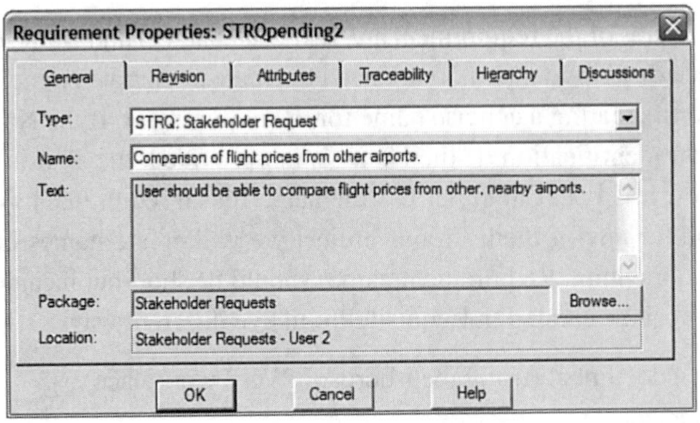

Figure 5.11   Requirement Properties dialog box: General tab.

3. Select STRQ as the requirement type.
4. If you want to set the attributes, click the Attributes tab to modify the attribute values, as shown in Figure 5.12.

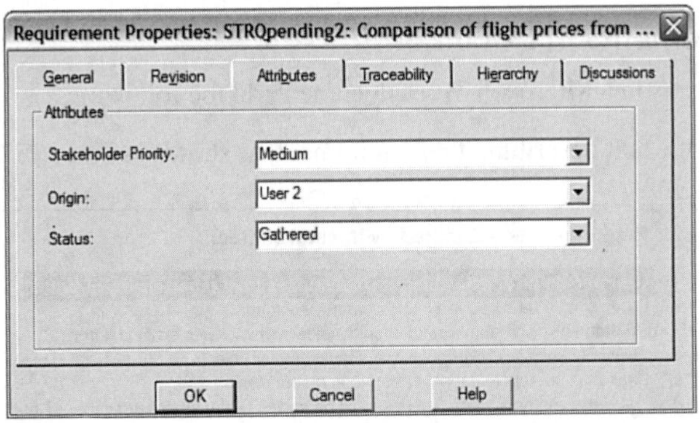

Figure 5.12   Requirement Properties dialog box: Attributes tab.

5. Click OK.

Requirement attributes can also be changed from a view and in the Explorer. Each requirement includes a prefix tag and a numeric value. RequisitePro assigns a unique tag to each requirement that is created. A requirement tag is a unique requirement identifier. The prefixes are associated with requirement types.

Until the document is saved, tags are displayed with the word "pending," as shown in Figure 5.13.

To save the document, in the Microsoft Word window, select RequisitePro > Document > Save (do not select File > Save).

After you save the document, tags contain prefixes describing the requirement type and consecutive numbers, as shown in Figure 5.14.

3. Requirements submitted by the stakeholder

1. [STRQpending2 User should be able to compare flight prices from other, nearby airports.]
2. [STRQpending3 Dates should be displayed in the dd/mm/yyyy format.]
3. [STRQpending4 On data entry screens system should indicate which fields are mandatory.]
4. [STRQpending5 Ability of canceling ticket purchase should be available.]
5. [STRQpending6 User shall be able to cancel car or hotel reservation.]
6. [STRQpending7 The outbound and return flights should be sorted by the smallest number of stops.]
7. [STRQpending8 User should be able to select seats.]
8. [STRQpending9 System shall have a natural language interface.]
9. [STRQpending10 System shall display a pop-up calendar when entering any date.]
10. [STRQpending11 User shall indicate if he needs one-way or return ticket by checking the check box.]

Figure 5.13   Pending requirements.

3. Requirements submitted by the stakeholder

1. [STRQ1 User should be able to compare flight prices from other, nearby airports.]
2. [STRQ2 Dates should be displayed in the dd/mm/yyyy format.]
3. [STRQ3 On data entry screens system should indicate which fields are mandatory.]
4. [STRQ4 Ability of canceling ticket purchase should be available.]
5. [STRQ5 User shall be able to cancel car or hotel reservation.]
6. [STRQ6 The outbound and return flights should be sorted by the smallest number of stops.]
7. [STRQ7 User should be able to select seats.]
8. [STRQ8 System shall have a natural language interface.]
9. [STRQ9 System shall display a pop-up calendar when entering any date.]
10. [STRQ10 User shall indicate if he needs one-way or return ticket by checking the check box.]

Figure 5.14   Saved requirements.

Requirements can be seen in the Explorer window, as shown in Figure 5.15.

When you are done with the first Stakeholder Requests document, you should create similar documents for other stakeholders.

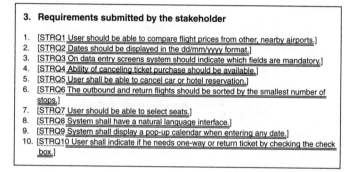

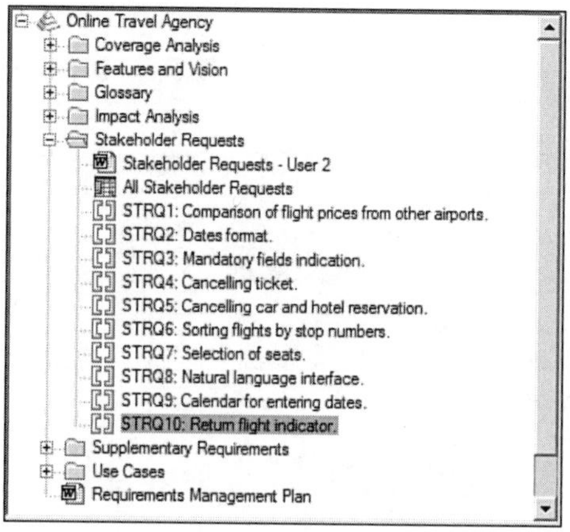

Figure 5.15   Explorer window showing STRQ requirements.

Changing Attributes of Requirement Types

By default, requirements of the type STRQ are shown in the documents in gray. If you feel that this color is too light, you can change it by updating attributes of requirement types. Let's change it to dark blue:

1. Position the cursor on the project name in Explorer.
2. Select File > Properties.
3. Select the Requirement Types tab.
4. Select the STRQ Requirement Type, as shown in Figure 5.16.

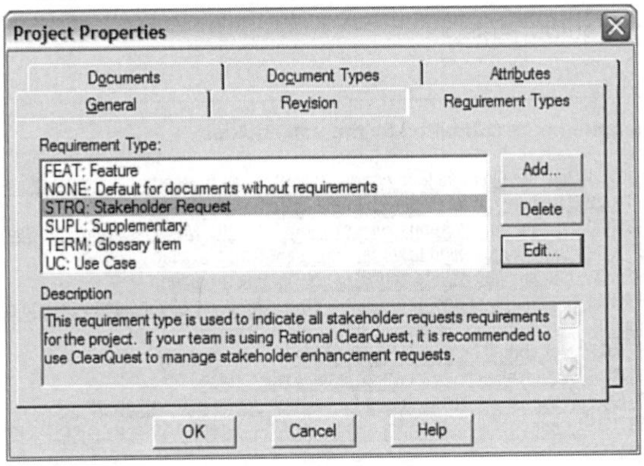

Figure 5.16   Selecting the STRQ requirement type.

5. Click Edit.
6. Change Requirement Color to Dark Blue, as shown in Figure 5.17.

    The following message box appears: "This function requires that the project be opened exclusively. Do you want to attempt to gain exclusive access to the project now?"

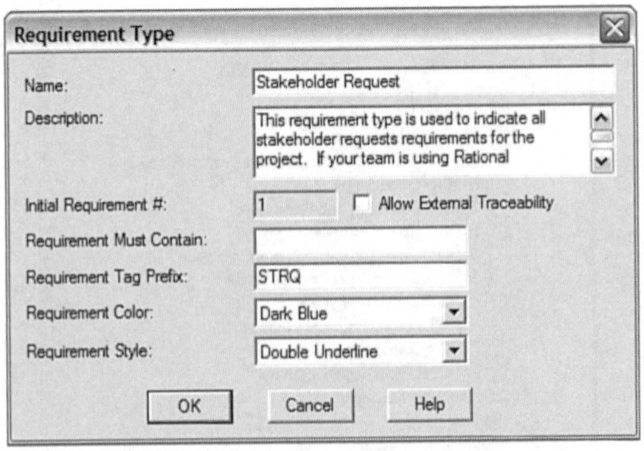

Figure 5.17   Changing Requirement Color to Dark Blue.

7. Click Yes to confirm opening the project exclusively. A confirmation message box appears.

8. Click OK in the message box.

9. Click OK in the Requirement Type dialog box.

10. Click OK on the Project Properties Screen.

The attribute representing the color of the STRQ requirement type is changed.

Adding a Requirement from the Explorer

If you decide that the project does not require Stakeholder Requests documents, but you need an STRQ requirement type, you can add the requirement from the View or from the Explorer.

To add a requirement from the Explorer, follow these steps:

1. Right-click the name of the package in which you want to create a requirement.

2. Select New > Requirement. The same Requirement Properties dialog box is displayed.

3. Fill in the necessary fields in the dialog, and click OK.

Modifying a Requirement in the Explorer

Regardless of how the requirement was created, you can modify it in the Explorer:

1. Right-click the requirement STRQ6 in the Explorer, and select Properties.

2. Make appropriate changes, and click OK.

Deleting a Requirement from the Explorer

To delete a requirement from the Explorer, do the following:

1. Highlight the requirement.

2. Right-click it and select Delete.

Requirements that are deleted cannot be restored. If you think that you may need to restore functionality, it is better to create an additional status called "Deleted." Requirements with status changed to Deleted can be reinstated by changing the status back to Proposed or Approved.

5.5 Using Views to Analyze Requirements

Views are used to display and manage requirements, their attributes, and their relationships with other requirements. You can sort and filter requirements to produce required reports. RequisitePro has three types of views:

- Attribute Matrix
- Traceability Matrix
- Traceability Tree

This section discusses the Attribute Matrix. The remaining two types are discussed in the next chapter.

Creating the Attribute Matrix View

After you have entered requirements from all stakeholders into the system, let's create a view showing all stakeholder requests. To create a new view that is not included in the template, do the following:

1. Right-click the package where you want to create a view (the Stakeholders Requests package is a good choice in this case), and select New > View. Alternatively, highlight the package where you want to create a view, and select File > New > View.

The View Properties dialog box appears, as shown in Figure 5.18.

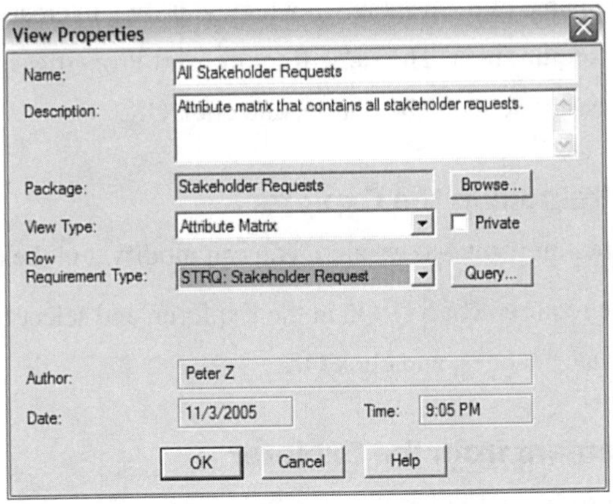

Figure 5.18   View Properties dialog box.

2. Name the view.
3. Select a View Type (Attribute Matrix, Traceability Matrix, or Traceability Tree)—in this case, Attribute Matrix.
4. Select a Row Requirement Type—in this case, STRQ.

   If you were creating a Traceability Matrix, you would also need to select the Column Requirement Type.
5. Click OK.

Opening a View

Many views are already predefined in the project templates. Because we have used a Use Case template, we already have an All Stakeholder Requests view in the Stakeholder Request package. We just need to open the view using the following steps:

1. Expand the Features and Vision folder.

2. Double-click the All Features view.

The Attribute Matrix displays all requirements of a specified type with their attributes. It is a spreadsheet-like display with requirement names in rows and attributes in columns, as shown in Figure 5.19.

Requirements:	Stakeholder Priority	Origin
STRQ1: Comparison of flight prices from other airports.	Medium	User 2
STRQ2: Dates format.	Medium	User 2
STRQ3: Mandatory fields indication.	Medium	User 2
STRQ4: Cancelling ticket.	Medium	User 2
STRQ5: Cancelling car and hotel reservation.	Medium	User 2
STRQ6: Sorting flights by stop numbers.	Medium	User 2
STRQ7: Selection of seats.	Medium	User 2
STRQ8: Natural language interface.	Medium	User 2
STRQ9: Calendar for entering dates.	Medium	User 2
STRQ10: Return flight indicator.	Medium	User 2
STRQ11: Comparison of prices from other airports	Medium	User 1
STRQ12: Airport Code and City search	Medium	User 1
STRQ13: Clear navigation	Medium	User 1
STRQ14: Storing client information	Medium	User 1
STRQ15: PayPal payments	Medium	User 1
STRQ16: Date format	Medium	User 1
STRQ17: Flight information	Medium	User 1
STRQ18: Sorting by price	Medium	User 1
STRQ19: Car rental comparison	Medium	User 1
STRQ20: Including taxes	Medium	User 1
STRQ21: Calendar	Medium	User 1
STRQ22: Main functionality	Medium	Travel Agency Owner
STRQ23: Online purchasing	Medium	Travel Agency Owner
STRQ24: Implementation guidelines	Medium	Travel Agency Owner
STRQ25: Userids and passwords for providers	Medium	Travel Agency Owner
STRQ26: Reliability	Medium	Travel Agency Owner
STRQ27: Development time	Medium	Travel Agency Owner
STRQ28: Userids and passwords for users	Medium	Travel Agency Owner
STRQ29: Reservation search	Medium	Customer Service Rep
STRQ30: Changing and cancelling reservation	Medium	Customer Service Rep
STRQ31: Submitting plain text	Medium	Content Manager
STRQ32: Storing content information	Medium	Content Manager
STRQ33: Browser selection	Medium	Developer
STRQ34: Airport map	Medium	Developer

Figure 5.19   An attribute matrix showing all stakeholder requests and their attributes.

To change a set of displayed attributes, do the following:

1. Position the cursor on the header row in the view pane, right-click, and select Displayed Attributes.

2. In the Attributes to Display list, select attributes that you want to see in a view, as shown in Figure 5.20.

Because during creation of the requirements we did not set priorities, we can do so now. To change the attributes of the requirement, do the following:

1. Right-click the appropriate cell, and select Set Value.

2. Select a value from the list, as shown in Figure 5.21.

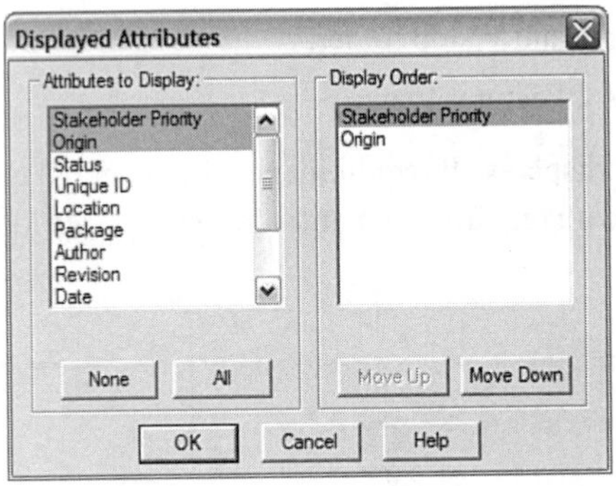

Figure 5.20   Selecting which attributes will be displayed in an attribute matrix.

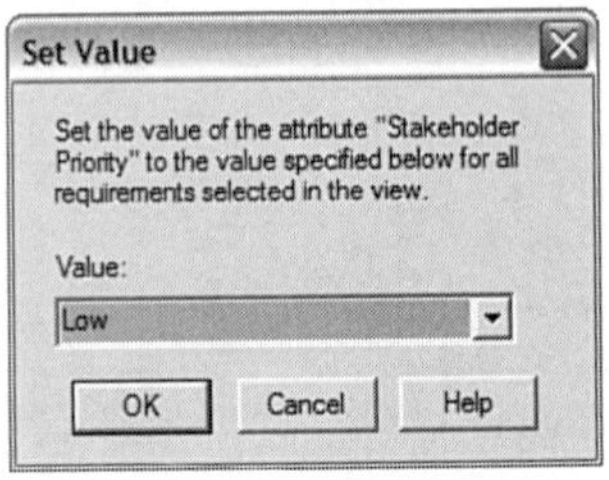

Figure 5.21   Setting an attribute value using the Set Value dialog box.

Another way of changing attributes of requirements is to double-click the appropriate cell in the spreadsheet and select the attribute from the drop-down, as shown in Figure 5.22.

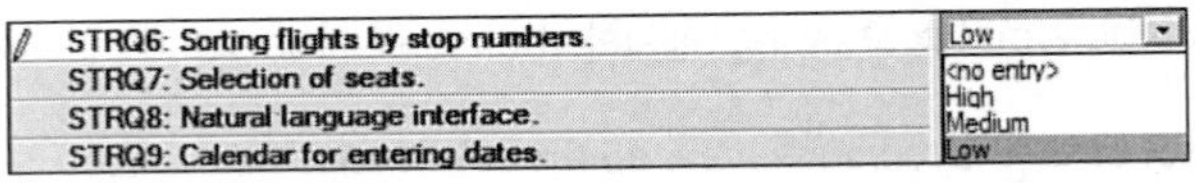

Figure 5.22   Setting an attribute value using the drop-down in the cell.

To change a Requirement Name or Text, right-click the requirement and select Properties.

Requirements can be created directly in the Attribute Matrix. However, it is not good practice to have some requirements of the same type created in documents and others only in a view. You can modify the requirement regardless of how it was created. If you change the text of a requirement in a view, this is also reflected in the document.

Exporting a View

We can export a view to a Microsoft Word document or a CSV file (that we can open in Microsoft Excel). This allows this information to be used outside the RequisitePro environment.

To export the attribute matrix that we have just created, do the following:

1. Select File > Export > Export to CSV.

2. Provide the filename.

3. Click the Save button.

The view is stored in a CSV file that you can open using Microsoft Excel, as shown in Figure 5.23.

	A	B	C	D	E
23	STRQ22	System should provide the opportunity to book the flight, purchase a ticket, reserve hotel, reserve car, and provide info about attractions.	Main functionality	High	Travel Agency Owner
24	STRQ23	User should be able to purchase a ticket online, without the necessity of calling the travel agent.	Online purchasing	High	Travel Agency Owner
25	STRQ24	System should follow implementation guidelines set up in the chain of our travel agencies.	Implementation guidelines	Medium	Travel Agency Owner
26	STRQ25	Hotel Providers, Car Providers, and Airline Representatives should have their ids and passwords to the pages where they can submit their offers.	Userids and passwords for providers	High	Travel Agency Owner
27	STRQ26	System must be available 24 hours a day with a reliability appropriate to commercial applications.	Reliability	Medium	Travel Agency Owner
28	STRQ27	System should be developed in 3 months.	Development time	Medium	Travel Agency Owner
29	STRQ28	Users shall pick ids and passwords while buying airline ticket.	Userids and passwords for users	High	Travel Agency Owner
30	STRQ29	The search facility should allow customer service representative to find a reservation based on: Last Name, Date, Destination City	Reservation search	Medium	Customer Service Rep
31	STRQ30	The customer service representative should be able to change reservation details or cancel a reservation.	Changing and cancelling reservation	High	Customer Service Rep
32	STRQ31	While submitting the content information, the Content Manager should be able to submit plain text without HTML tags.	Submitting plain text	Low	Content Manager
33	STRQ32	Content information should be stored in a text file.	Storing content information	Medium	Content Manager
34	STRQ33	System shall be fully tested under specific versions of most popular browsers only.	Browser selection	Medium	Developer

STRQ All Stakeholder Requests

Figure 5.23   Attribute Matrix exported to Excel.

Querying Requirements

You can query (filter and sort) information in an Attribute Matrix. To filter the rows, you can specify what criteria the displayed rows should fulfill. As an example, let's display only requirements that have priority High or Medium and an Origin of either User 1 or User 2.

1. Right-click the upper-left square of the view.

2. Select Query. The Query Row Requirements dialog box and Select Attribute dialog box are displayed.

3. Select Priority from the list of attributes, and click OK.

4. Select High and Medium from attribute values list, and click OK.

5. Click Add.

6. Select Origin from the list of attributes. Click OK.

7. Select User 1 and User 2 from the attribute values list, as shown in Figure 5.24. Click OK.

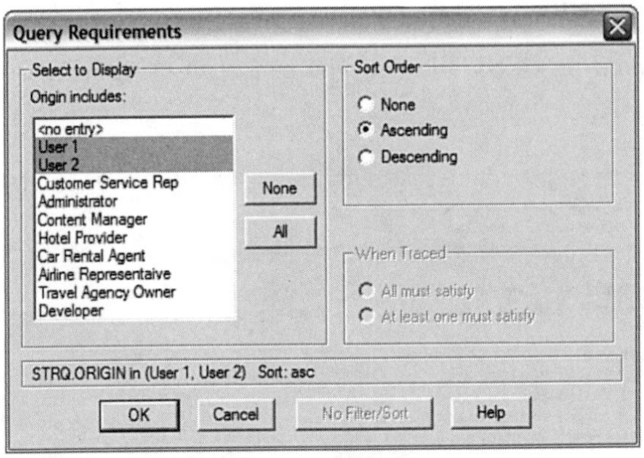

Figure 5.24   Selecting values of the attribute for the filter.

8. Accept all criteria by clicking OK, as shown in Figure 5.25.

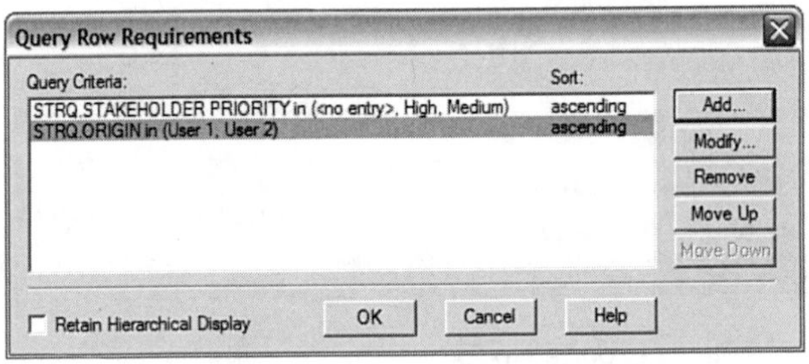

Figure 5.25   All query criteria (connected with an "AND" operator).

In the Query Requirements dialog box, you can also set Sort Order to Ascending or Descending for the given attribute.

To remove all filters and return to the original view, do the following:

1. Right-click the upper-left square of the view.

2. Select Query.

3. Click the Remove button in the Query Row Requirements dialog box until you delete all entries.

4. Click OK.

You can save results of a query in a view. The view will reflect the state at the time of the query. To reflect recent changes to the database, you need to select View > Refresh.

5.6 Summary

Stakeholder requests can be gathered through many different elicitation techniques. We have discussed 11 of them. Which technique you choose depends on the nature of the requirements and the type of stakeholder. It is good practice to record results in RequisitePro in the form of Stakeholder Requests documents and as requirements stored in the database. Having stakeholders' needs in the database lets you assign various attributes to them, such as priority or difficulty. It also lets you track the requirements and trace them to other requirement types.

References

[RUP04] *Rational Unified Process*, Version 2003.06.13, IBM, 2003.

[TAG04] Tague, Nancy. *The Quality Toolbox*, ASQ Quality Press, 2004.

[LAU02] Lauesen, Soren. *Software Requirements: Styles and Techniques*, Pearson Education, 2002.

CHAPTER 6

Developing a Vision Document

The Vision document is one of the three most important documents created in RequisitePro (the other two are the Use Cases and Supplementary Specification documents). The Vision document contains the following:

- A description of the problem being solved by the new system
- A high-level description of the solution
- A list of the system's main features

The Vision document may serve as a contract between a customer and developers for the technical requirements. The purpose of the Vision document is to

- Define the system's boundaries
- Identify constraints imposed on the system
- Gain agreement with the customer on the scope of the project
- Create a basis on which to define Use Cases and Supplementary Specification documents

The Vision is a repository for the requirements of type **Feature**, as shown in Figure 6.1. This chapter shows some examples of deriving features from needs and discusses attributes of features.

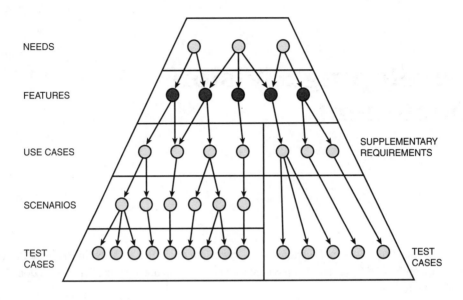

NEEDS

FEATURES

USE CASES

SUPPLEMENTARY
REQUIREMENTS

SCENARIOS

TEST
CASES

TEST
CASES

Figure 6.1   Features are on the second level of the pyramid.

6.1   The Structure of the Vision Document

Here are the contents of the Vision document as suggested by the RequisitePro template
[RUP04]:

10. Introduction
    1.1 Purpose
    1.2 Scope
    1.3 Definitions, Acronyms, and Abbreviations
    1.4 References
    1.5 Overview

2. Positioning
    2.1 Business Opportunity
    2.2 Problem Statement
    2.3 Product Position Statement

3. Stakeholder and User Descriptions
    3.1 Market Demographics
    3.2 Stakeholder Summary
    3.3 User Summary
    3.4 User Environment

You can tailor this table of contents to suit your project by removing entries that do not apply or by adding project-specific sections.

The Vision document is a repository for requirements of type Feature. They are listed in the section "Product Features." Other sections are usually free-form and do not contain any requirements.

6.2 Deriving Features from Stakeholder Needs

Features are derived from stakeholder requests. It is important to keep track of which feature was derived from which request, so when the stakeholder requests are stored in RequisitePro, they could be traced to the features implementing them.

Requests gathered from stakeholders do not necessarily have the attributes of a good requirement, as discussed in section 1.4, "Characteristics of a Good Requirement," in Chapter 1, "Requirements Management." Deriving features from stakeholder requests gives you a good opportunity to fix that. One approach is to go through all STRQ requirements and apply appropriate transformation to create one or more FEAT requirements.

The following transformations may be applied:

- Copy: If no changes are required, STRQ can be copied to FEAT exactly as is. It is okay to have different types of requirements with the same text. However, avoid requirements of the same type having the same text. In this case, requirements are redundant.

- Split: If the requirement is not atomic, we can split it into two or more requirements.

- Clarification: Clarification, or explanation, may be applied when the original requirement is unclear or ambiguous.

- Qualification: We achieve qualification by adding restrictions or conditions to the requirement. It may help to resolve contradictory requirements.

- Combination: Redundant or overlapping requirements may be combined into one.

- Generalization: If the requirement is not abstract, and it includes some unnecessary details, we may apply generalization.

- Cancellation: Sometimes the requirement needs to be deleted. This may happen when the requirement is infeasible, unnecessary, or inconsistent with another requirement.

- Completion: If the set of requirements is incomplete, we may need to add requirements at this stage.

- Correction: Correction may mean either rewording the requirement to fix grammar, spelling, or punctuation, or changing a portion of the requirement that is untrue.

- Unification: Requirements that use inconsistent vocabulary can be unified.

- Adding details: If the requirement is not precise enough, we may add details. This technique is often used to make testable requirements from untestable ones.

Chapter 5, "Requirements Elicitation," described requirements of the stakeholder request type. Let's analyze all the stakeholder requests gathered in Chapter 5 (one by one) and create features from them.

STRQ1   The user shall be able to compare flight prices from other, nearby airports.

This requirement is redundant with STRQ11. They can be combined into one requirement:

FEAT1   The user shall be able to compare flight prices from other, nearby airports (for outbound and inbound flights).

STRQ2 Dates shall be displayed in the dd/mm/yyyy format.

This requirement is inconsistent with STRQ 16, which requests the mm/dd/yyyy format. Requirement STRQ2 came from the user in France, and STRQ16 was supplied by the user in the U.S. The section "Brainstorming Sessions" in 5.2, "Techniques of Requirements Elicitation," Chapter 5, discusses how this issue was resolved. The requirements STRQ2 and STRQ16 were replaced by the following:

> *FEAT2   Dates shall be displayed according to the format stored in web browser settings.*

STRQ3 On data entry screens, the system shall indicate which fields are mandatory.

At some point the decision will be made as to how mandatory fields will be indicated as required fields. This decision can be made when creating a feature requirement, or slightly later, when supplementary requirements are derived from features. Let's assume we want to do this now, so we apply explanation to create a FEAT:

> *FEAT3   On data entry screens the system shall indicate which fields are mandatory by placing a star next to the field.*

STRQ4 The capability to cancel a ticket purchase should be available.

For consistency it is better to use standard constructs in requirements, such as "shall" instead of "should." Using different words such as "shall," "will," "should," and "could" may be wrongly interpreted as different levels of necessity. (For example, "will" might sound stronger than "shall," and "shall" might sound stronger than "should.")

Clarification is needed as to who shall be able to cancel ticket purchases (user, customer service representative, or administrator) and at what stage of the process this is required:

> *FEAT4   The user shall be able to cancel a ticket purchase any time before final confirmation of the purchase.*

STRQ5 The user shall be able to cancel a car or hotel reservation.

It is up to the system analyst to decide whether a specific requirement is atomic. In this case he decided that canceling a car or hotel room reservation can be considered the same requirement, so there is no need to split them:

> *FEAT5   The user shall be able to cancel a car or hotel reservation.*

STRQ6   The outbound and return flights shall be sorted by the smallest number of stops.

This terminology is inconsistent with STRQ11. The same concept is called "return flight" in STRQ6 and "inbound flight" in STRQ11. Let's assume that after consulting with authorities, we have decided to use the term "return flight." However, we already merged STRQ11 with STRQ1 in FEAT1. We need to go back to FEAT1 and change it for consistency:

> *FEAT1   The user shall be able to compare flight prices from other, nearby airports (for outbound and return flights).*

Because we have changed FEAT1 to be consistent with STRQ6, we can rewrite STRQ6 into FEAT6:

> *FEAT6   The outbound and return flights shall be sorted by the smallest number of stops.*

However, this contradicts STRQ18, which requests that flights be sorted by price. We may accommodate both requirements in one feature:

> *FEAT6   The user shall be able to choose if the flights shall be selected by the smallest number of stops or by price.*

As you can see, deriving features is an iterative process, and some requirements need to be changed a few times until they are consistent and nonredundant.

STRQ7   The user will be able to select seats.

For unification, we change "will" to "shall."
For the requirement to be completely stand-alone, we need to add some explanation:

> *FEAT7   While purchasing an airplane ticket, the user shall be able to select seats.*

STRQ8   The system shall have a natural-language interface.

At first glance this requirement is okay. However, after analyzing the scope of the system and time constraints, it was obvious that this requirement is unrealistic (infeasible). It is contradictory with STRQ27, which asks that the system be developed in three months. Implementing a natural-language interface would take more than three months. This requirement is canceled, and the user who provided this requirement is notified of the cancellation.

STRQ9   The system shall display a pop-up calendar when any date is entered.

This request overlaps with STRQ21, which asks for a calendar when the flight date is entered. Because STRQ9 is more generic (it mentions any date; that includes a hotel stay date or a car rental date), we will rewrite STRQ9 and cancel STRQ21. As a clarification, we may explicitly list all the dates:

> *FEAT8   The system shall display a pop-up calendar when any date is entered, such as a flight date, hotel stay date, or car rental date).*

STRQ10   The user shall indicate if he needs a one-way or return ticket by checking the checkbox.

This requirement contains unnecessary design. Details, such as whether to use a checkbox or radio button, should be left to the screen designer. In this case, a radio button may be more appropriate because options are exclusive. But at this stage such analysis and specific detail do not need to be done or included in the requirement:

> *FEAT9   The user shall have the opportunity to indicate if he needs a one-way or return ticket.*

STRQ11   For outbound and inbound flights, users shall be able to compare flight prices from other, nearby airports.

This request was combined into FEAT1, so it may be canceled.

STRQ12   Sometimes a user will enter an airport code, which the system will understand, but sometimes the closest city may replace it, so the user does not need to know the airport code, and it will still be understood by the system.

This sentence is complicated and unclear. We may replace it with a simpler one:

> *FEAT10   The system shall identify the airport based on either an airport code or a city name.*

STRQ13   The system shall have clear navigation.

This requirement is vague and is not precise enough to be testable. Two more concrete features were derived from it:

> *FEAT11   Separate tabs shall be available for the main functionality.*

> *FEAT12   On each page a Next button shall suggest a default flow.*

STRQ14   If the user purchased a ticket once, there shall not be a need to repeat the same information, such as address or credit card number.

In this request we clarify by adding "during future transactions":

> *FEAT13   If the user purchased a ticket once, there shall not be a need to repeat the same information (such as address or credit card number) during future transactions.*

STRQ15   Payment by PayPal shall be available.

This requirement is contradictory with STRQ41, which states that PayPal cannot be available. In this case, because for some reason the vendor cannot provide this service, we need to cancel the user's requirement.

STRQ16   Dates shall be displayed in the mm/dd/yyyy format.

This requirement was already incorporated into FEAT2.

STRQ17   The list of available flights shall include flight numbers, departure time, and arrival time for every leg of the flight.

There's nothing wrong with this one, so we just rewrite it:

FEAT14   The list of available flights shall include flight numbers, departure time, and arrival time for every leg of the flight.

STRQ18   It shall be sorted by price.

The word "It" refers to the preceding requirement. However, if the order of the requirements changes, this requirement will not be understandable.

To be independent, the requirement would need to be worded as follows:

The list of available flights shall be sorted by price.

However, we have already incorporated this requirement into FEAT6.

STRQ19   Comparison of car rental prices from different companies shall be provided.

This requirement is okay. We just need to remove the passive voice:

FEAT15   The system shall provide comparison of car rental prices from different companies.

STRQ20   Car rental prices shall show all applicable taxes (including 6% state tax).

The tax varies by state, so the provided 6% figure is incorrect. We can remove the words in parentheses, leaving the tax calculation to the designers:

FEAT16   Car rental prices shall show all applicable taxes.

STRQ21   A calendar shall be available to help with entering the flight date.

This requirement was incorporated into FEAT8.

STRQ22   The system shall provide the opportunity to book the flight, purchase a ticket, reserve a hotel room, reserve a car, and provide information about attractions.

This requirement is a combination of five atomic requirements, which makes traceability very difficult. This compound requirement will be split into five atomic ones:

> *FEAT17   The system shall provide an opportunity to book the flight.*
>
> *FEAT18   The system shall provide an opportunity to purchase an airplane ticket.*
>
> *FEAT19   The system shall provide an opportunity to reserve a hotel room.*
>
> *FEAT20   The system shall provide an opportunity to reserve a car.*
>
> *FEAT21   The system shall provide information about attractions in specific places.*

STRQ23   The user shall be able to purchase a ticket online, without the necessity of calling the travel agent.

Nothing is wrong here, so we can copy the requirement:

> *FEAT22   The user shall be able to purchase a ticket online, without the necessity of calling the travel agent.*

STRQ24   The system shall follow implementation guidelines set up in the chain of our travel agencies.

This requirement is unclear, unless another document is attached, describing implementation guidelines. Or all the guidelines can be explicitly listed. For example:

> *FEAT23   The system shall use J2EE architecture.*
>
> *FEAT24   If the architecture requires an application server, IBM WebSphere shall be used.*
>
> *FEAT25   If the system requires a database, Oracle shall be used.*

STRQ25   The pages where service providers can submit their offers shall be password-protected. Hotel providers, car providers, and airline representatives shall use assigned user IDs and passwords to access these pages.

Nothing is wrong here, so we can copy the requirement:

> *FEAT26   The pages where service providers can submit their offers shall be password-protected. Hotel providers, car providers, and airline representatives shall use assigned user IDs and passwords to access these pages.*

STRQ26   The system must be available 24 hours a day, with a degree of reliability appropriate to commercial applications.

This requirement is not precise enough to be tested. At some point we need to replace it with detailed requirements regarding reliability. We can do this now, while creating features, or we may wait until we create the Supplementary Specification. It is okay to make final decisions on nonfunctional requirements while deriving supplementary requirements from features. For now, we keep the requirement as is:

> *FEAT27   The system must be available 24 hours a day, with a degree of reliability appropriate to commercial applications.*

STRQ27   The system shall be developed in three months.

We may add an explanation about when this time calculation begins:

> *FEAT28   The system shall be developed three months from the date when the customer signs off on the Use Cases and Supplementary Specification.*

STRQ28   Users shall pick IDs and passwords while buying an airline ticket.

We can copy this requirement because there is nothing to fix:

> *FEAT29   Users shall pick IDs and passwords while buying an airline ticket.*

STRQ29   The search facility shall allow a customer service representative to find a reservation based on: Last Name, Destination City, Date, etc.

The "etc." is not precise enough. After confirming with the originator of this requirement that no other search criteria are required, the "etc." was removed.

> *FEAT30   The search facility shall allow a customer service representative to find a reservation based on the following: Last Name, Destination City, Date.*

STRQ30   The customer service representative shall be able to change reservation details or cancel a reservation.

Because this requirement is not atomic, we can split it into two:

> *FEAT31   The customer service representative shall be able to change reservation details.*
>
> *FEAT32   The customer service representative shall be able to cancel a reservation.*

STRQ31   While submitting the content information, the Content Manager shall be able to submit plain text without HTML tags.

This requirement is okay, so we just copy it:

> *FEAT33   While submitting the content information, the Content Manager shall be able to submit plain text without HTML tags.*

STRQ32   Content information shall be stored in a text file.

How the information is stored shall be transparent to the user, and it shall be the designer's or architect's decision. This requirement can be canceled. This suggestion, however, may be passed to the designer for consideration.

STRQ33   The system shall be fully tested under specific versions of the most popular browsers only.

After conveying to the customer that it is unrealistic to test the system on all available browsers, the customer agreed to limit the testing requirement to Internet Explorer and Netscape browsers:

> *FEAT34   The system shall be fully tested on the following browsers: Internet Explorer and Netscape.*

STRQ34   The system may display a map of to the airport.

This requirement came from a developer, who is neither a customer nor a user. After checking with the customer, it was confirmed that this requirement is unnecessary, so it was canceled.

STRQ35   The search facility shall allow a customer service representative to find a reservation based on: Last Name, Date.

Because STRQ35 is a subset of STRQ29, which was incorporated into FEAT30, we can cancel STRQ35.

STRQ36   All activity on the site shall be logged.

We add some details and explanation:

> *FEAT35   All transactions and errors shall be recorded and made available to the administrator.*

STRQ37   Various reports shall be available.

This requirement is imprecise. After additional interviews, details were added:

> *FEAT36   The following reports shall be available to the administrator:*
> *A list of all airline tickets purchased in the given time period.*
> *A list of all car reservations in the given time period.*
> *A list of all hotel room reservations in the given time period.*

STRQ38   While booking a hotel room, the customer shall provide the following information: town, stay dates, number of adults, number of children, room preferences.

This requirement is okay, so we just copy it:

> *FEAT37   While booking a hotel room, the customer shall provide the following information: town, stay dates, number of adults, number of children, room preferences.*

STRQ39   When providing the information about a hotel, the following information shall be displayed: address, phone, fax, e-mail, offered discounts, available methods of payment, etc.

The "etc." was removed:

> *FEAT38   When providing the information about a hotel, the following information shall be displayed: address, phone, fax, e-mail, offered discounts, and available methods of payment.*

STRQ40   The user shall be offered flight and hotel deals.

Some explanation is added:

> *FEAT39   The user shall be offered package deals consisting of flight and hotel stay.*

STRQ41   Only credit card payments shall be accepted. No checks, no PayPal.

Some rewording for clarification was applied:

> *FEAT40   While paying for the airplane ticket, only credit card payments shall be accepted. Checks and PayPal shall not be accepted.*

6.3   Attributes of Features

Attributes describe properties of requirements. They help organize and analyze the requirements in the project. We can create rules to decide, based on the attributes, which requirements to implement in the next iteration, phase, or release. For example, you may decide that in Elaboration you want to implement all requirements that have high Risk and high or medium Importance and all requirements that have high Importance and high or medium Difficulty.

Attributes can be either list-type (identified by the sets of predefined descriptive values such as High, Medium, and Low) or entry-type (text, time, date, numeric integer, numeric real).

The default attributes of features are as follows:

- Priority (usually used to determine order of implementation)
- Status (tracks the progress of requirement development—Proposed, Approved, Incorporated, and Validated)
- Difficulty (how difficult is implementing this requirement—the default values are High, Medium, and Low)
- Stability (the probability that the feature will not change during the project)
- Risk (the probability of issues related to this requirement—problems with implementation, missing deadlines, and so on)
- Planned iteration (for example, E1—the first iteration in the Elaboration phase)
- Actual iteration
- Origin (source of the requirement)
- Contact Name (usually the person responsible for this requirement)
- Enhancement Request
- Defect
- Author
- Location (in which document it resides)

This list may vary depending on the version of RequisitePro.

Very often we need to add attributes. Some examples follow.

We may want to have an attribute **Importance**, because it is not the same as **Priority**. It may help to manage the scope in case of delays. Values that can be used include Mandatory, Desirable, and Nice to have. In extreme situations multiple attributes may store these values, because **Importance according to the user** may not be the same as **Importance according to the project manager**.

Besides **Difficulty**, we may have an attribute called **Effort**. It is expressed in person-days and can provide a detailed estimate of how much time is required to implement the requirement.

To have a better cost estimate, we may add an attribute **Cost to implement**. It is useful if various resources come at significantly different prices (such as different hourly rates of consultants involved in the project). We may use this attribute to calculate cost/reward ratio, which we can store in the attributes **Cost/reward** or **Risk/reward**.

Instead of **Contact Name**, an attribute **Assigned To** is sometimes used.

Instead of **Planned iteration** and **Actual iteration**, we may have **Planned completion date** and **Actual completion date**.

Risk may be split into two separate attributes: **Risk probability** (what is the probability of problems) and **Risk impact** (if a problem occurs, how severe the impact is).

Described attributes may be used not only for features, but also for other requirements (such as use cases and supplementary requirements).

Adding a new attribute is so easy that you should not hesitate to do so if a custom attribute will help manage requirements of the particular type.

6.4   Creating the Vision Document in RequisitePro

The Vision document is included in the Use Case template, in the directory Features and Vision in the Explorer window. To open an existing document, do the following:

1. Expand Features and Vision.

2. Double-click the Vision document icon.

The Vision document template opens in the Word window.

If you are using a template that does not contain a Vision document, you can create it with the following steps:

1. In the Explorer, select the package where you want to place the Vision document.

2. Select File > New > Document. The Document Properties dialog box appears.

3. Type a name, description, and filename for the document.

4. From the Document Type drop-down list box, select Vision Document Type.

5. Click OK.

   The outline for the Vision document opens in Microsoft Word, as shown in Figure 6.2.

The template contains generic names such as <Company Name> or <Project Name>. Chapter 5 discussed how to replace them with actual values.

The document has the structure presented in section 6.1, "The Structure of the Vision Document." Fill in the appropriate sections with project-related information. Remove sections if they are not applicable. If needed, add new sections.

There is some flexibility with how to format the Product Features section. Different approaches are acceptable:

- Write requirements as separate, unnumbered sentences in section 5, Product Features, as shown in Figure 6.3.

- Number every requirement (5.1, 5.2, 5.3, and so on).

- Organize the requirements, and group them into numbered sections. For example, 5.1 Main functionality, 5.2 Functionality for the administrator, ... 5.9 Performance requirements. We can also have more granular groups, such as 5.1 Ordering airplane tickets, 5.2 Reserving a hotel room, 5.3 Reserving a car, and so on.

<Company Name>

<Project Name>
Vision

Version <1.0>

Figure 6.2 Vision document: initial template.

5. Product Features

User shall be able o compare flight prices form other, nearby airports (for outbound and return flights).

Dates shall be displayed according to the format stored in Web browser settings.

On data entry screens system shall indicate which fields are mandatory by placing a star next to the field.

Ability of canceling ticket purchase shall be available.

User shall be able to cancel car or hotel reservation.

Figure 6.3 Features listed in section 5 of the Vision document.

For simplicity, in our example we will use the first approach, but in a real project I would recommend grouping and organizing requirements.

6.5 Creating Features Requirements

After you have listed requirements in the Product Features section of the Vision document, you should store them in the database. This helps you manage requirement attributes in an Attribute Matrix and track traceability links between product features and software requirements.

To create a feature requirement, do the following:

1. Select (highlight) the text that defines the requirement, as shown in Figure 6.4.

   Do one of the following:

   • Right-click the text, and select "Create Requirement."

   • Select RequisitePro > Requirement > Create.

   • Click the New Requirement icon:

   The Requirement Properties dialog box appears.

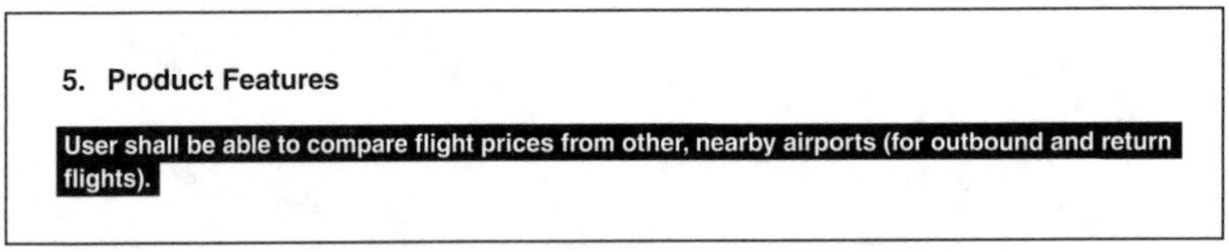

Figure 6.4   Highlighting the requirement.

2. Enter a requirement name. Because FEAT is the default requirement for a Vision document, the Type field should already be set to FEAT, as shown in Figure 6.5.

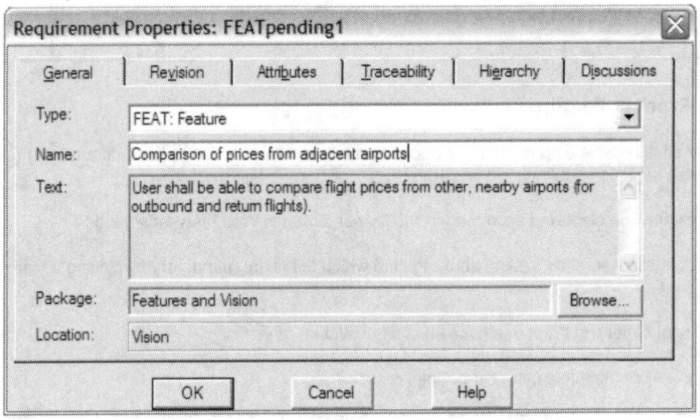

Figure 6.5   Requirement properties.

3. Click the Attributes tab, and set the requirements attributes (you can also do this any time later).

4. Click OK.

5. The tag FEATpending1 is assigned to the requirement, as shown in Figure 6.6. The word "pending" will be eliminated after you save the document.

5. Product Features

[FEATpending1 User shall be able to compare flight prices from other, nearby airports (for outbound and return flights).]

Figure 6.6   A pending requirement.

6. Select RequisitePro > Document > Save.

7. The tag is now called FEAT1, as shown in Figure 6.7.

5. Product Features

[FEAT1 User shall be able to compare flight prices from other, nearby airports (for outbound and return flights).]

Figure 6.7   The saved requirement.

8. Repeat these steps for each requirement described in the Product Features section of the Vision document. When you have finished, select RequisitePro > Document > Save.

RequisitePro assigns tags with consecutive numbers to all created requirements.

After product Features are stored in the database, they can be accessed from the Explorer, as shown in Figure 6.8.

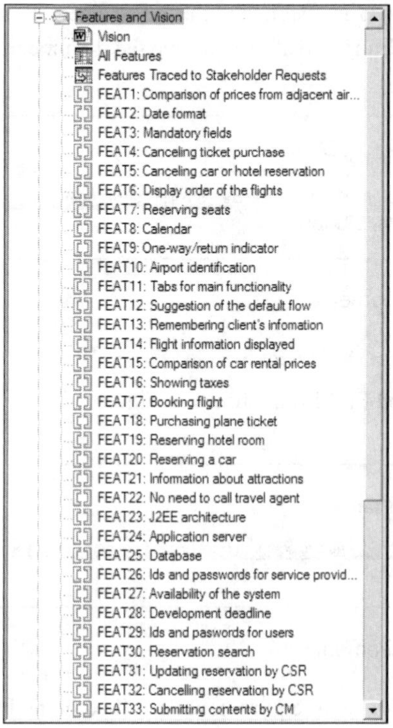

Figure 6.8   Features in the Explorer.

6.6   Traceability

Traceability is a technique used to provide relationships between requirements and design and implementation of a system. Thanks to traceability, we can follow the life of a requirement in both a forward and backward direction. This technique allows you to trace the origins of any requirement. When a requirement changes, traceability helps you analyze the impact of this change on other requirements.

The requirements pyramid was introduced in Chapter 1. Most often, we use traceability to capture relationships between requirements of adjacent layers:

- STRQ to FEAT
- FEAT to UC
- FEAT to SUPL

Usually a requirement becomes more specific as you move down the pyramid. For example:

Stakeholder Request: Data should be persistent.

Feature: A relational database should be used to store the data.

Supplementary Requirement: The Oracle 9i database should be used to store the data.

The main purposes of traceability are as follows:

- To verify that the implementation fulfills requirements (all requested functionality was implemented and tested)
- To verify that the application does only what was intended (all implemented functionality was requested)
- To help change management (analyze the impact of requirements change)

The traceability structure (which traceability items are traced to which) is established in the Requirements Management Plan.

You may find different interpretations of "Trace To" and "Trace From" in different sources. These interpretations determine in which direction the arrows point. Even the two sample projects included in RequisitePro (QuarterByte Savings Bank Example and Learning Project) use different conventions. In RequisitePro version 2003, the "Learning Project—Use Cases" requirements trace from derived requirement to source requirement. In "Learning Project—Traditional," requirements trace from source requirement to derived requirement. This book assumes that a source requirement is traced to a derived requirement, so STRQ is traced to FEAT, FEAT is traced to UC, and so on. Some recent publications and RequisitePro classes on rational.net use different interpretations. The derived requirement traces to a source requirement, so UC traces to FEAT, and FEAT traces to STRQ. However, it does not matter which convention you use in your project, as long as you use it consistently for every traceability in the same project.

The traceability structure described in this book and used in our sample project is shown in Figure 6.9.

Many projects use a simplified version of this structure, without scenarios and test cases, as shown in Figure 6.10.

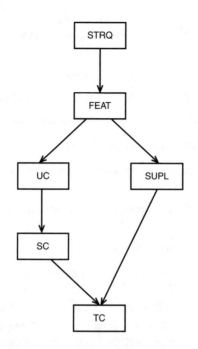

Figure 6.9 Traceability structure consistent with the pyramid from Figure 1.1.

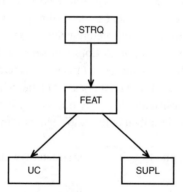

Figure 6.10 Traceability structure with stakeholder requests, features, use cases, and supplementary requirements.

Other projects may have additional traceability items—for example, PROB (Problems with existing solution)—traced to STRQ, as shown in Figure 6.11. This approach makes sense only if these items describe generic high-level problems such as "The current system is too complicated to learn" and not specific defects of the system. If the problem is related to defect management, it should be stored in ClearQuest and linked to the corresponding requirements in RequisitePro, rather than being created directly in RequisitePro.

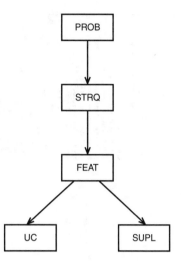

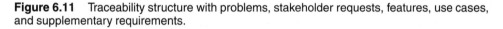

Figure 6.11 Traceability structure with problems, stakeholder requests, features, use cases, and supplementary requirements.

6.7 Views

RequisitePro provides a visual representation of traceability in two types of views: the Traceability Matrix and the Traceability Tree. The Traceability Matrix presents relationships between two requirement types. The Traceability Tree shows a view for the whole project.

The Traceability Matrix view shows relationships between requirements of the same or different types. The matrix is used to create, view, modify, and delete traceability relationships.

Accessing a Previously Created View

Some views are already created as part of a template that you chose while creating a project. For example, the Use Case template has a predefined view. Depending on the version of RequisitePro that you use, it may be located in different packages. In an older version the Traceability Matrix view called "Features to Stakeholders Requests" is in the "Features and Vision" package. In version 2003 it is called "Features Traced to Stakeholder Request" and is located in the "Coverage" analysis package. To display this view in the View workplace, do the following:

1. Double-click the view icon in the Explorer.

   The view opens. You may need to resize the parts of the view to see the full names of the requirements, as shown in Figure 6.12.

The Traceability Matrix contains all Features in rows and all Stakeholders Requests in columns. This view is used to create, modify, view, and delete traceability relationships.

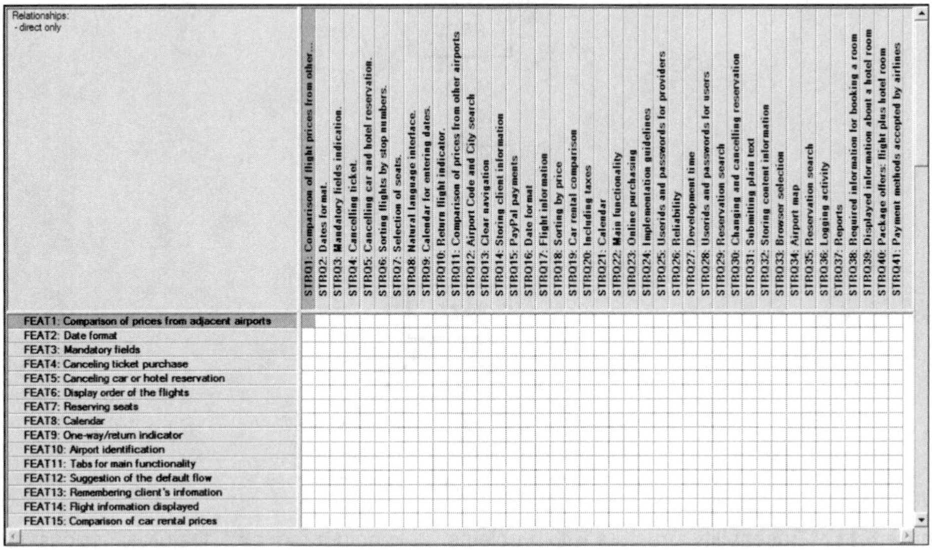

Figure 6.12   Traceability Matrix showing all features and stakeholder requests.

Setting a Traceability Link

To set a traceability link, do the following:

1. Right-click the intersection of a row and column.

2. Select the Traced From option. (If you use a different interpretation of the direction of traceability, select the Trace To option.)

   Figure 6.13 shows some traceability links between STRQ and FEAT.

Deleting a Traceability Link

To delete a traceability link, do the following:

1. Right-click the link.

2. Select Delete Trace.

Modifying Requirements in the View

You can modify requirements from the Matrix view:

1. Right-click a requirement (either row or column).

2. Select Properties.

3. Modify the properties.

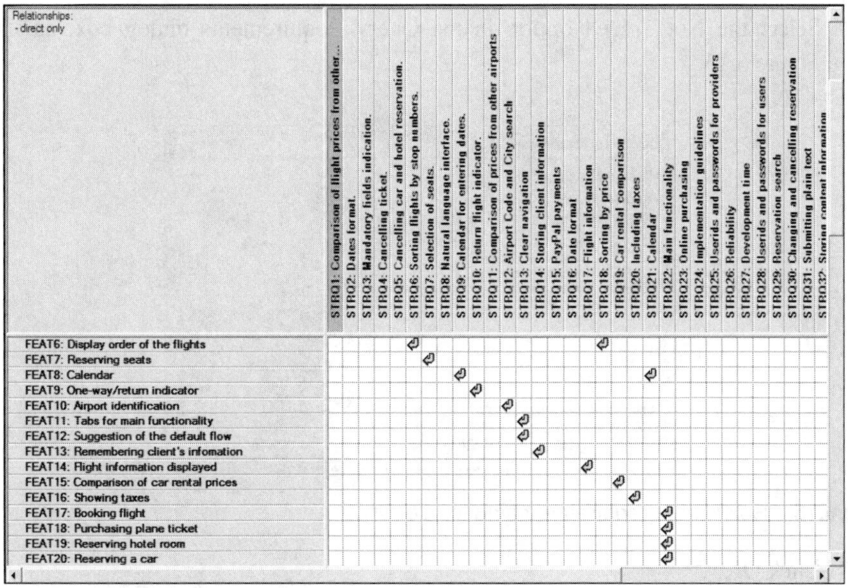

Figure 6.13 Traceability Matrix showing traceability links.

Queries

You can use queries to filter and sort information in any view. For example, let's display all STRQ requirements that are not traced to FEAT:

1. Right-click the upper-left square of the view.

2. Select Query Column Requirements.

3. Select the attribute Traced-to, as shown in Figure 6.14.

Figure 6.14 Selecting attributes for a filter.

4. Select the Not Traced option in the Query Requirements dialog box, as shown in Figure 6.15.

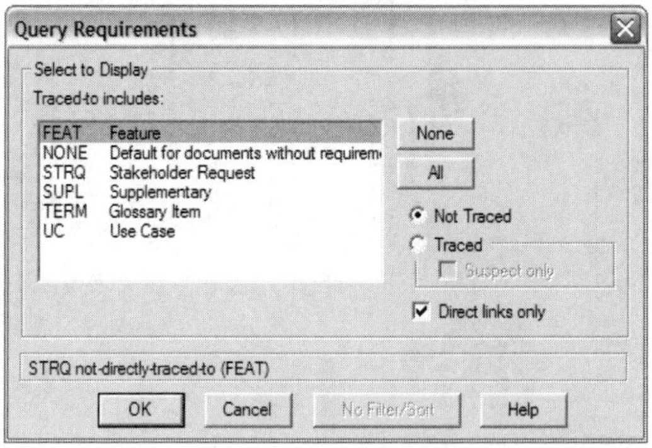

Figure 6.15   Selecting a requirement type for a query.

5. Click OK.

The Query Column Requirements dialog box is displayed with one criterion, as shown in Figure 6.16. You can add more filter criteria.

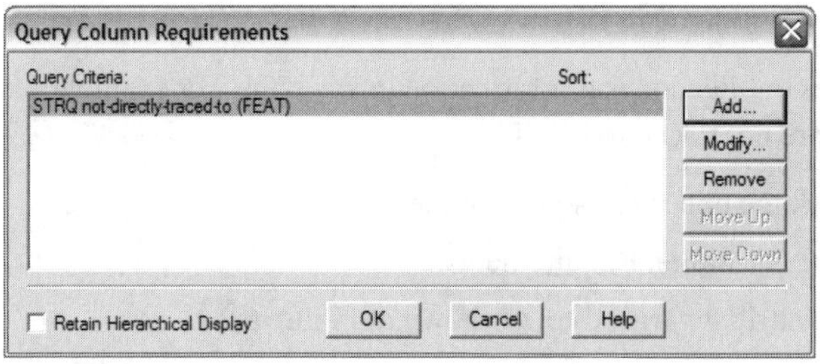

Figure 6.16   Query criteria.

6. Click OK.

The view displays only the columns that do not have a "trace-to" arrow, as shown in Figure 6.17. These stakeholder requests should be reviewed to be sure that only requirements that were canceled are shown.

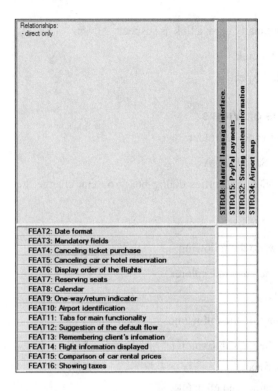

Figure 6.17 Output from a query.

Suspect Traceability

When the requirement is changed, RequisitePro automatically marks all the links related to this requirement as suspect. A suspect link means that related requirements should be analyzed because the change may affect them. Suspect links are marked with a diagonal red line in the Traceability Matrix and Traceability Tree:

After reviewing requirements flagged by a suspect link and incorporating the required changes, you should clear the link.

To remove suspect traceability, do the following:

1. Right-click the cell.

2. Select Clear Suspect.

You can also manually mark a link as suspect:

1. Right-click the link.
2. Select Mark Suspect.

Other Operations on Views

You can copy a view to another folder:

1. Select File > Save View As.
2. Update the View Properties dialog box. You can change the Name, Description, and Package.
3. Click OK.

To delete a view, do the following:

1. Right-click the view in Explorer.
2. Select Delete.

To rename a view, do the following:

1. Right-click the view in Explorer.
2. Select Properties.
3. Change the name, and click OK.

Traceability Tree

A Traceability Tree shows relationships to or from root requirements of a specific type. Branches of the tree can be collapsed or expanded. The Traceability Matrix shows only the traceability links between two requirement types, but the Traceability Tree displays all requirements in the project that are traced to or traced from a requirement.

Let's create a Traceability Tree to display STRQ and FEAT requirements:

1. Highlight the folder where you want to create a view (Features and Vision may be a choice for our view).
2. Select File > New > View.
3. In the View Properties dialog box, shown in Figure 6.18, enter a name for and description of the view.
4. Select View Type Traceability Tree (Traced into). There are two types of Traceability Trees: Traced into and Traced out of. The differences are shown in the following examples.

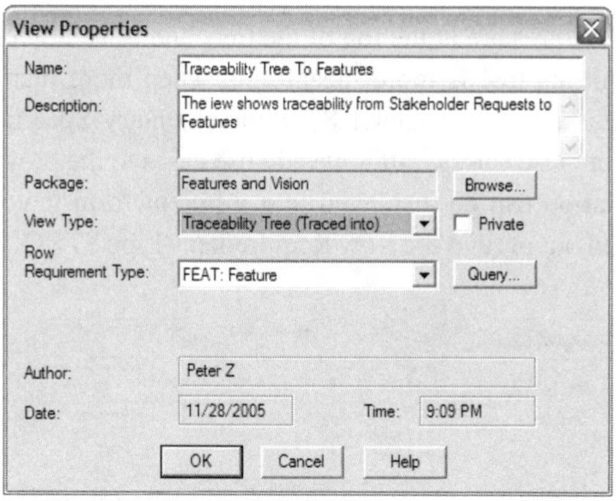

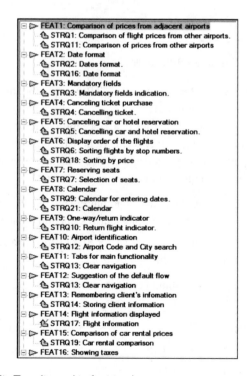

Figure 6.18   View properties for the Traceability Tree.

5. Select Row Requirement Type—in this case, FEAT.

6. Click OK. The Traceability Tree is displayed, as shown in Figure 6.19.

Figure 6.19   Traceability Tree (traced to features).

In this example, Features are at the top of the tree, and Stakeholder Requests are branches of the tree. The view in this tree is more meaningful when more than two requirement types are involved. We will view this in Chapter 8, "Supplementary Specification," and Chapter 9, "Creating Test Cases from Use Cases," after we add use cases to the project.

The same information can be displayed in a different form if you select the View Type Traceability Tree (Traced out of) and the Row Requirement Type STRQ, as shown in Figure 6.20.

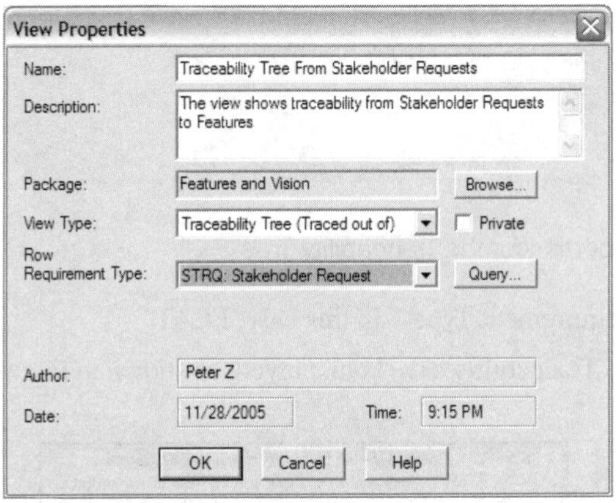

Figure 6.20   View properties for the Traceability Tree.

Now the Stakeholder Request Requirements (STRQ) are at the top of the tree, and Features form the branches, as shown in Figure 6.21.

You can view a requirement's properties in a Traceability Tree by highlighting the requirement. The properties are shown as view-only on the right part of the screen. To update properties, you need to open the Properties dialog box (right-click the requirement and select Properties).

Traceability views help you quickly find certain problems:

- A Use Case (UC) or Supplementary Requirement (SUPL) is not traced from any requirement (this means that you implemented something that was not requested).

- A Feature (FEAT) is not traced to any UC or SUPL (this means that you did not implement some requested functionality).

To help with this analysis, you should create views representing appropriate queries, such as these:

- All STRQ not traced to FEAT
- All FEAT not traced to US or SUPL
- All FEAT not traced from STRQ

- All UC not traced from FEAT
- All SUPL not traced from FEAT

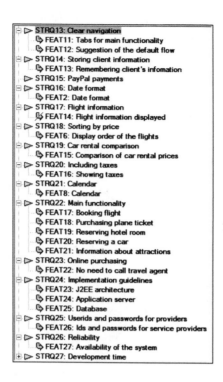

Figure 6.21 Traceability Tree (traced from stakeholder requests).

6.8 Summary

This chapter discussed how to derive features from stakeholder requests and how to present them in a Vision document. The structure of this document was presented. This chapter also introduced the concept of traceability and discussed how you can present it using RequisitePro views.

Reference

[RUP04] *Rational Unified Process*, Version 2003.06.13, IBM, 2003.

CHAPTER 7

Creating Use Cases

A **use case** is a description of a system in terms of a sequence of actions. It should yield an observable result or value for the actor interacting with the system. Following are some characteristics of use cases:

- They are initiated by an actor.
- They model an interaction between an actor and the system.
- They describe a sequence of actions.
- They capture functional requirements.
- They should provide some value to an actor.
- They represent a complete and meaningful flow of events.

The purpose of a use case is to facilitate agreement between developers, customers, and users about what the system should do. A use case may be used as a contract between developers and customers. It's also a basis for use case realizations, which play a major role in design. Furthermore, you can derive user documentation from use cases. Use cases may also be useful in planning the technical content of iterations and give system developers a better understanding of the system's purpose.

While creating use cases, we shall also define **scenarios**—specific paths through a use case. You can produce sequence diagrams, communication diagrams, and class diagrams from scenarios. They are also used as an input for test cases.

In the requirements pyramid, shown in Figure 7.1, use cases are one level below features, and scenarios are one level below use cases.

Use cases are a good way to express functional requirements of the system. The use case model contains all the use cases, actors who interact with use cases, and relationships between them. It defines interactions between the system and actors.

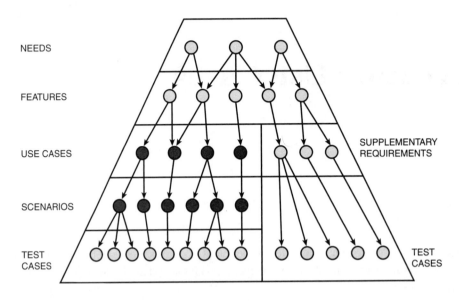

Figure 7.1   Use cases in the requirements pyramid.

7.1   Identifying Actors

An **actor** is someone or something that interacts with the system. It may be a person, but it also may be another system. Here are some examples:

- Users of the system
- Administrators
- Management
- People providing information for the system
- External systems providing data
- External systems that are notified

All stakeholders of the system are also candidates to be actors. Chapter 5, "Requirements Elicitation," identified the following stakeholders:

- Travel Agency Owner
- User 1 (from the U.S.)
- User 2 (from France)
- Developer
- Content Manager

- Customer Service Representative
- Administrator
- Hotel Provider, Car Rental Agent, Airline Representative

Let's review them and see who is also an actor:

- Travel Agency Owner may be an actor if he enacts some use cases specific to him. It depends on whether the owner has any specific privileges and if any system functionality is available only to the owner. If he has access to the same functionality as Administrator, there is no need to create a separate actor for Travel Agency Owner because actor Administrator covers it.

- User 1 and User 2 can be combined into one actor. Because the word "user" is too generic, let's call the person Traveler. Actor defines a role, not a specific person, so there is only one actor for all people having the same role.

- We still need an actor called User, who will comprise all people having access to the system. Use cases, such as Register or Log In, will be applicable to this actor. Many actors will inherit functionality from User.

- Developer is not an actor, because after the system is created, developers do not interact with it.

- Content Manager is an actor who provides the content through an interface.

- Customer Service Representative is an actor who has special access to the system information.

- Administrator is an actor who performs administrative tasks.

- Hotel Provider, Car Rental Agent, and Airline Representative may be considered three separate actors or one actor called Service Provider. It depends on how the use cases they perform differ. The decision may be made later in the process.

An additional actor is the *Airline Reservation System*. It does not initiate any use cases, but it receives the information generated during the reservation process.

Some use cases may be initiated not by a person, but according to a schedule (such as a nightly batch initiated every day at a specific hour). In this case we can show on the diagrams an actor Timer initiating these use cases. You can also call this actor System Clock, Time, or any other name that clearly indicates that the use case will start at a specific moment.

7.2 Identifying Use Cases

Here are some questions that can help identify use cases:

- What functionality does each actor expect from the system?
- Do actors need to be informed about the events occurring in the system?

- What information do actors need to supply to the system?
- What information do actors need to receive from the system?
- About what events outside the system does the system need to be notified?

Use cases can be identified during a requirements workshop.
Here are some guidelines for creating use cases:

- Each use case shall interact with at least one actor.
- Each use case shall be initiated by an actor.
- The names of use cases shall be meaningful. Use *Search Reservation* and *Search Traveler* rather than *Search 1* and *Search 2*. Never have two use cases with the same name. Names shall be understood not only by the development team, but also by customers and users.
- Use cases shall describe functionality, not the implementation. "Create Session Bean" is not a good use case.
- It shall be clear who initiates the use case.

Also keep in mind that use cases cannot be too small or too big. For example, *Submit credit card information* is not a correct use case because it does not represent a complete flow of events and does not provide any value to the actor. It is just one step in the bigger use case *Purchase a ticket*. If the use case has only one or two steps, it is probably not a correct use case.

As another example, the use case *Maintain administrative tasks* is too generic and may be split into a few meaningful use cases such as *Run report* or *Update user information*.

The following use cases were found for each of the actors in our project:

- **User**
  - Register
  - Log in
- **Traveler**
  - Book a flight
  - Purchase a ticket
  - Reserve a hotel room
  - Find attractions
  - Reserve a car
- **Customer Service Representative**
  - Log in
  - Change reservation
  - Delete reservation
  - Search reservation

- **Administrator**
  - Register user
  - Search for a user
  - Update user information
  - Log in
  - Run report
- **Content Manager**
  - Log in
  - Submit information
- **Hotel Provider**
  - Log in
  - Submit information

- **Car Provider**
  - Log in
  - Submit information

- **Airline Representative**
  - Log in
  - Submit information

The Airline Reservation System does not initiate any use cases.

7.3   Use Case Diagrams

Use case diagrams represent actors, use cases, and the relationships between them. You can design these diagrams using IBM Rational Rose, IBM Rational Software Architect, Microsoft Visio, and many other tools.

In a use case diagram, shown in Figure 7.2, actors are represented as stick figures, and use cases are represented as ovals. The solid arrow indicates a communication path between an actor and a use case.

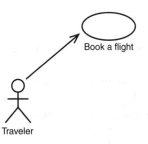

Figure 7.2   An actor and a use case.

Use case diagrams illustrate relationships in the use case model. For small systems, the whole use case model may be presented in one diagram. For big systems, we need to split the whole system into many diagrams. There are no strict rules about how the model should be split. Here are some options for what can be grouped in one diagram:

- All use cases initiated by the same actor or group of actors
- Use cases that are usually executed in a given sentence
- Use cases related to the same type of tasks (such as administrative tasks)

Figures 7.3 through 7.5 present initial use case diagrams for the Online Travel Agency project.

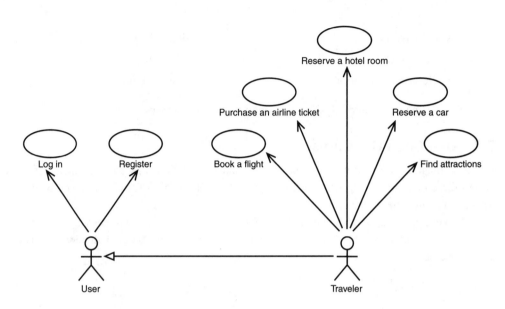

Figure 7.3   Use cases initiated by actors Traveler and User.

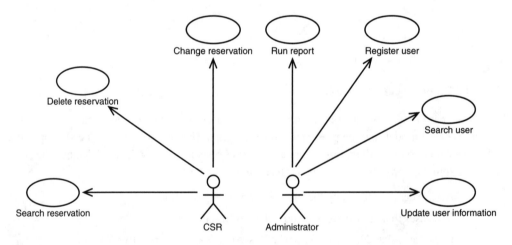

Figure 7.4   Use cases for actors Customer Service Representative and Administrator.

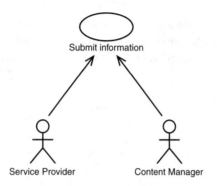

Figure 7.5   A use case initiated by the Service Provider and Content Manager.

7.4   Structuring the Use Case Model

After the initial use case model is done, we can structure it. The main purpose of structuring the model is to remove any redundancy, making the use cases easier to understand and maintain. First, we need to analyze use cases and find any parts of the flows that contain similar steps. Then we can apply some of the three types of relationships between use cases:

- Include
- Extend
- Generalization

We can apply generalization to use cases as well as to actors.

If two use cases are always activated in the same sequence, we may consider combining them. For example, because use case *Purchase an airline ticket* comes after *Book a flight*, we have decided to merge them.

If the use case is too complicated, we can consider splitting it. One technique to decide when a use case should be split is to look at alternatives. When there is an alternative path for an alternative path, usually this means that the use case is becoming too complex. This is a sign that the use case is a candidate to be split into two different use cases, one extending the base use case.

However, if the use case has many steps that are always performed together in the same sequence, it should not be split into two use cases.

Include Relationship

If a significant part of the flow is used in more than one use case, it is a good candidate to be extracted as a separate use case that is connected with an *include* relationship. The use case instance will contain a base use case as well as the included one. The included use case should be self-contained and cannot make any assumptions about which use case is including it.

To show this relationship in a use case diagram, you need to create a dependency between the two use cases (using a dashed arrow) and then assign an include stereotype to the dependency, as shown in Figure 7.6. The direction of the arrow is from the base use case to the included use case.

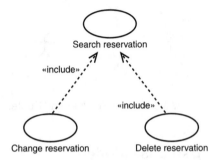

Figure 7.6   An include relationship between two use cases.

Extend Relationship

If some part of the use case is optional or conditional, to make the model more clear, we can extract it as a separate use case that is connected with an **extend** relationship. Reading the extending use case shall not be necessary to understand the purpose of the base use case.

To show an extend relationship in a use case diagram, create a dependency between the use cases, and then assign an extend stereotype to the dependency. The arrow points to the base use case, as shown in Figure 7.7.

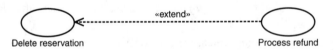

Figure 7.7   An extend relationship between two use cases.

Generalization Relationship Between Use Cases

If two or more use cases are similar, we can extract similarities into the base use case. Derived use cases can add behavior and modify behavior defined in the base use case. The parent use case does not need to know what children are specializations of it. However, because this technique may be hard for stakeholders to understand, IBM Rational suggests avoiding using use case generalization.

Figure 7.8 shows how use case generalization is presented in use case diagrams.

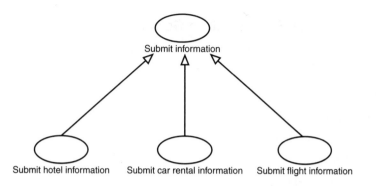

Figure 7.8   Generalization between use cases.

Generalization Relationship Between Actors

Generalization can be also used between actors. It is especially useful if a set of actors initiate the same use cases. Figure 7.9 shows how actor generalization is presented in use case diagrams.

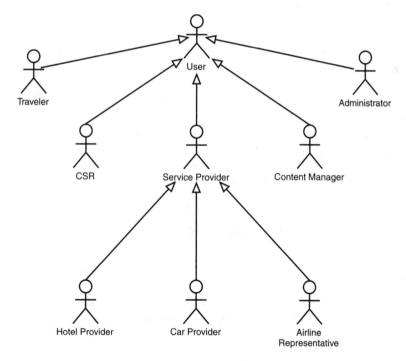

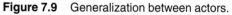

Figure 7.9   Generalization between actors.

7.5   The Use Case Specification Document

This book uses the following format for a Use Case Specification document:

1. Brief description
2. Basic flow
3. Alternative flows

    3.1 Alternative flow 1

    3.2 Alternative flow 2

4. Special requirements
5. Preconditions
6. Postconditions
7. Extension points
8. Context diagram
9. Activity diagram
10. State machine diagrams
11. Scenarios

This outline contains some differences compared to a use case template included in RequisitePro:

- Basic flow and alternative flows are split into separate sections to avoid three levels of numbering.
- Context, activity, and state machine diagrams are added.
- Scenarios are added.

The following sections discuss all parts of a use case.

Brief Description

The description shall clearly explain its purpose. You shall also mention all the actors who interact with the use case.

Basic Flow

The **basic flow** contains the most popular sequence of actions—the steps that happen when everything goes correctly. In our Online Travel Agency project, the basic flow of the use case *Book a flight* might look like this:

B1.   Traveler enters the site's URL.

B2.   System displays the home page.

B3.   Traveler enters the following:

  • Departure airport, date, time

  • Arrival airport, date, time

  • Number of traveling adults and children

  Traveler selects "Search flights."

B4.   System displays outbound flights sorted by price.

B5.   Traveler selects a flight.

B6.   System displays return flights.

B7.   Traveler selects a return flight.

B8.   System displays details of the flight.

B9.   Traveler confirms the flight.

B10. User provides a userid and password to proceed with buying a ticket.

B11. Traveler provides passenger information.

B12. System displays available seats.

B13. Traveler selects seats.

B14. Traveler provides credit card information and billing address.

B15. System provides a confirmation number.

Alternative Flows

Alternative flows represent variations of the flow, including less usual cases and error conditions. The following questions can help find alternative flows:

  • What other action can be taken at each step of the basic flow?

  • What errors can occur in each step (wrong data, missing data, connection problems)?

  • Is there a behavior that can happen at any time (such as exit, print, help)?

  • Will any conditions (such as a specific combination of entered data) significantly change the flow?

In the literature you will find two words used to describe these flows. Some sources use the word **alternative**, and others use **alternate**. Both words are correct, and they are used as synonyms.

This book uses the following convention to name the flows:

  • Basic flow: B

  • Alternative flows: A1, A2, A3,...

  • Steps in a basic flow: B1, B2, B3,...

- Steps in alternative flow 1: A1.1, A1.2, A1.3,...
- Steps in alternative flow 2: A2.1, A2.2, A2.3,...

There is no universal standard for how to number the steps in a use case. Some people use sequential numbers 1, 2, 3..., and others use 2.1, 2.2, 2.3... (because it is in section 2 of the document). Some people do not number steps at all. I do not recommend this approach because that would make it difficult to refer to specific steps.

Here are the alternative flows for the use case *Book a flight*:

A1.   Comparison of flights from nearby airports

    A1.1.   In step B3 the Traveler selects the option "Compare surrounding airports."

    A1.2.   The system shows a list of airports within 100 miles of the departure and destination airports.

    A1.3.   The Traveler selects which airports shall be considered.

    A1.4.   The flow returns to step B4 of the basic flow.

A2.   Sorting the flights

    A2.1.   After step B4 the Traveler changes the sorting of the flights.

    A2.2.   The system presents the flights sorted by a selected criterion.

    A2.3.   The flow returns to step B5 of the basic flow.

A3.   Saving the itinerary

    A3.1.   After step B8 the Traveler selects an option to save the itinerary and exit.

    A3.2.   The system returns to the home page.

    A3.3.   The use case ends.

A4.   Going back to return flight selection

    A4.1.   After step B8 the Traveler returns to return flight selection.

    A4.2.   The flow returns to step B6 of the basic flow.

A5.   Going back to outbound flight selection

    A5.1.   After step B8 the Traveler returns to outbound flight selection.

    A5.2.   The flow returns to step B4 of the basic flow.

A6.   New user

    A6.1.   After step B9 the Traveler selects the option New User.

    A6.2.   The system prompts for user information.

    A6.3.   The Traveler registers by providing first and last name, address, e-mail address, and selected password.

    A6.4.   The system confirms that the e-mail address is unique and will be treated as the user ID.

    A6.5.   The flow returns to step B11 of the basic flow.

A7. *New user ID is not available*

    A7.1. After step A6.3 of alternative flow A6, the system returns a message that the supplied e-mail ID is already taken.

    A7.2. The Traveler provides a new e-mail address.

    A7.3. The flow returns to step A6.4.

A8. *Wrong password*

    A8.1. After step B10 of the basic flow, the system returns an error message saying that the password is wrong.

    A8.2. The Traveler supplies the correct combination of e-mail and password.

    A8.3. The flow returns to step B11 of the basic flow.

The alternative flows shall have unique sequences of actions; they cannot differ just in data. For example, if alternative flow A1 had no extra step in which the Traveler selects airports, it would not be a good candidate for an alternative flow:

A1. *Comparison of flights from nearby airports*

    A1.1. In step B3 the Traveler selects the option "Compare surrounding airports."

    A1.2. The system displays outbound flights that include flights from airports within 100 miles of the selected departure and destination airports.

    A1.3. Flow returns to step B5 of the basic flow.

This flow should not be extracted as a separate alternative flow because the sequence of steps is the same as in the basic flow. The difference is only in the data. On the input screen an additional option is selected, and on the output screen additional flights are presented. However, this case should be considered as a separate test case while deriving test cases from this use case (see Chapter 10, "Creating Test Cases from Supplementary Requirements").

While structuring the use case model, we may consider making two changes:

- Because the functionality of logging in may be used in other use cases, step B10 and alternative flow A8 can be extracted into a separate use case called *Login*.

- Because we have an alternative flow (A7) of another alternative flow (A6), the structure of the use case becomes quite complex. To avoid this, we can extract the functionality of A6 and A7 into a separate use case called *Register*.

Special Requirements

The Special Requirements section contains all the requirements related to this use case that were not covered by the flows of events. Usually these are nonfunctional requirements. However, if a requirement is generic and applies to many use cases, it shall be described in a Supplementary Specification.

Preconditions

A **precondition** is the system's state before the use case can start. For example, a precondition to the use case *Search reservation* may be *Administrator must be logged into the system.*

Postconditions

A **postcondition** is the system's state after the use case ends. Unless it's specifically mentioned, a postcondition shall be valid for any alternative flows, not just for the basic flow.

Extension Points

An **extension** point is a place from which an extending use case can be invoked. For example, the use case *Delete reservation* may have the following extension:

> Name: Process refund
>
> Location: After step B5 of the basic flow

Context Diagram

A **context diagram**, shown in Figure 7.10, is part of a use case diagram showing the relationships of this particular use case to actors and other use cases. All use cases having include, extend, or generalization relationships with the given use case should also be shown on the context diagram.

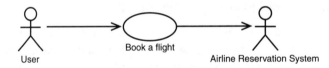

Figure 7.10   A context diagram for the use case *Book a flight.*

The context diagram and the activity diagram are not necessary, but they help you visualize the use case and its position in the project.

Activity Diagram

An **activity diagram**, shown in Figure 7.11, is similar to a flow chart. It can be used to graphically represent flows in the use case. Boxes with rounded corners represent activity states, arrows represent transitions, and branches are modeled as diamonds. One activity diagram should contain the basic flow and all alternative flows. Steps that do not have any branches in between may be combined.

It is good practice to represent a basic flow as a straight line, while portraying alternative flows as loops or branches.

Activity diagrams can be created easily using various modeling tools, such as Rational Rose, Rational Software Architect, Rational Data Architect, Rational Software Modeler.

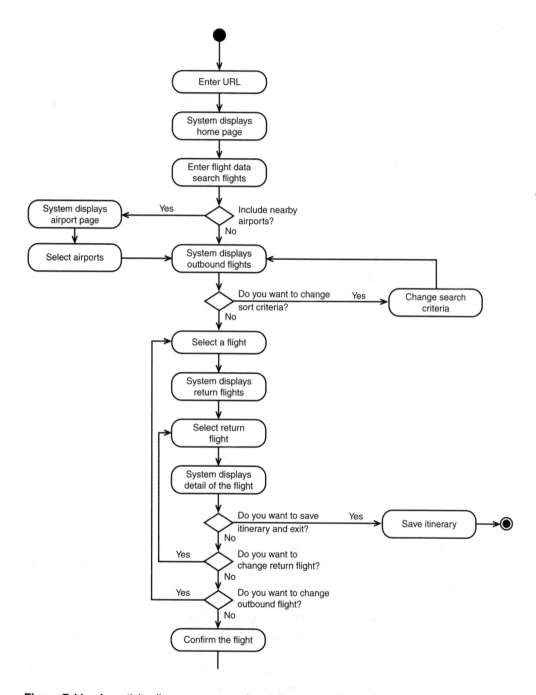

Figure 7.11   An activity diagram representing the use case *Book a flight. (continues)*

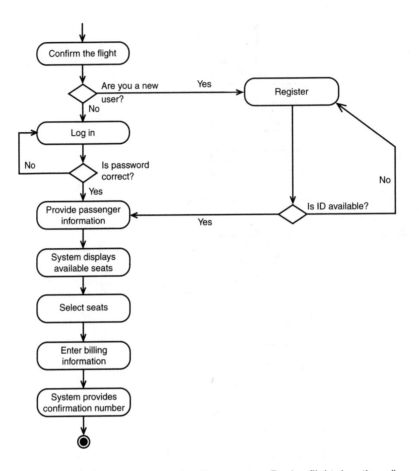

Figure 7.11   An activity diagram representing the use case *Book a flight. (continued)*

State Machine Diagrams

Sometimes we may need to describe the behavior of objects that act differently depending on their state. In this case we can use UML 2 **state machine diagrams** [AMB04]. In previous versions of UML, these diagrams were called state chart diagrams, and in other modeling languages, they are called state-transition diagrams or just state diagrams.

UML state machine diagrams depict the various states that an object may be in and the transitions between those states. For example, an object Flight may be in the state Reserved or Booked.

The rounded rectangles represent states. The arrows represent transitions from one state to another triggered by an event. Dark circles represent initial and final states.

This section of the use case document is optional.

Scenarios

A **scenario** is an instance of a use case. It describes one specific path through the flow of events. It is important to identify all valid scenarios for every use case. They will be used for analysis and design, as well as to derive test cases from the use cases. The next section discusses how to find all the scenarios.

7.6 Scenarios

To find all the scenarios, we need to identify all paths through the given use case. Figure 7.12 shows a hypothetical graph representing a use case with a basic flow B and alternative flows A1, A2, A3, and A4. To find all scenarios, we need to draw all possible lines through this graph.

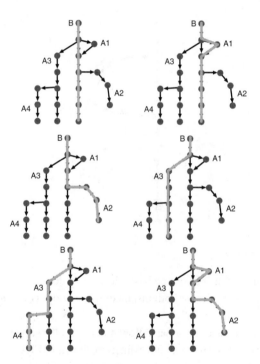

Figure 7.12   Finding scenarios in a use case.

There is one scenario for a basic flow, one scenario for each alternative flow, and one scenario for each combination of alternative flows. There are more scenarios than alternative flows because there is one for A1, another one for A2, and one scenario that will be a combination of these two.

The easiest way to describe a scenario is to provide a sequence of alternative flows. For example, do flow A3 and then A4:

SC5: A3, A4

We do not need to add B showing the basic flow because almost all scenarios start with the basic flow anyway.

Another way to describe a scenario is to list all its steps, but this is both more difficult and unnecessarily detailed:

SC5: B1, B2, A3.1, A3.2, A3.3, A4.1, A4.4, A4.3

What should you do if you have infinite loops (loops going backwards)? Theoretically, this would generate an infinite number of scenarios. Figure 7.13 shows an infinite loop.

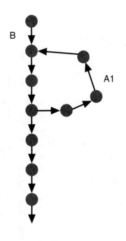

Figure 7.13   An infinite loop.

The reasonable approach is to do the basic flow once, do a loop once, and then do a loop a second time. If the program works for both instances of the loop, you can assume it will work for many loops.

The *Book a flight* use case has a basic flow and eight alternative flows, as shown in Table 7.1. Figure 7.14 was derived from the activity diagram shown in Figure 7.11. Five of the alternative flows are going backwards, and the other three are going forward. If you wanted to describe all possible alternative flow combinations, you would have a few thousand scenarios. Obviously you do not need to do all of them.

Table 7.1 Flows in the *Book a Flight* Use Case

Flow ID	Name
B	Basic flow
A1	Comparison of flights from nearby airports
A2	Sorting the flights
A3	Saving the itinerary and exiting
A4	Going back to return flight selection
A5	Going back to outbound flight selection
A6	New user
A7	New user ID is not available
A8	Wrong password

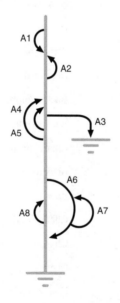

Figure 7.14 A diagram showing basic and alternative flows.

Choose which scenarios represent a reasonable subset of these eight thousand scenarios. Usually it is wise to select a basic flow, one scenario covering each alternative flow, and some reasonable combinations of alternative flows. Using the flows from Table 7.1, it probably will not make sense to add a scenario that contains both flows A1 and A8 because they are so far apart on the diagram that they do not have any influence on each other. But it makes sense to do A1 and A2 because they are immediately after each other and may be related.

Table 7.2 illustrates the selected scenarios: one representing the basic flow, eight representing each alternative flow, and 13 reflecting some combination of the flows.

Table 7.2   Scenarios Selected for Testing in the *Book a Flight* Use Case

Number	Sequence of Flows	Description
Scenario 1	B	
Scenario 2	A1	Nearby airports
Scenario 3	A2	Sorting
Scenario 4	A3	Saving and exiting
Scenario 5	A4	Back to return flight selection
Scenario 6	A5	Back to outbound flight selection
Scenario 7	A6	New user
Scenario 8	A6, A7	User ID not available
Scenario 9	A8	Wrong password
Scenario 10	A1, A2	Nearby airport, then sorting
Scenario 11	A1, A5	Back to outbound flight selection with nearby airports
Scenario 12	A1, A4	Back to return flight with nearby airports
Scenario 13	A2, A2	Changing sorting sequence twice
Scenario 14	A4, A3	Back to return flight, then save
Scenario 15	A4, A5	Back to return flight, then back to beginning
Scenario 16	A5, A4	Change outbound flight, then change return flight
Scenario 17	A5, A3	Change outbound flight, then save
Scenario 18	A4, A4	Change return flight twice
Scenario 19	A5, A5, A4	Change outbound flight twice, then return flight once
Scenario 20	A5, A5, A3	Change outbound flight twice, then save
Scenario 21	A6, A7, A7	Unavailable ID twice
Scenario 22	A8, A8	Wrong password twice

7.7   Use Cases in RequisitePro

The Use Case Specification document is created from a template containing parts discussed in the preceding section. If you do not have access to RequisitePro, you can create this document in Microsoft Word. Using RequisitePro, however, gives you much more functionality, such as creating requirements of the type of use case, setting traceability, and producing related reports.

You do not need to finish the whole document at once. Creating a use case is an iterative process. As soon as the use case is identified, you can create an associated document with a brief description indicating its purpose. In the next iteration an outline can be added, then all the steps, and finally a detailed description of each step. A detailed analysis of all stages of the use case life-cycle is presented in the book *Use Case Modeling* by Kurt Bittner and Ian Spence [BIT02].

Creating the Use Case Specification

To create a Use Case Specification document in RequisitePro, you need to apply steps similar to those you used previously to create Stakeholder Requests and Vision documents:

1. In the Explorer, select the Use Cases package.

2. Select File > New > Document.

3. Fill in the fields in the Document Properties dialog box, shown in Figure 7.15. Click OK.

The outline of the document opens in Word.

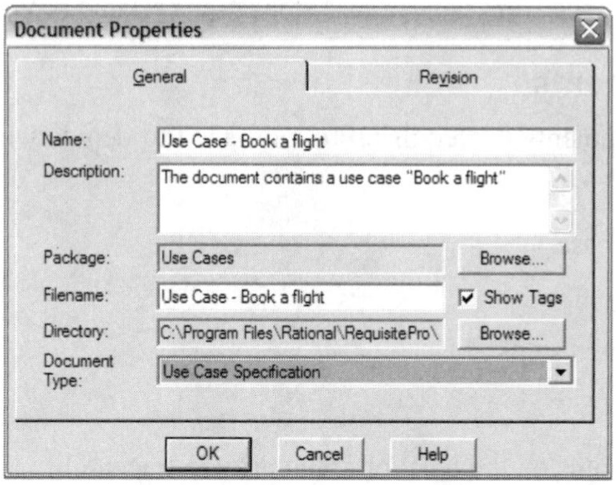

Figure 7.15   Document Properties dialog box for the use case *Book a flight*.

4. Fill out all parts of the document as discussed in section 7.5.

Prototype screens can be included to visualize some steps. However, the purpose of these screens is not to design a GUI, just to clarify what objects interact with an actor. The screen can also show sample input values.

One of the fastest ways to create such screens is to use Microsoft Excel to create a spreadsheet, and then cut and paste it into the use case document, as shown in Figure 7.16.

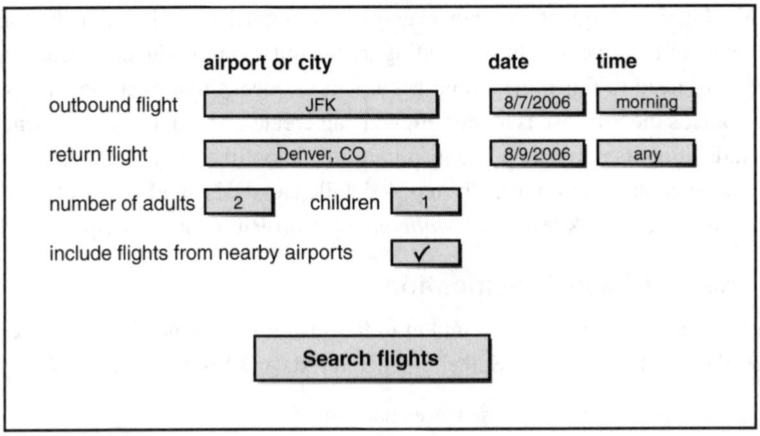

Figure 7.16   Screen prototype.

More sophisticated prototype screens may be created using Visio, Microsoft PowerPoint, Visual Basic, and many other tools.

To make updates and revisions easier, you can separate the prototype screens from the use case flow. In this case you would create an additional section (for example, Prototype Screens) and provide a clear reference from the use case steps to the related screen shots.

Creating Requirements

Before capturing requirements in RequisitePro, you need to decide what will be treated as one requirement:

- The whole use case
- Each alternative flow
- A group of related steps
- Each step

This decision depends on the level of granularity in traceability that you want to maintain. The advantage of capturing whole use cases only is limited overhead, but that approach may not be precise enough to check if all features are correctly assigned. Capturing every step as a separate requirement provides precise traceability, but it costs a lot in overhead and may obscure the main functionality with many details. Usually, treating basic and alternative flows as atomic requirements is a balanced solution. However, this decision may vary for different projects.

The process of creating use case requirements is the same one we used for STRQ and FEAT requirements:

1. Highlight the use case name.

2. Right-click and select New Requirement, or select RequisitePro > Requirement > New, or click the New Requirement icon: 🔳

   The Requirement Properties dialog box appears. On the General tab you do not need to enter anything: Type shows up by default as "UC: Use Case." There is no need to provide a Name because the Text can be used for requirement identification.

3. Click OK in the Requirements Properties dialog box.

Instead of highlighting just the use case name, you can have the requirement include the entire flow. This will allow automatic change detection if someone adds, removes, or updates any step. Any modification will result in a suspect link. You can then use the headline as the name and the flow as the description for the requirement. If you only make the headline a requirement, you need to manually mark the suspect links when you modify the flow description.

RequisitePro provides an opportunity to set a hierarchy of requirements. This is very helpful, especially in structuring the use case requirements. You can define each use case as a parent and attach all alternative flows as children. To create a child requirement, follow these steps:

1. Highlight the alternative flow name, as shown in Figure 7.17.

---

3. Alternative Flows

4.1 **A1. Comparison of flights from nearby airports.**
   A1.1. In step B3 user selects an option comp are surrounding airports."

   A1.2. The system shows a list of airports within 100 miles from the departure and destination airports.

   A1.3. The user selects which airports shall be considered.

   A1.4. Flow returns to step B4 of the basic flow.

Figure 7.17   Highlighting requirement text.

2. Right-click and select New Requirement, or select RequisitePro > Requirement > New, or click the New Requirement icon.

   The Requirement Properties dialog box appears.

3. Select the Hierarchy tab.

4. In the Parent list box, select <choose parent>.

   The Parent Requirement Browser dialog box appears, as shown in Figure 7.18.

5. Select the parent requirement.

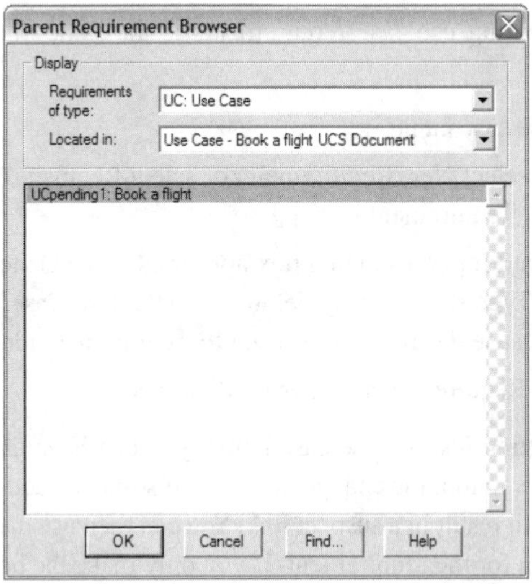

Figure 7.18   Selecting the use case name in the Parent Requirement Browser dialog box.

6. Click OK in the Parent Requirement Browser dialog box.

7. Click OK in the Requirement Properties dialog box, as shown in Figure 7.19.

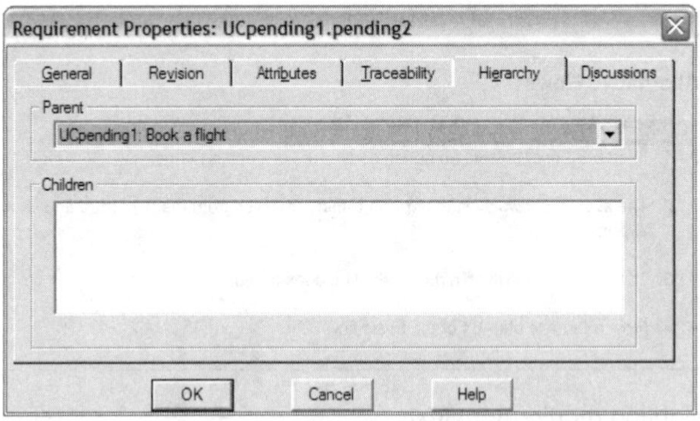

Figure 7.19   The Hierarchy tab in the Requirement Properties dialog box.

After saving the document, RequisitePro assigns a unique number to a requirement. In the case of child requirements, the number consists of the parent number, a dot, and the consecutive child number, as shown in Figure 7.20. The hierarchy of requirements can be seen in the Explorer, as shown in Figure 7.21.

---

3. **Alternative Flows**

A1.[*UC1.1 Comparison of flights from nearby airports*.]
A1.1. In step B3 user selects an option "compare surrounding airports."

A1.2. The system shows a list of airports within 100 miles from the departure and destination
        airports.

A1.3. The user selects which airports shall be considered.

A1.4. Flow returns to step B4 of the basic flow.

Figure 7.20   Child requirements numbering.

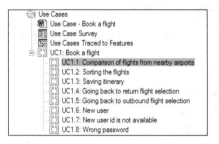

Figure 7.21   Use case hierarchy shown in the Explorer.

7.8   Creating a New Requirement Type in RequisitePro

Depending on how precisely you want to track traceability in RequisitePro, you can enter all scenarios into the system, or you may set traceability directly from use cases to test cases. The advantage of entering scenarios is more granular traceability. The disadvantage is that it creates more overhead. This section uses the approach of entering all the scenarios.

Scenario is not a standard requirement type in RequisitePro, so you need to add it as a new requirement type by following these steps:

1. In the Explorer, right-click the project and select Properties.

2. Select the Requirement Types tab.

3. Click Add.

4. Fill in the appropriate fields, as shown in Figure 7.22:

    Name: Scenario

    Requirement Tag Prefix: Can be anything, but preferably should be something meaningful, such as SC

    Requirement Color: Accept the default (Blue), or select another

    Requirement Style: Accept the default (Double Underline), or select another

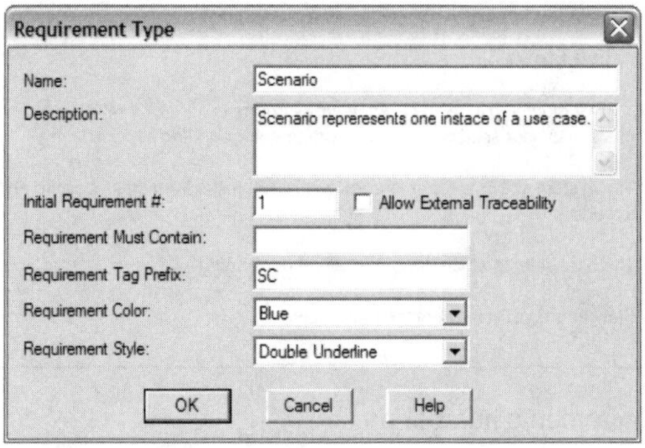

Figure 7.22   Adding a requirement type Scenario.

5. Click OK. The scenario should appear on the Requirement Types tab, as shown in Figure 7.23.

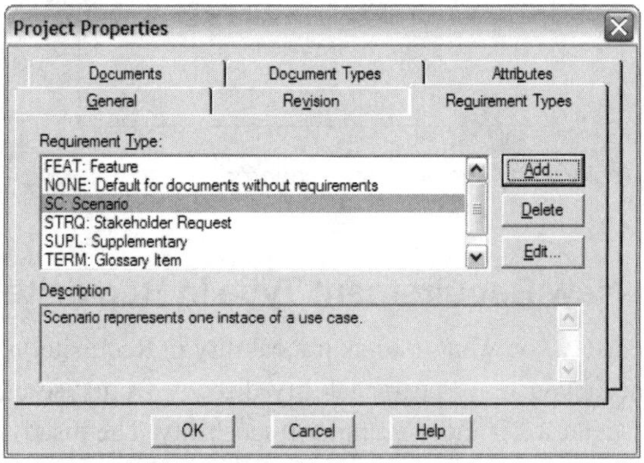

Figure 7.23   Scenario added to the list of requirement types.

7.9   Summary

Use cases play an important role in the software development process. They

- Help users and system analysts agree on the system's functionality.
- May be used as a contract between customer and development team.
- Are a basis for system design, documentation, and test cases.

The first step in use case modeling is identifying actors and use cases and presenting them on the use case diagrams.

To remove redundancy in the use case model, you can extract some use cases and apply one of three relationships: include, extend, or generalization. However, you need to be careful not to create unnecessary relationships that will only obscure the model. If you can express the functionality using only nonredundant alternative flows, extracting use cases and applying relationships is unnecessary. You especially should avoid long chains of include and extend relationships.

The use case is described in the Use Case Specification document. Its parts were described in section 7.5. The most important part is the description of a basic flow and alternative flows as a sequence of actors interacting with the system.

Creating the Use Case Specification document and requirements for the use case type follows the same steps we discussed for creating other documents and requirements.

This chapter introduced the requirements hierarchy. It helps organize requirements by establishing parent-child relationships. Hierarchy is quite often used for use case requirements because we can create alternative flows or separate steps as children of the main use case.

Use cases are a very convenient tool for capturing functional requirements. However, many requirements cannot be easily captured in the use case. They are stored in the Supplementary Specification, described in Chapter 8, "Supplementary Specification."

References

[AMB04] Ambler, Scott. *The Object Primer: Agile Model-Driven Development with UML 2.0*, Third Edition.

[BIT02] Bittner, Kurt, and Ian Spence. *Use Case Modeling*, Boston: Addison-Wesley Professional, 2002.

Supplementary Specification

The Supplementary Specification captures all requirements that cannot be expressed in use cases. This does not mean, however, that all functional requirements are in use cases and that all non-functional requirements are in the Supplementary Specification. The Use Case Specification also contains nonfunctional requirements if they apply to only one use case. The Supplementary Specification contains all generic functional requirements that are not associated with any specific use case. Table 8.1 illustrates what type of requirement is found in which document.

Table 8.1   Allocation of Software Requirements Between the Use Case Specification and Supplementary Specification

Requirement Type	Use Case Specification	Supplementary Specification
Functional	Basic flow and alternative flows related to a specific use case.	Functional requirements related to more than one use case.
Nonfunctional	Nonfunctional specification related to only one use case.	Nonfunctional requirements related to many use cases.

A common impression is that functional requirements are only in the Use Case Specification and that nonfunctional requirements are in the Supplementary Specification. This may be because

- Nonfunctional requirements usually apply to the system as a whole and not to any specific use case (so they are in the Supplementary Specification).
- Functional requirements are most often related to a specific flow of events (so they are in the Use Case Specification).

Supplementary requirements are also called architectural requirements [EEL01] or quality factors [LAU02]. These concepts are not completely synonymous with supplementary requirements, but they mean almost the same thing in the context of the software development process.

Recently the name of the artifact was changed in Rational Unified Process (RUP) from "Supplementary Specification" to the plural "Supplementary Specifications" to reflect the fact that we may use more than one document to capture supplementary requirements.

In the requirements pyramid, supplementary requirements are on the same level as use cases, as shown in Figure 8.1.

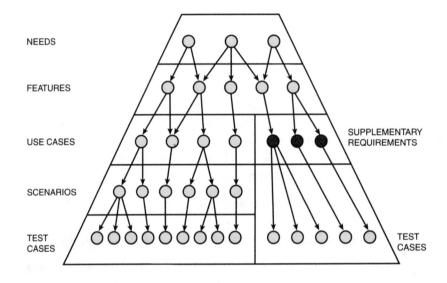

Figure 8.1   The location of supplementary requirements in the requirements pyramid.

8.1   Eliciting Supplementary Requirements

Gathering supplementary requirements is quite a challenging task because of the following:

- Customers often forget about these requirements and do not provide them unless asked.
- Customers are usually unaware of the cost of improving specific metrics.
- Nontechnical users often have trouble understanding the implications of some technical requirements.
- Some requirements are difficult to measure, such as "The system must be easy to learn."

The following approach suggested by Peter Eeles [EEL01] addresses these problems:

1. Create a list of all categories of supplementary requirements.
2. For each category, create one or more questions.

3. Explain to the customer the impact and cost of each decision.

4. Capture the customer's response to each question.

5. Assign priority or weight to each requirement.

In step 3, while explaining the impact, we need to mention the cost (a longer development time equals greater development cost).

Section 8.2 presents a sample checklist of requirements.

Most often these types of requirements are gathered using interviews and questionnaires. Usually they do not change too much while being transformed from needs to features to supplementary requirements. Eeles suggests that you create a new type of requirement, Supplementary Stakeholder's Request (SSTRQ), and distinguish this type of requirement from those already at the stakeholder requests level (the top level, called *needs* in Figure 8.1).

8.2 Classification of Supplementary Requirements

Many attempts have been made to classify supplementary requirements. One of the first classifications was published by McCall and Matsumoto [MCC80]. It is shown in Table 8.2. The International Organization for Standardization uses the classification shown in Table 8.3 [ISO91].

Table 8.2 Classification Proposed by McCall and Matsumoto

Category	Subcategory
Operation	Integrity
	Correctness
	Reliability
	Usability
	Efficiency
Revision	Maintainability
	Testability
	Flexibility
Transition	Portability
	Interoperability
	Reusability

Table 8.3   Classification Used by ISO

Category	Subcategory
Functionality	Accuracy
	Security
	Interoperability
	Suitability
	Compliance
Reliability	Maturity
	Fault tolerance
	Recoverability
Usability	Usability
Efficiency	Efficiency
Maintainability	Testability
	Changeability
	Analyzability
	Stability
Portability	Adaptability
	Conformance
	Replaceability

This book follows the classification proposed by Robert Grady [GRA92] and adapted by Rational Software. This classification is called FURPS+, which stands for Functionality, Usability, Reliability, Performance, and Supportability. The + is a placeholder for the various types of constraints: Design, Implementation, Interface, and Physical. The Software Specifications template found in the RUP [RUP04] also contains the following separate sections:

- Online User Documentation and Help System Requirements
- Purchased Components
- Licensing Requirements
- Legal, Copyright, and Other Notices
- Applicable Standards

There is some flexibility in placing these requirements:

- Online User Documentation and Help System Requirements can be included in Functionality Requirements.
- Purchased Components can be described in Implementation Constraints.
- Licensing Requirements can be combined with Legal and Copyright requirements.
- Applicable Standards can be described in Implementation Constraints or the Compliance section.

The RUP template does not list Implementation and Physical requirements as separate sections because they may be described in the Design Constraints section.

The classification proposed in this chapter is an attempt to cover many types of requirements (gathered from various classifications) and present them consistently with the FURPS+ structure (see Table 8.4). This classification includes five categories covered by FURPS, four categories covered by +, and two categories from the RUP template.

Table 8.4 Categories of Supplemental Requirements

Category	Subcategory
Functionality	
Usability	Accessibility
	Aesthetics
	UI consistency
	Ergonomics
	Ease of use
Reliability	Availability
	Robustness
	Accuracy
	Recoverability
	Fault tolerance
	Safety
	Security
	Correctness
Performance	Throughput
	Response time
	Recovery time
	Startup/shutdown time
	Capacity
	Utilization of resources

Category	Subcategory
Supportability	Testability
	Adaptability
	Maintainability
	Compatibility
	Configurability
	Upgradeability
	Installability
	Scalability
	Portability
	Reusability
	Interoperability
	Compliance
	Replaceability
	Changeability
	Analyzability
	Localizability
Design constraints	
Implementation requirements	
Interface requirements	
Physical requirements	
Documentation requirements	
Licensing and legal requirements	

The following sections describe each category. None of them is obligatory. Many of them can be omitted if they are not applicable. However, a requirement should be excluded as the result of a planned decision of a customer and a system analyst, not because its importance was not analyzed.

Functionality

This section contains functional requirements that were not captured in any of the use cases. It usually includes some generic functions available from many places in the system. Examples include printing, online help, and reports.

Example: Online help shall be available from the menu on every page.

However, if the functionality is more complicated and cannot easily be expressed in a few sentences, we may need to create additional use cases to describe it.

Usability

The concept of usability is multifaceted. This section defines usability requirements in several areas:

- **Accessibility**

  Ease of access to and use of specific functionality.

  Example: Booking an airplane ticket functionality shall be available from the home page.

  Example: Renting a car functionality shall be available after no more than one click from the home page.

- **Aesthetics**

  Aesthetics of the user interface and description of "look and feel."

  Example: Multiple entry fields on one page shall be vertically aligned.

- **UI consistency**

  Consistency of the user interface, both within the system and with other systems.

  Example: User interface shall be consistent with IBM CUA standard. [CUA91a] [CUA91b]

  To avoid ambiguity, when we mention a standard, it is worth providing a reference to a source where this standard is described.

- **Ergonomics**

  Ergonomic aspects of the user interface (avoiding unnecessary clicks, avoiding uncomfortable movements with the mouse, and so on).

  Example: When a dialog box is opened, the focus shall be on the first entry field in the dialog box.

- **Ease of use**

  Ease of learning and using the system.

  Example: No technical skills (except for using the browser) shall be required to use the system.

Example: Service provider shall be able to learn to use the system in one hour.

Example: Average time of booking a hotel room shall be no longer than ten minutes.

If you do not want to create this special section, these requirements can also be inserted in the Accessibility section.

Reliability

This section covers the various aspects of system dependability:

- **Availability**

  Percentage of time the system is available, mean time between errors.

  Example: Mean Time Between Failures (MTBF) shall be at least 30 days.

  Example: System shall be available 99.93% of the time.

- **Robustness**

  Capability of the system to resist external disturbance, such as invalid input or shortage of resources.

  Example: For every invalid input from the user, the system shall display a meaningful error message explaining what format of input is expected.

- **Accuracy**

  Preciseness with which the system calculates values.

  Example: Currency amounts shall be calculated and stored with accuracy of two decimal places.

- **Recoverability**

  How elegantly the system recovers from a failure. In this section we are concerned about elegance and lack of side effects, while time of recovery is described in the Performance section. However, it is also okay to combine both aspects of recovery in one place.

- **Fault tolerance**

  Sensitivity of the system to failure of some of its parts.

- **Safety**

  Any threats to users, data, system components, or interoperating systems presented by use of the system.

- **Security**

  Level of protection regarding access to specific parts of the system.

  Example: Password shall be required to access administrator screens.

- **Correctness**

  How error- or defect-free the system shall be.

Example: When returning a list of flights, the system cannot miss any direct flight or any flight with only one stopover.

Example: After releasing to production, the system shall have zero critical defects, zero significant defects, and no more than 20 minor defects.

Ideally the system shall not have any defects. This goal, however, is often unrealistic within the available time constraints.

Performance

This section covers the various indicators of system performance.

- **Throughput**

  The rate at which the system performs its tasks. This can be expressed, for example, in the number of transactions per minute.

  Example: The system shall accommodate 1,000 booked flights per minute.

- **Response time**

  How fast the system responds to events.

  Example: Average system response time should be less than two seconds.

  Example: Average time of returning a list of flights shall not be greater than ten seconds.

  The second requirement is related to one specific system response when the user searches matching flights in the use case *Book a flight*. In this situation it is better to insert it into the Special Requirements section in the Use Case Specification. Requirements in this section take precedence over generic requirements from the Supplementary Specification.

- **Recovery time**

  How fast the system recovers from failure. It is important to distinguish between the time when the system becomes operational from the user's point of view (usually because a redundant system resumes operations) and the time when the problem is actually fixed. Although switching to a redundant system is usually done automatically, fixing the original problem quite often requires human intervention.

  Example: In case of a system failure, a redundant system shall resume operations within 30 seconds.

  Example: Average repair time shall be less than one hour.

- **Startup/shutdown time**

  The length of time it takes to start up and shut down.

  Example: The system shall be operational within one minute of starting up.

- **Capacity**

  The number of users that the system can accommodate.

  Example: The system shall accommodate 5,000 concurrent users.

- **Utilization of resources**

  Utilization of memory, disk space, database storage, and so on.

  Example: The system shall store in the database no more than one million transactions. If the database grows over this limit, old transactions shall be backed up and deleted from the operational database.

  These requirements may also be described under Implementation Requirements.

Supportability

Supportability is concerned with numerous aspects of sustaining and modifying the system.

- **Testability**

  How easy it is to test the system. Is integration with any testing tools required?

  Example: The user interface shall not contain any components that would prevent automated testing using IBM Rational Robot and IBM Rational Functional Tester.

- **Adaptability**

  How easily the system adapts to new environments.

  Example: Deployment time on a new version of WebSphere Application Server shall be no longer than one day.

- **Maintainability**

  How easy it is to locate and repair errors.

  Example: An error log containing information about all critical errors shall be accessible to the system administrator over the Internet so that it can be checked remotely at any time.

- **Compatibility**

  The system's degree of compatibility with previous versions of the system, with the system it is replacing, and with interfaces.

  Example: After the system is in production, subsequent versions of the system shall be backward-compatible. All transactions entered in previous versions shall be available in the new version.

- **Configurability**

  How configurable the system is after it is installed. What features shall be configurable?

- **Upgradeability**

  How easy it is to expand the system with new features.

  Example: No installation on the client's workstation shall be required. All system upgrades and new releases should be done on the server.

  Configurability and upgradeability are sometimes called flexibility.

- **Installability**

  Ease of system installation.

  Example: Installing a new version of the system shall not require any installation on users' workstations.

- **Scalability**

  How easy the system scales data volume or users.

  What volume of users the system shall support over time.

  Example: After six months of operation, the system shall be able to accommodate an additional 5,000 users.

- **Portability**

  How easy it is to move to another software or hardware platform.

  Example: Changing the system database in the future shall not require rewriting application logic.

- **Reusability**

  How easy it is to reuse parts in other systems.

  Example: The system's main functionality (booking the flight, purchasing an airplane ticket, reserving a hotel room, reserving a car) shall be encapsulated in components that can be reused in a client/server (non-Internet) application.

- **Interoperability**

  How easy it is to cooperate with other systems.

  Interoperability is the ability of products, systems, or business processes to work together to accomplish a common task.

  Example: The system shall automatically book a ticket with the Airline Reservation System without the necessity of human intervention.

- **Compliance**

  How well the system meets standards and regulations.

  Ex: Gathering personal information of a person purchasing airplane tickets shall be in compliance with the Patriot Act.

- **Replaceability**

  How easy it is to replace system components.

- **Changeability**

  How easy it is to change the system's functionality.

- **Analyzability**

  How easy it is to analyze the system.

- **Auditability**

  How easy it is to audit the system's operation.

- **Localizability**

  The languages the system supports. How easy it is to expand the system with a new language.

  Example: The application shall be available in English, French, and Spanish.

Design Constraints

Requirements related to the system's design and architecture.

Example: The system shall be based on J2EE architecture.

Implementation Requirements

Examples of implementation requirements include the following:

- Computer languages used to develop the system
- Operating systems and their versions
- Databases being used
- Third-party components
- Resource limits: memory, disk space
- Coding standards

Interface Requirements

This section describes various interfaces:

- User interfaces
- Hardware interfaces
- Software interfaces
- Communications interfaces

Physical Requirements

Physical requirements are usually related only to hardware on which the system is deployed. It can specify, for example, the device's shape, size, or weight. It is not applicable to web-based applications.

Documentation Requirements

Requirements related to the documentation may contain

- Printed documentation
- Documentation available on CD
- Documents available online
- Online Help

Example: The Administrator's Guide shall be available as a PDF document.

The online portion of these requirements (including Help) is sometimes provided in the Functionality section of the Supplementary Specification.

Licensing and Legal Requirements

This section contains legal, regulatory, and licensing requirements.

Example: On the pages that gather the user's personal data, there shall be a link to a page describing the privacy policy.

8.3 Deriving Supplementary Requirements from Features

Many features that were defined in the Vision document become supplementary requirements. Including them in the Supplementary Specification provides an opportunity to add more details and organize the requirements by inserting them in the appropriate section. One approach is to go through all the features, identify which ones were not addressed in use cases, and translate them into supplementary requirements. Quite often no changes are necessary, and we can use the same wording as in features.

Out of all the features derived in Chapter 6, "Developing a Vision Document," fifteen are nonfunctional requirements that were not reflected in any of the use cases. Let's analyze each of them and use them as a basis for creating supplementary requirements:

FEAT2   Dates shall be displayed according to the format stored in web browser settings.

FEAT3   On data entry screens, the system shall indicate which fields are mandatory by placing a star next to the field.

FEAT8   The system shall display a pop-up calendar when any date is entered, such as a flight date, hotel stay date, or car rental date.

FEAT11   Separate tabs shall be available for the main functionality.

FEAT12   On each page a Next button shall suggest a default flow.

All of these features are usability requirements and can be moved to supplementary requirements without any changes. By default, RequisitePro adds the SUPL prefix to all supplementary requirements, along with a consecutive number. In this chapter we will prefix requirements with SUPL without a number.

Let's continue going through all the features.

FEAT23   The system shall use J2EE architecture.

This requirement is a design constraint. It can be rewritten as is.

The next two requirements are implementation constraints:

FEAT24   If the architecture requires an application server, IBM WebSphere shall be used.

FEAT25   If the system requires a database, Oracle shall be used.

If we do not have a separate section for implementation requirements, these two requirements will be in design constraints. At this stage of the project, quite often the system architect has already made basic architecture decisions, and we know that an application server and relational database are required, so we can remove conditions from these statements:

SUPL   IBM WebSphere shall be used as an application server.

SUPL   Oracle shall be used as a database.

The next feature specifies on which browser the application shall work:

FEAT34   The system shall be fully tested on the following browsers: Internet Explorer and Netscape.

This requirement shall be qualified by versions of the software:

SUPL   The system shall be fully tested on the following browsers: Internet Explorer (version 6.0 and newer) and Netscape (version 6 and newer).

Next is a reliability/availability requirement:

FEAT27   The system must be available 24 hours a day, with a degree of reliability appropriate to commercial applications.

Because this is too generic, while transforming it into supplementary requirements we can split it into more precise statements:

SUPL   The system shall be available 24 hours a day, 7 days a week.

SUPL   The average time between failures shall be at least 20 hours.

SUPL   The system may be unavailable no more than one minute per 24 hours.

SUPL   The system shall be available 99.93% of the time.

The last two requirements are equivalent. They express the same measurement in a different way. It is enough to include only one of them.

Next is a supportability/maintainability requirement, but it can also be treated as a usability requirement:

FEAT35   All transactions and errors shall be recorded and made available to the administrator.

Because the error log and transaction log probably will be implemented separately, for traceability purposes it is better to split this requirement into two:

SUPL   All system errors shall be recorded and made available to the administrator.

SUPL   All transactions (ticket purchase, making a reservation, updating a reservation, and canceling a reservation) shall be recorded and made available to the administrator.

The next two are reliability/security requirements:

FEAT26   The pages where service providers can submit their offers shall be password-protected. Hotel providers, car providers, and airline representatives shall use assigned user IDs and passwords to access these pages.

FEAT29   Users shall pick IDs and passwords while buying an airline ticket.

The next requirement is quite complex:

FEAT36   The following reports shall be available to the administrator:
A list of all airline tickets purchased in the given time period.
A list of all car reservations in the given time period.
A list of all hotel room reservations in the given time period.

This requirement requires some explanation. For example, the following aspects of the requirement need elaboration:

- From where the reports shall be available
- What search attributes shall be available
- How to select available reports

In this situation it is better to create a separate use case rather than to include the requirement in the Supplementary Specification.

The next requirement does not describe the system itself, but the way in which the system is produced:

FEAT28   The system shall be developed three months from the date when the customer signs off on the Use Cases and Supplementary Specification.

The best place to have this type of restriction is in a contract or statement of work, not in system requirements documents. However, if we want to include it in the Supplementary Specification, we can create a separate section called Development Process Requirements. Here are some other requirements that may fall into the same category:

Example: Development shall be done at the customer's premises.

Example: The testing team shall include at least two manual testers and two testers proficient in Rational Robot.

Example: The system shall be developed using the RUP.

8.4   Attributes of Supplementary Requirements

The default attributes of supplementary requirements are

- Priority
- Status
- Difficulty
- Stability
- Risk
- Contact Name

- Author
- Location
- Enhancement Request
- Defect
- Obsolete

This list may vary slightly depending on the version of RequisitePro.

Some requirements (especially performance-related) may vary, depending on the number of users. In this case we can use a method suggested by Mark Lines: create a table with performance requirements by number of simultaneous users to show acceptable degradation. Table 8.5 shows an example. You may need a separate table for each relevant use case transaction.

Table 8.5   Differentiating Requirements Depending on the Number of Concurrent Users

Number of Simultaneous Users	Maximum Transaction Time (in Seconds)
1 to 10	3
11 to 50	5
51 to 100	7
More than 100	10

This section discusses two other attributes that may be useful for supplementary requirements.

Importance

Whereas all functional requirements are usually truly required in the system, nonfunctional requirements may have different levels of importance. For example, some of them are mandatory:

The application shall be available for Internet Explorer browser users.

If Internet Explorer is not supported, the majority of Internet users will not be able to use the application.

Some requirements are desirable:

Subsequent screens shall appear in less than two seconds.

If it is not two seconds but four seconds, users will be less happy, but they will still be able to use the application.

Some requirements are not so important:

The system shall be operational within one minute of starting up.

The system is restarted only once in a few days, and the system administrator is the only person who waits during this time, so even if it lasts five or ten minutes, this is not a big deal.

Understanding the levels of importance will help you correctly allocate the resources to design and implement appropriate solutions with a reasonable cost.

To store the levels of importance, we may create a new attribute called *Importance* having three possible values:

- Mandatory
- Desirable
- Nice to have

If you do not want to create a new attribute, you may use *Priority* to store these values (however, priority and importance are not exactly synonyms).

Satisfaction Shape

Another attribute that is applicable to supplementary requirements is **satisfaction shape**. This attribute describes how customers' satisfaction changes with the fulfillment of required metrics.

Satisfaction shape may have the following values:

- Sharp: The metrics used in the requirement shall be fulfilled exactly as described. The measurement cannot be even slightly worse.
- Medium: The value of measurement shall be quite close to expected values. However, a small discrepancy is okay.
- Linear: The better the result, the better the satisfaction; however, there are no strict expected values.

Let's analyze some examples.

Sharp Satisfaction Shape

Imagine a real-time system for sorting packages. Packages are moving on the conveyor belt. The system scans an address label on the package and, based on the destination, instructs the diverter to divert to an appropriate belt. The requirement is that the system shall calculate the diverter's proper action within one second. If it fails, the package moves past the diverter.

In this case the response time shall be less than one second, otherwise the whole system will not work. However, it does not matter if this is done in 0.99 seconds or 0.5 seconds. There is no additional value in having a shorter response time.

Figure 8.2 shows the satisfaction shape for this requirement. For all values less than one second the satisfaction is one, and for all values greater than one second the satisfaction is zero.

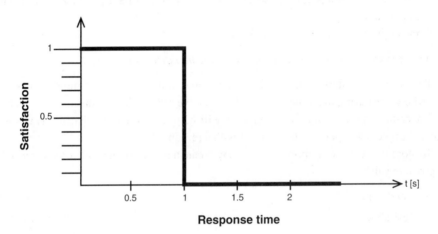

Figure 8.2   Sharp satisfaction shape.

Medium Satisfaction Shape

Let's assume that in some systems the batch files and process transactions from the previous day are run at midnight. At 8 a.m. a person comes to the office who is supposed to analyze results from night batches. This means that the batch processing shall be done in eight hours. If it is done in 8.5 hours, this is not a big deal, but nine or ten hours is a problem. The satisfaction shape may look like Figure 8.3.

Whether the value of the satisfaction line is decreasing or increasing depends on the requirement. For example, for the requirement "The system shall accommodate 5,000 concurrent users," the higher the satisfaction values are, the greater the number of users on the horizontal axis, as shown in Figure 8.4.

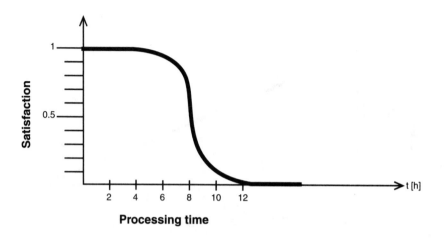

Processing time

Figure 8.3 Medium satisfaction shape for the processing time requirement.

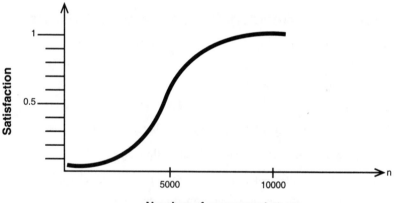

Number of concurrent users

Figure 8.4 Medium satisfaction shape for the number of concurrent users requirement.

The line does not need to be symmetric.

Linear Satisfaction Shape

The reports shall be displayed in 20 seconds or less. Twenty seconds is just a reasonable figure providing a good expectation per cost ratio (see Figure 8.5).

Importance does not necessarily go with the satisfaction shape. For example, the number of concurrent users is very important, but it is not sharp. There is no big difference between 4,900 and 5,100 users.

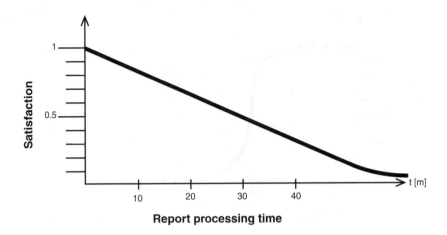

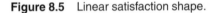

Report processing time

Figure 8.5   Linear satisfaction shape.

8.5   Entering Supplementary Requirements in RequisitePro

As with any other requirements, we can enter supplementary requirements in RequisitePro in three different ways:

- Directly from the Explorer
- From a view
- Create the Supplementary Specification, and then add requirements from the document

To add requirements from the Explorer, do the following:

1. Right-click the Supplementary Requirements package and select New > Requirement.
2. Fill in the fields in the Requirement Properties dialog box.

In some templates the view All Supplementary Requirements is already created. If you work with a template that does not have this view predefined, do the following to create a view:

1. Right-click the Supplementary Requirements package and select New >View.
2. In the View Properties dialog box, shown in Figure 8.6, the View Type should be Attribute Matrix, and the Row Requirement Type should be SUPL.

Adding requirements from a view involves the following steps:

1. In the Explorer window, double-click the view All Supplementary Requirements.
2. In the View window, click the last row, with the text <Click here to create a requirement>.
3. Enter a Name and Text.

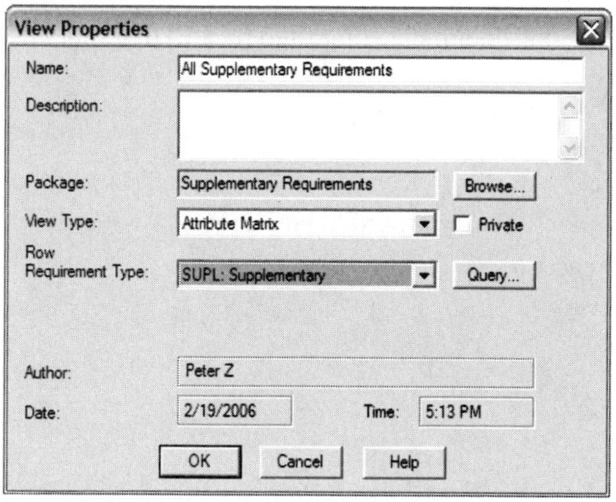

Figure 8.6   View Properties dialog box.

A big advantage of the third approach (creating the Supplementary Specification and then adding requirements from it) is that we can print an entire document and use it to communicate with the customer. Sometimes this document is even used as part of a contract with the customer.

To create the Supplementary Specification (or, if you follow current RUP naming conventions, you will call it Supplementary Specifications, with an "s" at the end), do the following:

1. Right-click the Supplementary Requirements package and select New > Document.

2. Fill in the fields of the Document Properties dialog box, as shown in Figure 8.7.

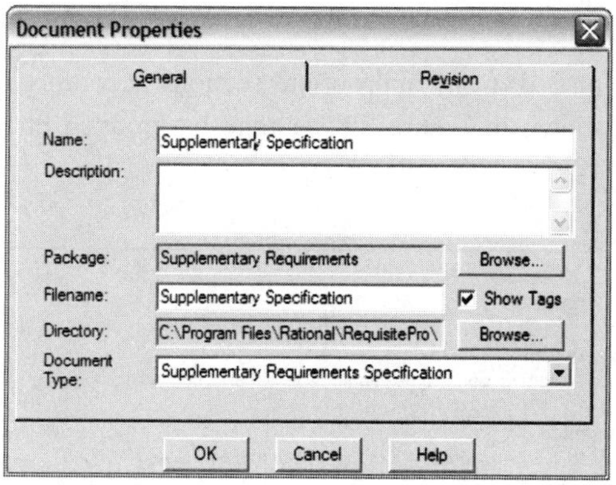

Figure 8.7   Document Properties dialog box.

Here is the format of this document suggested by a RUP template [RUP04]:

1. Introduction
   1.1   Purpose
   1.2   Scope
   1.3   Definitions, Acronyms, and Abbreviations
   1.4   References
   1.5   Overview
2. Functionality
3. Usability
4. Reliability
5. Performance
6. Supportability
7. Design Constraints
8. Online User Documentation and Help System Requirements
9. Purchased Components
10. Interfaces
    10.1   User Interfaces
    10.2   Hardware Interfaces
    10.3   Software Interfaces
    10.4   Communications Interfaces
11. Licensing Requirements
12. Legal, Copyright, and Other Notices
13. Applicable Standards

Requirements are placed in the appropriate sections according to the type. They can be labeled individually, as shown in Figure 8.8, or may be grouped in related sets, as shown in Figure 8.9.

---

5. Performance

5.1 Response Time
Average system response time should be less than 2 seconds.

5.2 Throughput
System shall accommodate 1000 booked per minute.

5.3 Recovery Time
In case of a system failure, redundant system shall resume operations within 30 seconds.
Average repair time shall be less than 1 hour.

Figure 8.8   Each requirement has its own header.

> **5. Reliability**
>
> **4.1 Availability**
> The system shall be available 24 hours a day, 7 days a week.
> Average time between failures shall exceed 20 hours.
> System may be unavailable no more than 1 minute per 24 hours.
> Each downtime can't exceed 30 seconds. Complete server redundancy should be implemented.

Figure 8.9   Multiple requirements are combined under one header.

After writing requirements as plain text in a Microsoft Word document, you should add them to the database:

1. Highlight the text describing the requirement.

2. Select RequisitePro > Requirement > New, or right-click the text and select Create Requirement, or click the New Requirement icon on the toolbar.

3. Fill in the fields of the Requirement Properties dialog box on the General tab, as shown in Figure 8.10. Select SUPL as the requirement Type.

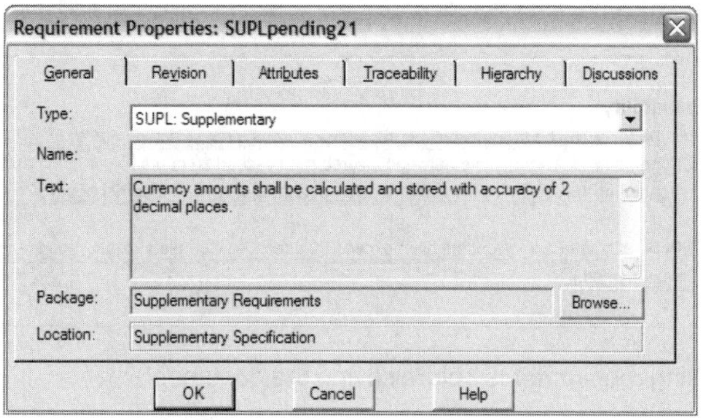

Figure 8.10   Requirement Properties dialog box.

4. If you want to set the attributes at this time, click the Attributes tab to modify the attribute values (you can also do this later).

5. If you want to set the attributes at this time, click the Traceability tab to add the requirement from which this one is traced (you can also do this later).

When you save a requirement to a database, you can highlight the whole description, or you can highlight only one sentence summarizing the requirement. If the whole idea is expressed in one sentence, and the rest only clarifies the requirement, it is enough to save one sentence, as shown in Figure 8.11. However, if multiple sentences are necessary to understand the requirement, it is okay to insert a longer description, as shown in Figure 8.12. The advantage of highlighting the whole description is that this allows automatic suspect detection when the requirement is modified.

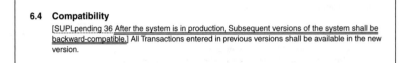

6.4 Compatibility

[SUPLpending 36 After the system is in production, Subsequent versions of the system shall be backward-compatible.] All Transactions entered in previous versions shall be available in the new version.

Figure 8.11   Saving only the first sentence of the requirement to the database.

5.6 Utilization of resources

[SUPLpending 32 System shall store in the database no more than 1 million transactions. If the database grows over this limit, old transactions shall be backed up and deleted from operational database.]

Figure 8.12   Saving multiple sentences describing the requirement to the database.

When the requirements are stored in the database, but the document is not saved, they are labeled with the SUPLpending prefix, as shown in Figure 8.13. After the document is saved, the prefix changes to SUPL, as shown in Figure 8.14.

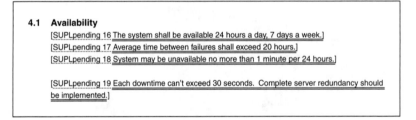

4.1 Availability

[SUPLpending 16 The system shall be available 24 hours a day, 7 days a week.]
[SUPLpending 17 Average time between failures shall exceed 20 hours.]
[SUPLpending 18 System may be unavailable no more than 1 minute per 24 hours.]

[SUPLpending 19 Each downtime can't exceed 30 seconds. Complete server redundancy should be implemented.]

Figure 8.13   Labeling requirements before saving the document.

4.1 Availability

[SUPL16 The system shall be available 24 hours a day 7 days a week.]
[SUPL17 Average time between failures shall exceed 20 hours.]
[SUPL18 System may be unavailable no more than 1 minute per 24 hours.]
[SUPL19 Each downtime can't exceed 30 seconds. Complete server redundancy should be implemented.]

Figure 8.14   Labeling requirements after saving the document.

After all the requirements have been saved to the database, they appear in the Explorer window, as shown in Figure 8.15.

Figure 8.15   Supplementary requirements in the RequisitePro Explorer.

8.6   Traceability to Supplementary Requirements

Most supplementary requirements are traced from features. Depending on the project guidelines, we may also allow them to be traced directly from stakeholder requests. We can also allow requirements to be added directly on the supplementary requirements level. However, these decisions should be made while developing the Requirements Management Plan; they should not be made ad hoc while finalizing the Supplementary Specification.

Setting the Type Attribute for Features

To facilitate setting traceability from features to supplementary requirements, it is worth setting values of the *Type* attribute for features. Depending on the version of RequisitePro that you use, this attribute may already be defined. In version 2003.06.13 this attribute has the following values:

- Functional (non-use case)
- Usability
- Reliability
- Performance
- Supportability

- Design Constraint
- Implementation Reqt
- Physical Reqt
- Interface Reqt

You can use these predefined values, or you can change to a set that better fits your needs. For example, if you want less granularity, you may use only four values:

- Functional: UC specific
- Functional: Generic
- Non-functional: UC specific
- Non-functional: Generic

To handle these four options, you can either set a type of attribute to *List (Single Value)* and enter them as listed here, or set a type of attribute to *List (Multiple Value)* and specify the following options (see Figure 8.16):

- Functional
- Non-functional
- UC specific
- Generic

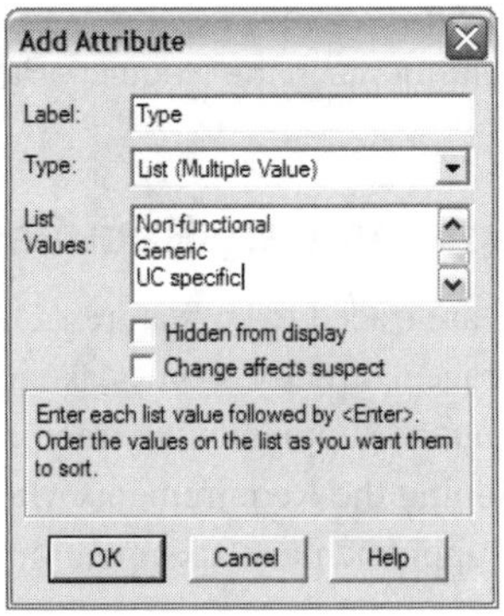

Figure 8.16   An attribute with a multiple-value list.

For multiple-value lists you can enter more than one value, such as *Functional* and *UC specific*. However, be sure that you enter a valid combination of attribute values. For example, you would not enter *UC specific* with *Generic*.

If you did not set the *Type* attribute while entering features, you can do so now. The fastest way to set attributes of multiple requirements is from a view. First, check if the required attribute is in the view. If the attribute *Type* does not show up in the spreadsheet, you need to add it to the view by following these steps:

1. Right-click the title row of the view and select Displayed Attributes.
2. In the left window, select the attributes that you want to see in the view, as shown in Figure 8.17.

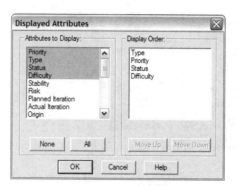

Figure 8.17   Setting which attribute shall appear in the view.

3. In the right window you can set the order in which the attributes will appear.

To set attributes of multiple requirements, follow these steps:

1. Double-click the All Features view in the Features and Vision package.

2. Double-click a cell at the intersection of the column Type and row with a requirement that you want to update.

3. Select an appropriate value from the list box, as shown in Figure 8.18.

Figure 8.18   Setting attribute values from the view.

Setting Traceability

If the view with the Traceability Matrix from FEAT to SUPL is not set up already, you can create it by following these steps:

1. Right-click the Supplementary Requirements package and select New > View.

2. Fill in the fields of the View Properties dialog box, as shown in Figure 8.19. View Type should be Traceability Matrix, Row Requirement Type should be SUPL, and Column Requirement Type should be FEAT.

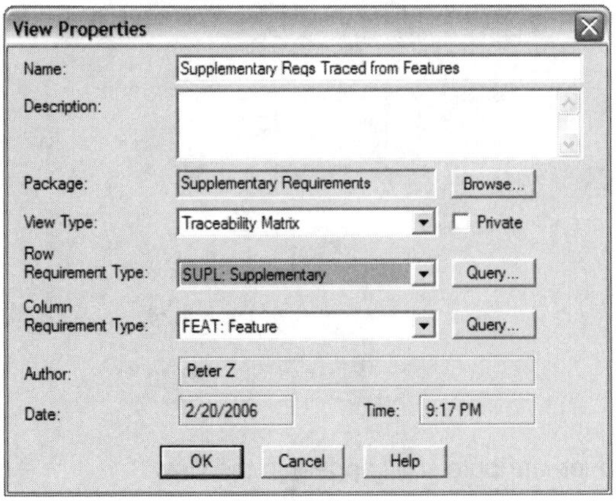

Figure 8.19   View Properties dialog box for the Traceability Matrix.

This view can also be set with FEAT requirements in rows and SUPL in columns.

Because in this matrix we do not need to include the features that were already taken care of in use cases, we can query only features that are not use case specific:

1. Click the Query button next to FEAT.

2. In the Select Attribute dialog box, shown in Figure 8.20, select Type as the attribute's name.

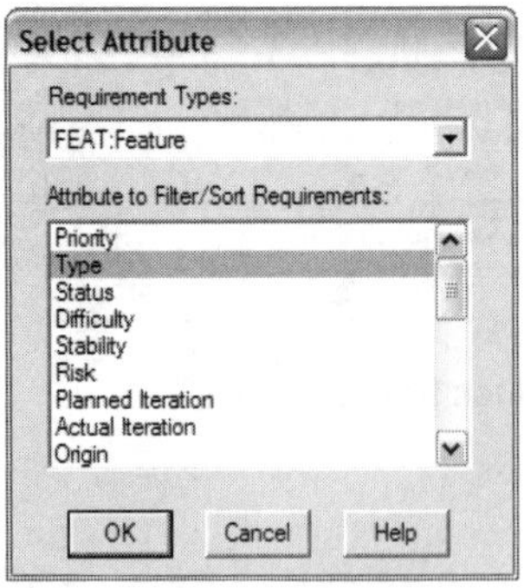

Figure 8.20   Selecting the attribute on which we want to filter.

3. Click OK in the Select Attribute dialog box.

4. In the Query Requirements dialog box, shown in Figure 8.21, select in the left window applicable values.

5. Click OK in the Query Requirements dialog box.

6. Click OK in the Query Column Requirements dialog box, as shown in Figure 8.22.

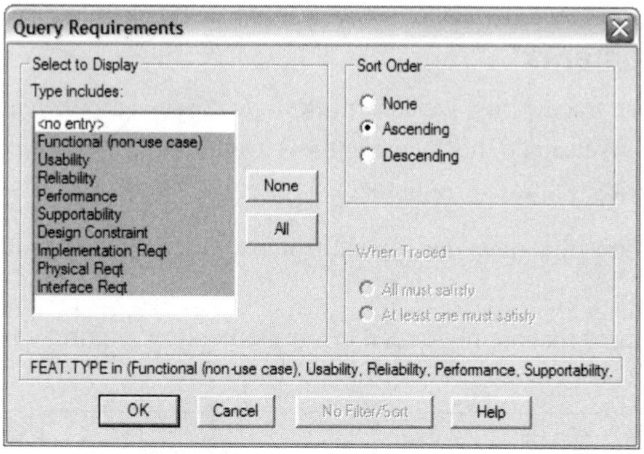

Figure 8.21   Selecting values of the attribute which we want to filter.

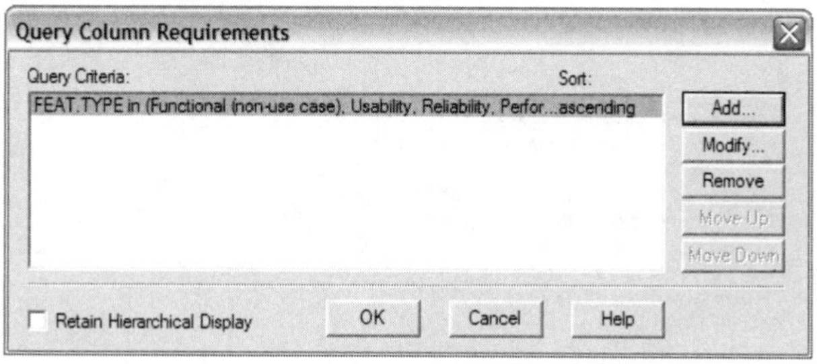

Figure 8.22   Adding query criteria on the Query Column Requirements dialog box.

7. Click OK in the View Properties dialog box (refer to Figure 8.19).

The view displays only features having one of the selected values of the attribute *Type*. To set the traceability, follow these steps:

1. Right-click the intersection of the related feature and supplementary requirement.

2. Select Trace From (or Trace To, depending on what you have in the rows, and depending on your interpretation of *trace to* and *trace from*).

After setting traceability, you can analyze it either on the Traceability Matrix (see Figure 8.23) or on the Traceability Tree (see Figure 8.24). The Traceability Tree lets you see the path all the way from stakeholder requests.

Querying Requirements

After we have set all the traceability, we can check if we covered all the features related to supplementary requirements. We can do this by using the Attribute Matrix or Traceability Matrix view.

We need to filter the features simultaneously on two criteria:

Filter 1: Features that have the Type attribute applicable to the supplementary requirement.

Filter 2: Features that are not traced to supplementary requirements.

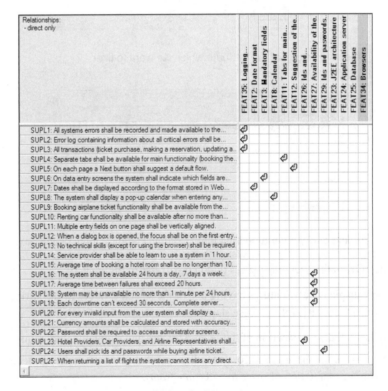

Figure 8.23   Traceability Matrix from FEAT to SUPL.

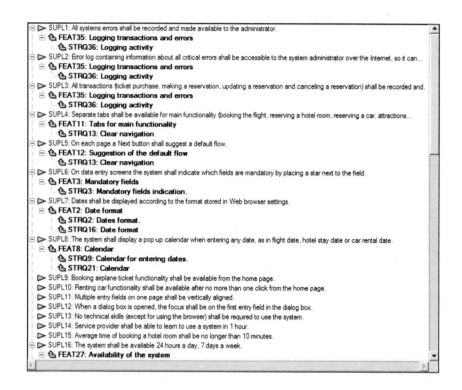

Figure 8.24   Traceability Tree to SUPL.

In the view Traceability Requirements Traced From Features, the first filter is already applied to column requirements, so we only need to set a second one:

1. Select View > Query Column Requirements.

2. Click the Add button in the Query Column Requirements dialog box.

3. Select Traced-to in the Select Attribute dialog box, as shown in Figure 8.25.

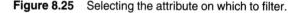

Figure 8.25   Selecting the attribute on which to filter.

4. Click OK in the Select Attribute dialog box.

5. Select SUPL in the left window of the Query Requirements dialog box, as shown in Figure 8.26.

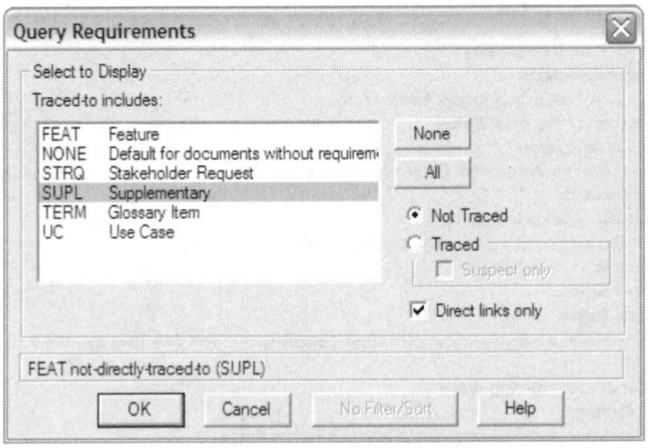

Figure 8.26   Selecting what traceability we are interested in.

6. Select the Not Traced radio button.

7. Click OK in the Query Requirements dialog box.

8. Click OK in the Query Column Requirements dialog box, which now shows both filters (see Figure 8.27).

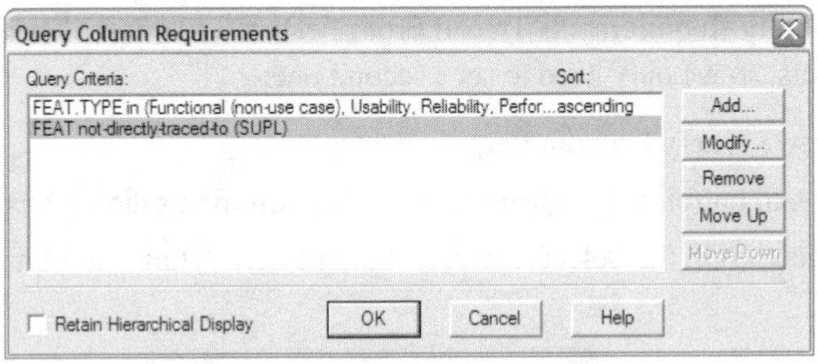

Figure 8.27   All filters applied to the requirements.

We expect to have an empty view, as shown in Figure 8.28. If any feature is shown on the view, it requires careful analysis. This probably means that we forgot to add supplementary requirements satisfying this feature, or we made a mistake either setting traceability or setting the Type attribute.

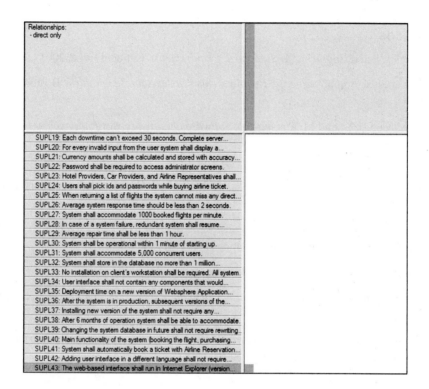

Figure 8.28   An empty view after applying both conditions.

8.7   Summary

Depending on the scope, software requirements can reside either in Use Case Specifications or in Supplementary Specifications. Supplementary requirements together with use cases capture all the system's software requirements. The majority of supplementary requirements are nonfunctional. They deal with usability, reliability, performance, supportability, and design constraints.

A common way of eliciting supplementary requirements is through interviews and questionnaires using a predefined list of questions. The list organizes requirements according to a chosen classification, such as FURPS+ [GRA92].

Because a small improvement in performance or reliability may be quite costly in terms of required resources, it is worth capturing the importance and satisfaction shape of each requirement. Analyzing these attributes may help you optimally allocate the resources and direct the efforts where they are required the most.

After capturing all requirements in RequisitePro, we should set traceability from features (and, if needed, from the stakeholder requests). Next, we can run queries that check if all applicable features are covered by supplementary requirements.

References

[EEL01] Eeles, Peter. *Capturing Architectural Requirements*, Rational Edge, 2001.

[LAU02] Lauesen, Soren. *Software Requirements: Styles and Techniques*, Boston: Addison-Wesley, 2002.

[MCC80] McCall, J.A., and M. Matsumoto. *Software Quality Metrics Enhancements*, Rome Air Development Center, 1980.

[ISO91] ISO/IEC TR 9126, *Information Technology, software product evaluation, quality characteristics and guidelines for their use*. International Organization for Standardization, Geneva, 1991.

[GRA92] Grady, Robert. *Practical Software Metrics for Project Management and Process Improvement*, Upper Saddle River, NJ: Prentice Hall, 1992.

[RUP04] *Rational Unified Process*, Version 2003.06.13, IBM, 2003.

[CUA91a] *Systems Application Architecture Common User Access Guide to User Interface Design*, SC34-4289, IBM Corporation, 1991.

[CUA91b] *Systems Application Architecture Common User Access Advanced Interface Design Reference*, SC34-4290, IBM Corporation, 1991.

CHAPTER 9

Creating Test Cases from Use Cases

This chapter describes how to create functional test cases from use cases. In many projects the importance of this step is not recognized. Often the testers are given a printout of a Use Case Specification and then perform ad hoc manual testing. However, if we neglect formal creation of test cases, we may end up with poor coverage of a testing universe while performing many duplicate tests.

Presented here is a formal method that facilitates achieving quite good coverage using a reasonable number of test cases. This approach was introduced by Jim Heumann [HEU01a] [HEU01b]. It requires creating scenarios. Scenarios were introduced in Chapter 7, "Creating Use Cases." Test cases are located in the pyramid one level below scenarios, as shown in Figure 9.1.

Because this chapter introduces a new document type that is not defined in standard RequisitePro templates, section 9.3 shows how to create a new document type in RequisitePro. If we want to avoid any overhead related to creating and maintaining a new requirement type and a new document type, we can link the requirements to test cases in a test management tool (such as ClearQuest Test Manager). However, creating new types is so easy and quick, and I feel it is worth having everything in the RequisitePro environment.

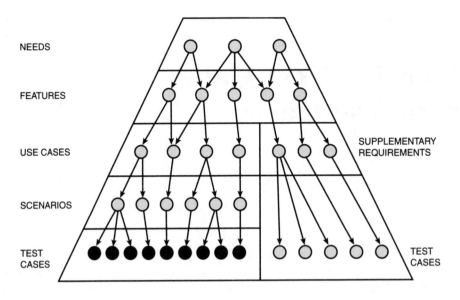

Figure 9.1   Deriving test cases from scenarios.

9.1   Creating Test Cases

When we have all the scenarios derived in Chapter 7, we need to create the test cases. Four steps are involved:

1. Identify variables for each use case step.
2. Identify significantly different options for each variable.
3. Combine options to be tested into test cases.
4. Assign values to variables.

The following sections describe the details of these steps.

Step 1: Identify Variables for Each Use Case Step

First, we need to identify all input variables in all the steps in the given scenario. For example, if in some step the user enters a user ID and password, there are two variables. One variable is the *user ID*, and the second is the *password*. The variable can also be a selection that the user can make (such as selecting a flight from a list).

Here are the variables from the *Book a flight* use case:

- B3. User enters flight information:
    - Departure airport
    - Departure date

- Arrival airport
- Return date
- Number of traveling adults
- Number of traveling children
- B5. User selects a flight.
  - Outbound flight
- B7. User selects a return flight.
  - Return flight
- B10. User provides user ID and password to proceed buying a ticket.
  - User ID
  - Password
- B11. User provides passenger information:
  - First name
  - Last name
  - Sex
  - Date of birth
- B13. User selects seats.
  - Seats
- B14. User provides credit card information and billing address:
  - Credit card type
  - Credit card number
  - Expiration date
  - Name on the card
  - Address
  - City
  - State
  - Zip code
  - Country

The number of variables may depend on the values entered in the previous steps. If in step B3 *Number of traveling adults* = 2 and *Number of traveling children* = 1, step B11 will contain three sets of data—one for each passenger. If in step B5 the selected flight has a stopover, in step B13 the seats need to be selected for each leg of the flight.

Step 2: Identify Significantly Different Options for Each Variable

Options are "significantly different" if they may trigger different system behavior.

For example, if we select a *user ID*, which is supposed to be six to ten characters long, the following entries are significantly different:

- **Alex** is too short, and we expect an error message to appear.
- **Alexandria** is a valid user ID.
- **Alexandrena** is too long, and we expect the system to prevent us from entering a user ID that long.

However, *Alexandria* and *JohnGordon* are not significantly different because both are valid user IDs that should cause the system to react in the same way.

The following guidelines describe some specific cases.

An option can be considered significantly different if

- It triggers a different process flow (usually an alternative flow).

  Example: Entering an invalid password shall trigger Alternative Flow 2.

- It triggers a different error message.

  Example: If an e-mail is too long, the message shall be "E-mail should have no more than 50 characters."

  Example: If an e-mail address does not contain the @, the message shall be "Invalid e-mail address."

- It causes a different appearance of the user interface.

  Example: If Method of Payment is a credit card, the screen shall display fields where the user can enter credit card number, expiration date, and cardholder name.

- It causes different selections to be available in drop-down lists.

  Example: The customer registration screen shall contain drop-down lists Country and State/Province. State/Province shall be populated based on the country selected: for the U.S. it shall contain all the states, for Canada all the provinces, and for other countries it shall be dimmed.

  This requirement creates three significantly different options:

  - U.S.
  - Canada
  - Any other country

- It is an input to a business rule.

  Example: If the order is placed after 6 p.m., and the user selects Overnight Shipment, a message shall inform the user that the book will arrive after tomorrow.

This business rule triggers two separate options:

- Overnight Shipment, order placed before 6 p.m.
- Overnight Shipment, order placed after 6 p.m.

- It is a border condition.

  Example: Password should have at least six characters.

  In this case we should test the following:

  - Password with five characters
  - Password with six characters

- Something needs to be changed versus using the default.

  Example: On the credit card payment screen, the cardholder's name shall be populated with the name of the person placing the order. The user shall be able to keep this default value or insert another one.

  This creates two separate options:

  - Keep the default cardholder's name
  - Change the cardholder's name to a different one

- The entry format is not clearly defined or enforced, and it may be interpreted differently by various users.

  Example: The phone entry field shall accept free-form text.

  Phone numbers are written differently by different people:

  - Using parentheses: (973) 123-4567
  - Using dashes: 973-123-4567
  - Plain number with spaces: 973 123 4567
  - No spaces: 9731234567

  All reasonable formats shall be tested.

- Regular cases differ in different countries.

  Credit card expiration date format may be different in the U.S. and in Europe.

- If you are testing numbers, you may consider the following significantly different options:

  - Regular number, reasonable from the application's point of view
  - Zero
  - Negative number
  - A number with two decimals
  - The biggest number that can be entered (for instance, 99999999999999—as many nines as can fit in the entry field)

Many options are application-specific. For example, different options for selecting a flight might include the following:

- Select a direct flight
- Select a flight with one stopover
- Select a flight with two stopovers
- Select a flight that arrives the next day
- Select a flight that arrives two days after the departure date

If you wonder how the last option is possible, check any evening flight from the U.S. to Australia.

Quite often significantly different options include combinations of more than one value. On the screen where we enter outbound and return flight dates, we have the following combinations:

- Return date later than the departure date (regular case)
- Return date equal to the departure date (border condition—valid depending on the flight times)
- Return date before the departure date (error)
- Any of the dates are not specified (error)

Depending on the specific rules imposed by the Airline Reservation System, we may have additional options, such as "Return date over one year later than the outbound date."

Let's find some options worth testing for all variables in a basic flow of the *Book a flight* use case:

- B3. User enters flight information.
  - Departure airport

    Valid airport code

    Valid town and state

    Valid town and foreign country

    Invalid airport code

    Nonexisting airport code

    Blank
  - Departure date

    Valid date in the future set manually

    Valid date in the future set from a calendar

    Date in the past

    Today's date

February 30 or 31

Not set

- Arrival airport

    Valid airport code

    Valid town and state

    Valid town and foreign country

    Invalid airport code

    Nonexisting airport code

    Blank

- Return date

    Reasonable date, one week after departure date

    Reasonable date set from calendar

    Date equal to the departure date

    Future date before the departure date

    Date in the past

    February 30 or 31

- Number of traveling adults

    0

    1

    2

    Maximum allowed

- Number of traveling children

    0 (with number of adults = 0)

    0 (with number of adults > 0)

    1 (with number of adults = 0)

    2 (with number of adults > 0)

    Maximum allowed

- B5. User selects a flight.

    - Outbound flight

        Any direct flight

        Flight with one stopover

        Flight with maximum number of stopovers

        Cheapest flight

Flight arriving the next day (if there are any)

Flight arriving in two days (if there are any)

- B7. User selects a return flight.
  - Return flight

    Same as for the outbound flight

- B10. User provides user ID and password to proceed buying a ticket.
  - User ID

    Valid user ID

    User ID containing invalid characters

    Nonexisting user ID

    Blank

  - Password

    Correct password (with correct user ID)

    Incorrect password (with correct user ID)

    Valid password (with incorrect user ID)

    Password containing invalid characters

    Blank

- B11. User provides passenger information.
  - First name

    Valid first name

    Long name (maximum number of characters allowed)

    One character longer than allowed

    One character

    Blank

    Two names with a space in between (such as Anna Maria)

  - Last name

    Regular last name

    Long name (maximum number of characters allowed)

    Name containing an apostrophe (such as D'Artagnan)

    One character longer than allowed

    One character

    Blank

    Two words with a space in between

- Sex

  M

  F

- Date of birth

  Valid date

  Future date

  Recent date for an adult

  Remote date for a child

  Invalid date

- B13. User selects seats.

  - Seats

    Accept default allocation

    Window seat

    Middle seat

    Aisle seat

    Two seats next to each other

    Two seats separate from each other

    Select only one seat when two passengers are traveling

- B14. User provides credit card information and billing address.

  - Credit card type

    One option for each available card

  - Credit card number

    Valid number for a given type

    Invalid number for a given type

    Invalid number for any card

    String containing letters

    String containing special characters

    Blank

  - Expiration date

    Valid future date

    Date in the past

    Wrong date for a valid card

    Invalid date

- Name on the card

    Accept the default (passenger's name)

    Overwrite the default

    Valid name, but not an owner of this card

    Blank

    Maximum number of letters allowed

- Address

    Valid address

    Maximum string allowed

    Blank

    Valid address, but not a billing address for this card

- City

    Valid city

    Maximum string allowed

    Blank

- State

    Correct state

    No state selected

- Zip code

    Valid zip code

    String containing invalid characters

    Four-digit number

    Six-digit number

    Blank

- Country

    U.S.

    Valid country, but not U.S.

    Nonexisting country, maximum string allowed

    Blank

Step 3: Combine Options to Be Tested into Test Cases

The preceding section identified all significantly different options worth testing. Now we need to combine them in the sequence of test case steps. One way to do so is to create a Test Case Allocation Matrix. The rows of this matrix contain all the variables for all the steps that require the user's input. The first column contains the step number, the second column contains the name of the variable, and the remaining columns contain tests cases. You can label them T1, T2, and so on. You need to estimate how many test cases will cover this scenario. A rough estimate may be the biggest number of significantly different options identified for a variable. If you estimate incorrectly, it's no problem because you can add or remove a column while filling the matrix. Usually from five to seven test cases cover typical scenarios. However, some application-specific cases require more test cases. We need to create one matrix per scenario selected for testing. Table 9.1 shows the Test Case Allocation Matrix for the basic flow of the *Book a flight* use case.

Table 9.1   Test Case Allocation Matrix with All the Variables for the Use Case *Book a Flight*

Step	Variable	T1	T2	T3	T4	T5	T6
B3	Departure airport						
B3	Departure date						
B3	Arrival airport						
B3	Return date						
B3	Number of traveling adults						
B3	Number of traveling children						
B5	Outbound flight						
B7	Return flight						
B10	User ID						
B10	Password						
B11	First name						
B11	Last name						
B11	Sex						
B11	Date of birth						
B11	First name of the second passenger						
B11	Last name of the second passenger						
B11	Sex of the second passenger						
B11	Date of birth of the second passenger						
B11	First name of the third passenger						
B11	Last name of the third passenger						

(continues)

Table 9.1   Test Case Allocation Matrix with All the Variables for the Use Case *Book a Flight*
(continued)

Step	Variable	T1	T2	T3	T4	T5	T6
B11	Sex of the third passenger						
B11	Date of birth of the third passenger						
B13	Outbound seats for the first leg						
B13	Outbound seats for the second leg						
B13	Outbound seats for the third leg						
B13	Return seats for the first leg						
B13	Return seats for the second leg						
B13	Return seats for the third leg						
B14	Credit card type						
B14	Credit card number						
B14	Expiration date						
B14	Name on the card						
B14	Address						
B14	City						
B14	State						
B14	Zip code						
B14	Country						

For each row, enter all the options that need to be tested for this variable. In the first row is the variable *Departure airport*. In each column we enter a different option to be tested, as shown in Table 9.2.

Table 9.2   Entering Selected Options into the Test Case Allocation Matrix

Step	Variable	T1	T2	T3	T4	T5	T6
B3	Departure airport	Valid airport code	Valid town and state	Valid town and foreign country	Invalid	Nonexisting	Blank

Some of the options are invalid because we are performing "negative testing" to see if the system displays the correct error message (or prevents the user from entering incorrect data). So as not to break the test case, we add additional blank rows—where we enter some valid options for all entries in the previous row where we expect the system to reject the entered value. For second-choice options, use a reasonable combination of all valid options from the previous row, and the most popular options. For example, the variable *Departure airport* has three valid options: a valid airport code, a valid town/state, and a valid town/country. We can use all three of them in the line with second choices. However, because a foreign country is used as a departure location much less often than a domestic airport, and we already tested this option in T3, for a second-choice option in T6 again, we have selected a valid airport code (see Table 9.3). However, for *Arrival airport*, we have selected the second time *Valid town and foreign country* because often we do not know a foreign airport code, so we specify the town and country instead (see Table 9.4). When we have the same option a few times, for each of them we can later select different values (see the section "Step 4: Assign Values to Variables"). For example, *Valid airport code* may be EWR in test case T1, LAX in T4, and JFK in T6.

Table 9.3 Entering Second Choices for Invalid Options

Step	Variable	T1	T2	T3	T4	T5	T6
B3	Departure airport	Valid airport code	Valid town and state	Valid town and foreign country	Invalid	Nonexisting	Blank

Table 9.4 Options for Arrival Airport (Previous Rows Are Not Shown)

Step	Variable	T1	T2	T3	T4	T5	T6
B3	Departure airport	Valid airport code	Valid town and state	Valid town and foreign country	Invalid	Nonexisting	Blank
					Valid airport code	Valid town and state	Valid town and foreign country

We continue filling the matrix. For each row, when adding an option to be tested, be sure that it does not contradict any of the values that were entered previously in the given column. As fillers, you can use any valid options or some unusual combinations that have not been tested so far. For example, *Valid date a week from now* and *Valid date over one year from now* are not significantly different, because they should trigger the same behavior. But because we have an available cell in the Test Case Allocation Matrix, we can use it to add some unusual variations to be sure that system performs correctly in these cases, as shown in Table 9.5.

Table 9.5   Filling Subsequent Rows in the Test Case Allocation Matrix

Step	Variable	T1	T2	T3	T4	T5	T6
B3	Departure airport	Valid airport code	Valid town and state	Valid town and foreign country	Invalid	Nonexisting	Blank
					Valid airport code	Valid town and state	Valid town and foreign country
B3	Departure date	Valid set manually	Valid, from calendar	Past	Today	Invalid	Not set
				Valid, over one year from now		Valid, set manually	Valid, from calendar

Often we need to check the options that were set a few steps ago. For example, while setting the return date, we need to be sure that these options are in sync with the departure dates that were previously set (see Table 9.6). Also, while setting the number of travelers, we need to account for different combinations of adults and kids, as shown in Table 9.7. The option 0/0 is not allowed, so as a second choice we added 1/max to add a case with the maximum allowed number of children. The case 0/1 probably will trigger a message explaining under what conditions a child is allowed to travel without an accompanying adult.

Table 9.6   Options for a Return Date

Step	Variable	T1	T2	T3	T4	T5	T6
B3	Departure date	Valid set manually	Valid, from calendar	Past	Today	Invalid	Not set
				Valid, over one year from now		Valid, set manually	Valid, from calendar
				Valid one week after departure	Valid, from calendar		Valid, set manually

Table 9.7 Options for Number of Adults and Kids

Step	Variable	T1	T2	T3	T4	T5	T6
B3	Number of traveling adults	1	2	0	1	0	Maximum allowed
				1			
B3	Number of traveling children	0	1	0	2	1	1
				Maximum allowed			

Sometimes the number of options to be tested is smaller than the number of columns, as shown in Table 9.8. Fill the remaining cells either with the most popular options or with some slightly different but valid options.

Table 9.8 Options for User ID and Password

Step	Variable	T1	T2	T3	T4	T5	T6
B10	User Id	Valid	Invalid	Nonexisting	Blank	Valid, using maximum number of letters	
			Valid	Valid	Valid		
B10	Password	Correct	Incorrect	Invalid	Blank	Incorrect	
			Correct	Correct	Correct	Correct	

Sometimes there are more options than the number of columns we initially allocated. Before adding a new column, analyze whether some of the options can be moved to the next row. Because some of the options will result in an error message, we can move some valid options to a "second-chance row." In Table 9.9 the option "Two words" does not fit in the same row with the other six options, but because "Longer than allowed" is one of the invalid options, in this test case we can retry the last name containing two words.

Table 9.9   Seven Options for Last Name (the Seventh Option Is Moved to a "Second-Chance Row")

Step	Variable	T1	T2	T3	T4	T5	T6
B11	Last name	Regular	Maximum length	With an apostrophe	Longer than allowed	One character	Blank
					Two words		Regular

Some rows are not filled for every column. In our example the rows with information related to the second passenger apply only to the test cases in which the number of passengers is greater than one, the rows with the information related to the third passenger apply only to the test cases in which the number of passengers is greater than two, and so forth (see Table 9.10). For test cases in which we have many passengers, we do not need to test all negative cases for each passenger. If some unusual option worked correctly for the first three passengers, it probably will work for the remaining three.

Some cells may not be filled when a test case is created. In the test case in which we test "Next day arrival," we do not know up front how many stopovers the flight will have, so rows related to selecting seats for the second or third legs may be filled at the time of testing if the selected flight has more than one leg (see Table 9.11).

Table 9.10   Filling in the Passenger's Information Depends on How Many Passengers Are Being Used in the Specific Test Case

Step	Variable	T1	T2	T3	T4	T5	T6
B3	Number of traveling adults	1	2	0	1	0	Maximum
				1			
B3	Number of traveling children	0	1	0	2	1	1
				Maximum			
			Correct	Correct	Correct	Correct	
B11	First name	Regular	Maximum length	Longer than allowed	One character	Blank	With space
				Regular		Regular	

Step	Variable	T1	T2	T3	T4	T5	T6
B11	Last name	Regular	Maximum length	With an apostrophe	Longer than Allowed	One Character	Blank
					Two words		Regular
B11	Sex	M	F	Not set	M	F	Not set
				M			F
B11	Date of birth	Valid	Future	Invalid	Last year	Over 20 years ago	Valid
			Valid	Valid	Valid	Valid	
B11	First name of the second passenger		Regular	Maximum length	Longer than allowed		Blank
					One character		With space
B11	Last name of the second passenger		Maximum length	With an apostrophe	Longer than allowed		Blank
					One character		Two words
B11	Sex of the second passenger		M	F	Not set		M
					F		
B11	Date of birth of the second passenger		Future	Invalid	Last year		Valid
			Valid	Valid	Valid		
B11	First name of the third passenger		Maximum length	With space	Regular		Regular

(continues)

Table 9.10   Filling in the Passenger's Information Depends on How Many Passengers Are Being Used in the Specific Test Case *(continued)*

Step	Variable	T1	T2	T3	T4	T5	T6
B11	Last name of the third passenger		Maximum length	With an apostrophe	Two words		Regular
B11	Sex of the third passenger		M	F	M		F
B11	Date of birth of the third passenger		Valid	Valid	Valid		Valid
B11	First name of the fourth passenger			Valid			Valid
B11	Last name of the fourth passenger			Valid			Valid
B11	Sex of the fourth passenger			F			M
B11	Date of birth of the fourth passenger			Valid			Valid
B11	First name of the fifth passenger			Valid			Valid
B11	Last name of the fifth passenger			Valid			Valid
B11	Sex of the fifth passenger			M			F
B11	Date of birth of the fifth passenger			Valid			Valid

Step	Variable	T1	T2	T3	T4	T5	T6
B11	First name of the sixth passenger			Valid			Valid
B11	Last name of the sixth passenger			Valid			Valid
B11	Sex of the sixth passenger			F			M
B11	Date of birth of the sixth passenger			Valid			Valid

Table 9.11 Filling in the Seat Selection Depends on How Many Passengers Are Being Used in the Specific Test Case and How Many Stopovers the Selected Flight Has

Step	Variable	T1	T2	T3	T4	T5	T6
B3	Number of traveling adults	1	2	0	1	0	Maximum
				1			
B3	Number of traveling children	0	1	0	2	1	1
				Maximum			
B5	Outbound flight	Direct	1 stopover	Maximum stopovers	The cheapest	Next-day arrival	Arrival in 2 days
B7	Return flight	Direct	1 stopover	Maximum stopovers	The cheapest	Next-day arrival	Arrival in 2 days
B13	Outbound seats for the first leg	Window	3 seats next to each other	Accept the default	2 seats together, 3rd in another row	Aisle	2 seats selected, the rest not selected
B13	Outbound seats for the second leg		Only one seat selected	All seats next to the window, different rows			
B13	Outbound seats for the third leg			Accept the default			

Step 4: Assign Values to Variables

In this step, you replace placeholders such as "a very long last name" or "a long phone number with extension" with actual values, such as "Georgiamistopolis" and "011-48 (242) 425-3456 ext. 1234," respectively.

In this step we also split all the test cases from the Test Case Allocation Matrix, creating a separate table for each test case.

For Test Case 1 of *Book a flight*, the test case is represented by the matrix shown in Table 9.12. In addition to the rows from Test Case Allocation Matrix, we have added some rows representing actions. For example, *B3 Search flights* means that we are selecting an action that initiates searching for flights. Usually this involves clicking a button with a name representing the action. However, at this stage we try to avoid decisions about whether it is clicking a button, clicking a link, or selecting a menu option. The user interface designer will decide which control represents the selection later in the process.

For the rows representing input variables, the expected result is usually either accepted or rejected. For the rows representing actions, the expected result is often the appearance of a new screen or dialog box.

Table 9.12   Test Case

Step	Variable	T1	Expected Result	Actual Result	Pass/ Fail	Com- ments
B3	Departure airport	EWR	Accept			
B3	Departure date	39166	Accept			
B3	Arrival airport	LAX	Accept			
B3	Return date	39179	Accept			
B3	Number of traveling adults	1	Accept			
B3	Number of traveling children	0	Accept			
B3	Search flights	Search flights	List of flights			
B5	Outbound flight	Select direct flight	List of flights			
B7	Return flight	Select direct flight	Login screen			
B10	User ID	User1	Accept			
B10	Password	Password	Accept			
B10	Login	Login	Passenger data screen			

Step	Variable	T1	Expected Result	Actual Result	Pass/ Fail	Com- ments
B11	First name	John	Accept			
B11	Last name	Smith	Accept			
B11	Sex	M	Accept			
B11	Date of birth	Valid	Accept			
B11	Submit	Submit	Seat selection screen			
B13	Outbound seats	Window	Accept			
B13	Submit	Submit	Seat selection screen			
B13	Return seats	Window	Accept			
B13	Submit	Submit	Seat selection screen			
B14	Credit card type	Visa	Accept			
B14	Credit card number	4123456789012340	Accept			
B14	Expiration date	01/01/2009	Accept			
B14	Name on the card	John Smith	Accept			
B14	Address	1 Main St.	Accept			
B14	City	New York	Accept			
B14	State	NY	Accept			
B14	Zip code	10001	Accept			
B14	Country	USA	Accept			
B14	Submit	Submit	Confirmation number			

This document will be given to a tester. The tester will follow the directions from columns 2 and 3 and record the results in columns 5, 6, and 7.

While creating scenarios and test cases, you can give feedback to the use case designers and refine the requirements. This can help you find any gaps in requirements early in the process.

9.2   Business Rules

The preceding section often referred to the field's required length or the allowable values for some parameter. How do you know the minimum and maximum allowable length of a field? This requirement can come from different sources. Sometimes it comes from the business analyst or a customer. For example, if we enter a Dun & Bradstreet number that identifies a company, that number should always be nine digits long. It is a business requirement.

Quite often, however, the requirement does not come from the customer or the user. If you ask the customer how big the last name field should be, he might say he does not care and ask you to make it whatever is reasonable. In this case it is a design step rather than a requirement step to decide how long the variable should be.

We call this type of requirement business rules. Distinguishing them from other requirements provides additional flexibility because business rules may change over time. For example, an Account Number may have eight digits when a system is developed but change to nine digits a year later.

There is a question about where business rules should be documented. One place to add this kind of requirement is in a section called Special Requirements in the use case. This is appropriate if these rules are specific to this use case. Another place where you can put this kind of requirement is in the glossary or data dictionary.

Another good option is to specify a separate Business Rules (BR) document. You can then define BR as a distinct requirement type. Then, the step in the use case could be worded in this fashion: "System validates the Account Information according to BR*nnn*," where *nnn* is a business rule number. This puts the business rules in a context, which is very useful for the developer. Using the OOAD (Object Oriented Analysis and Design) approach, they know in which method for a particular class the validation needs to occur.

9.3   Creating a New Document Type

The Test Case document type is not part of a standard RequisitePro template. We need to create a new document type. Follow these steps:

1. Create the required document template in Microsoft Word.
2. Save this outline as a template with the extension .dot, such as testcases.dot.
3. Create a text file containing three lines:
   - Title
   - Description
   - Name of the file that contains the outline
4. Save the test file with the same name as the outline, but with the extension .def, such as testcases.def.

Here is a sample .def file:

```
Test Cases Outline

The outline to be used for deriving Test Cases from Use Cases.

testcases.dot
```

5. Put .dot and .def files in the directory ProgramFiles\Rational\RequisitePro\outlines.

6. Open the Project Properties dialog box (right-click the project name and select Properties, or highlight the project name and select File > Properties).

7. Select the tab Document Types.

8. Click the Add button.

9. Fill in the fields of the Document Type dialog box, as shown in Figure 9.2:

Name: This name will appear in a list box of available document types in the New Documents dialog box while a document is being created.

Description: Any meaningful description.

File Extension: You can choose any extension, but make it meaningful (such as TCD for a Test Case Design document).

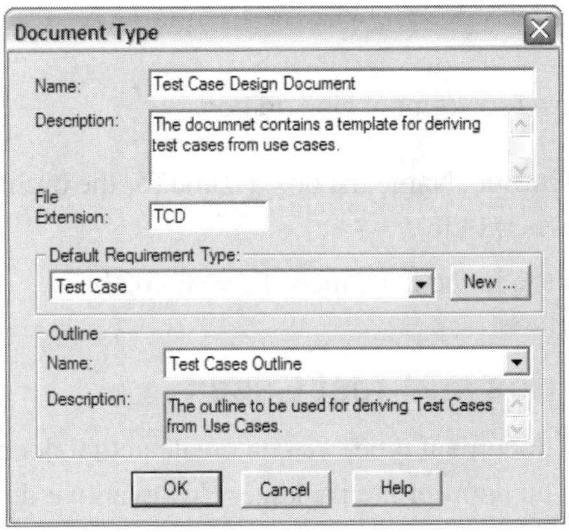

Figure 9.2 Defining a new document type.

10. Select the Default Requirement Type.

If you already added Test Case to the list of requirement types used in the project (using the method described in section 9.3), select it in the list box.

If you did not create a test case requirement yet, follow these steps to add it now:

a. Click the New button.

b. Fill in the fields of the Requirement Type dialog box, as shown in Figure 9.3:

Name: Test Case

Requirement Tag Prefix: TC

Requirement Color: Accept the default (Blue) or select another

Requirement Style: Accept the default (Double Underline) or select another

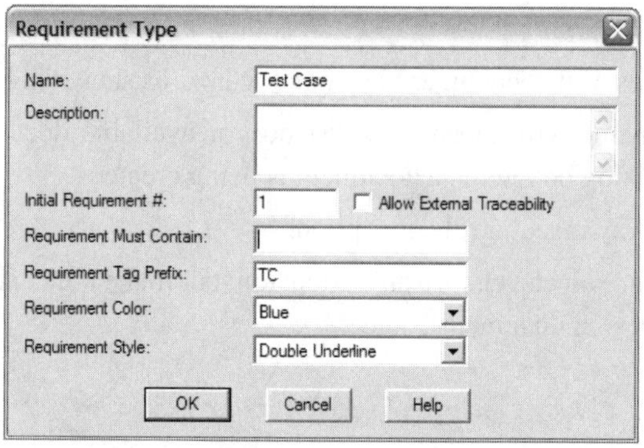

Figure 9.3   Adding a new requirement type ad hoc.

11. Select from the Outline, Name list box a name for the outline (it was defined in the first line of the testcases.txt file).

12. Click the OK button in the Document Type dialog box.

9.4   Adding Scenarios and Test Cases

After we have added a new document type, we can create actual documents. It is a good practice to create each document in an appropriate package. However, we do not have a default package for scenarios and test cases. We can create two separate packages—one for scenarios, and another for test cases—or we can combine them.

Creating a New Package

Let's create a new package. We can create separate packages for scenarios and test cases, or we can have one package to store both types of requirements.

To create a new package, follow these steps:

1. Right-click the project name and select New > Package.

2. Fill in the fields of the dialog box, as shown in Figure 9.4.

3. Click OK.

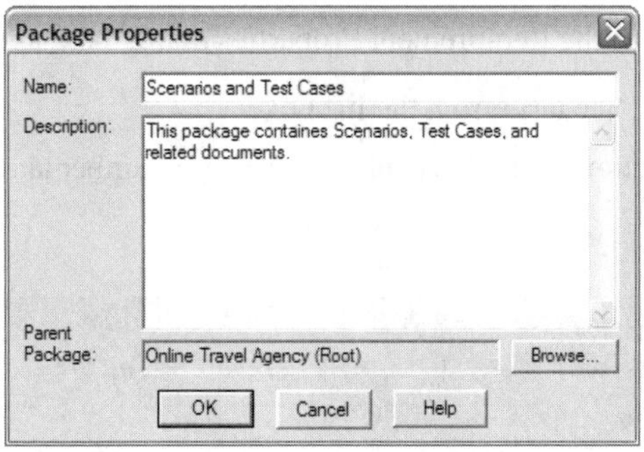

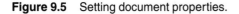

Figure 9.4   Creating a new package.

Creating a Document

Now we can create a document in this package. Do the following:

1. Right-click the package Scenarios and Test Cases and select New > Document.
2. Fill in the fields of the Document Properties dialog box, as shown in Figure 9.5.

   In the Document Type, select from the list box a name that was assigned in the Document Type dialog box (refer to Figure 9.2).
3. Use the document as a template to create test cases.

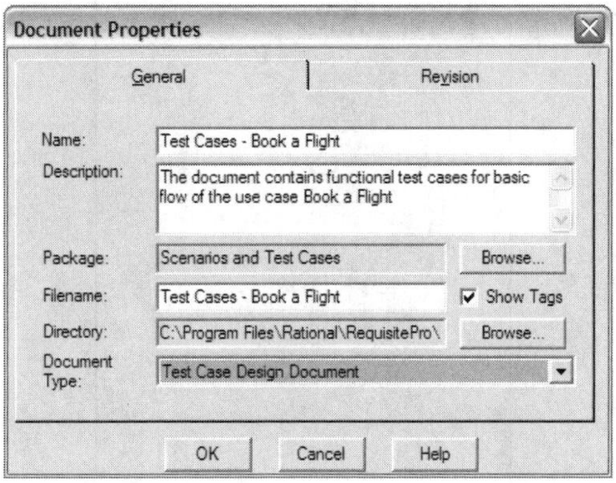

Figure 9.5   Setting document properties.

Adding Requirements from the Explorer

Section 5.4 described how to insert requirements from a document. This section shows how to add requirements from the Explorer:

1. Right-click the Supplementary Requirements package and select New > Requirement.

2. Fill in the fields of the Requirement Properties dialog box, as shown in Figure 9.6:

Type: Select SC: Scenario from the list box.

Name: You can name scenarios using the use case number and a sequence of flows (such as UC1, A6, A7).

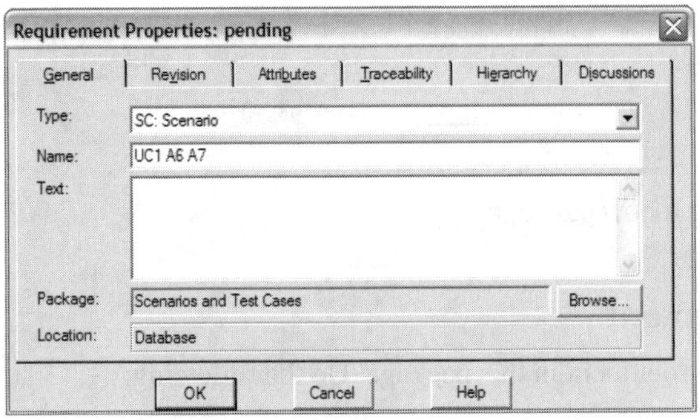

Figure 9.6   Filling the Requirement Properties dialog box for scenarios.

Entered scenarios appear in the Explorer, as shown in Figure 9.7.

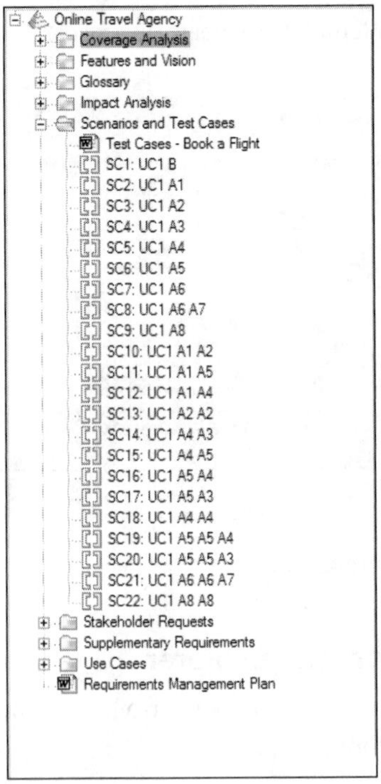

Figure 9.7   Scenarios in the Explorer.

We can enter the test cases in the same way. We need to assign a name for each test case. We can name the test cases with the scenario number and subsequent test case number:

SC1 TC5   (scenario 1, test case 5)

Or we can include the use case number in the name:

UC1 SC1 TC5   (use case 1, scenario 1, test case 5)

9.5   Setting Traceability

Mapping use cases to scenarios is a one-to-many or many-to-many relationship, depending on what we saved as use case requirements. If we have stored only full use cases, one use case will correspond to many scenarios (one or more). If we stored each flow or each step as a separate requirement, the relationship between use cases and scenarios will be many-to-many.

As discussed in previous chapters, to set traceability, we need to create a Traceability Matrix (see Figure 9.8). Then we can set traceability by placing arrows in the appropriate cells, as shown in Figure 9.9.

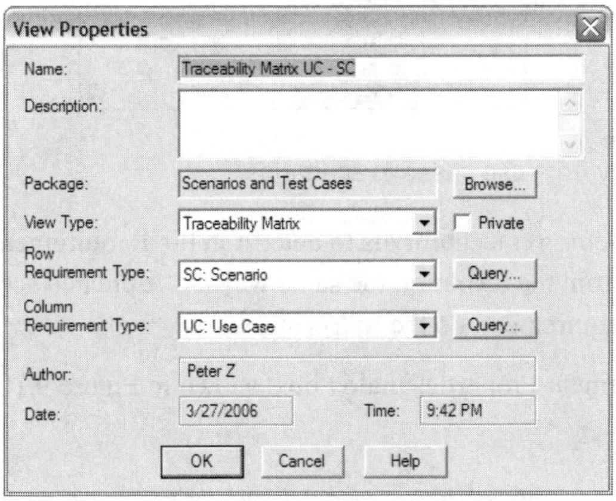

Figure 9.8   View Properties dialog box for creating a Traceability Matrix between use cases and scenarios.

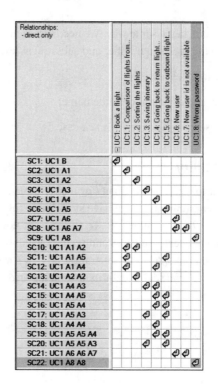

Figure 9.9   Traceability from use cases to scenarios.

Another way of setting traceability is to enter it in the Requirement Properties dialog box. Let's create test cases from the Explorer, the same way as we created scenarios. To set traceability while creating the requirement, do the following:

1. In the Requirement Properties dialog box, shown in Figure 9.10, select the Traceability tab.

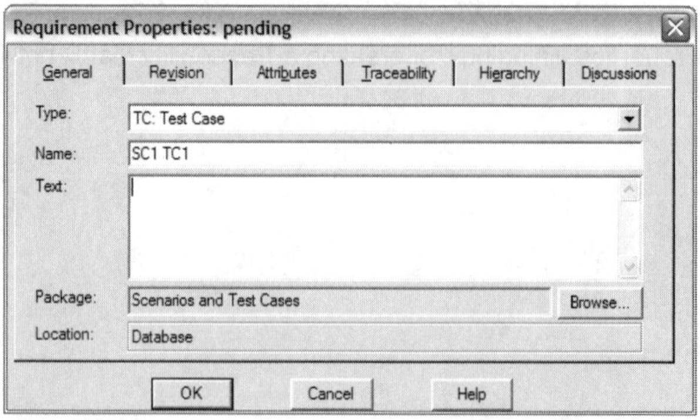

Figure 9.10   Requirement Properties dialog box for test cases.

2. Click Add next to the From entry field, as shown in Figure 9.11.

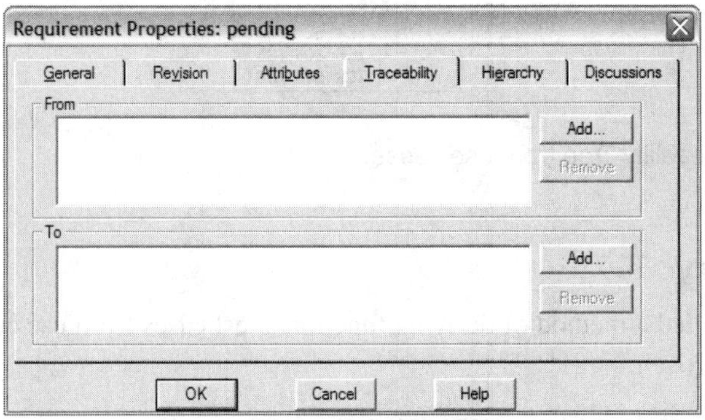

Figure 9.11   Requirement Properties dialog box for test cases.

3. Select a scenario from which this test case is traced, as shown in Figure 9.12.

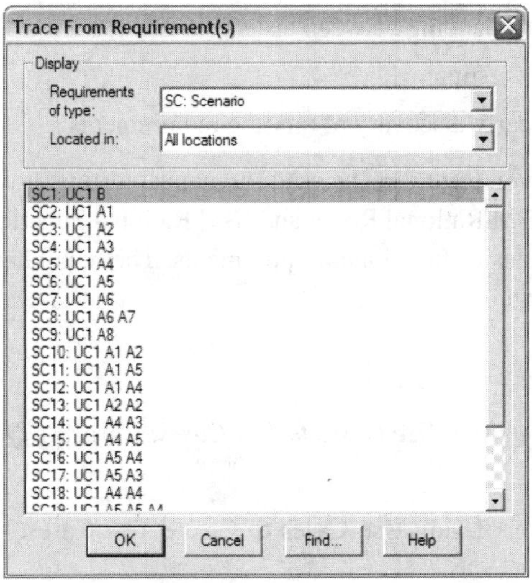

Figure 9.12   Setting traceability from the dialog box.

4. Click OK in the Trace From Requirement(s) dialog box.

After setting the traceability between scenarios and test cases, we can create a traceability tree that shows traceability all the way from use cases to the test cases, as shown in Figure 9.13. Creating the traceability tree was discussed in Chapter 6, "Developing a Vision Document."

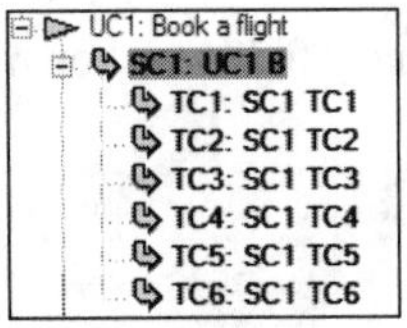

Figure 9.13   Traceability Tree from use cases.

9.6   Summary

This chapter presented a method of deriving functional test cases from use cases. Here are some benefits of this approach:

- Test cases are derived in a more automatic way
- Duplicate testing is avoided
- Better test coverage is achieved
- Easier monitoring of testing progress
- Easier workload balancing between testers
- Easier regression testing
- Contribution to early discovery of missing requirements

The test cases that you create can be used for manual testing, as well as for automated testing using tools, such as IBM Rational Robot and IBM Rational Functional Tester.

This approach applies to functional requirements. The next chapter discusses how to test nonfunctional requirements.

References

[HEU01a] Heumann, Jim. *From Use Cases to Test Cases: Ensuring Quality from the Beginning*, RUC, 2001.

[HEU01b] Heumann, Jim. "Using Use Cases to Create Test Cases." *The Rational Edge*, June 2001.

CHAPTER 10

Creating Test Cases from Supplementary Requirements

The preceding chapter introduced a method that can be applied to any use case to derive test cases. This chapter discusses deriving a test case from supplementary requirements (see Figure 10.1). With supplementary requirements, however, there is no unified approach, because various requirements are different in nature, and testing them requires quite different methods. This chapter presents the following methods of creating test cases:

- Executing selected test cases in different environments
- Adding an additional check to all use cases
- Checking and modifying specific use cases
- Performing the exercise
- Checklist
- Analysis
- White-box testing
- Automated testing

This chapter also covers using IBM Rational Robot and IBM Rational Test Manager for automated testing. The most recent tool from IBM, replacing previous versions of Test Manager, is called ClearQuest Test Manager. These tools can also be used for functional testing, not only for the performance testing described in this chapter.

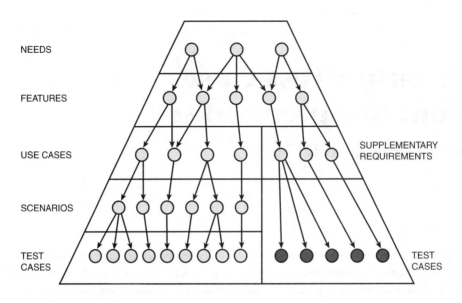

Figure 10.1   Deriving test cases from supplementary requirements.

10.1   Executing Selected Test Cases in Different Environments

Some requirements request that the application shall work in different environments:

> *The web-based interface shall run in Internet Explorer (version 6.0 and newer) and Netscape (version 6 and newer).*

The best approach to addressing this type of requirement is to select some big test case (in our case it may be one of the test cases related to a basic flow of the *Book a flight* use case) and execute it in different environments. This means that one full test case will be executed using the Internet Explorer (IE) browser and then using the Netscape browser.

Quite often a requirement is related to operating systems on which the application should run:

> *The system shall run on Windows XP, Windows Vista, and Solaris 10 operating systems.*

In case of Internet applications, however, the operating system is not that important, as it is in the case of desktop and client/server applications.

A variation of this case is if we need to test the application in the same environment, but with a different setup:

> *Dates shall be displayed according to the format stored in the web browser settings.*

In this case the testing involves the following steps:

1. Check the web browser settings.
2. Run the full test script for these settings.

3. Change the web browser settings (for example, to the French way of displaying the date).

4. Run the full test script for the new settings.

Figure 10.2 shows this approach. The selected scenario is tested in different environments, so we have one test case per environment.

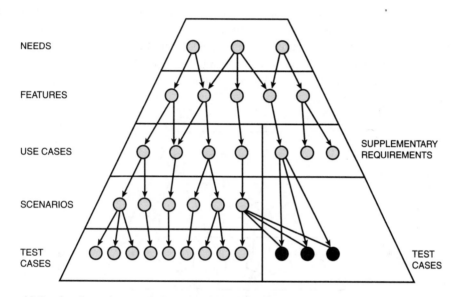

Figure 10.2 A selected scenario is executed in different environments.

10.2 Adding an Additional Check to All Use Cases

Many requirements describe appearance or behavior of some controls in the user interface. Here are some examples:

> *On each page a Next button shall suggest a default flow.*
>
> *On data entry screens the system shall indicate which fields are mandatory by placing a star next to the field.*
>
> *The system shall display a pop-up calendar when any date is entered, as in flight date, hotel stay date, or car rental date.*
>
> *Multiple entry fields on one page shall be vertically aligned.*
>
> *When a dialog box is opened, the focus shall be on the first entry field in the dialog box.*
>
> *For every invalid input from the user, the system shall display a meaningful error message, explaining what format is expected for the input.*

Currency amounts shall be calculated and stored with accuracy of two decimal places.

Each feature of the system should be described in online help, available from the menu on every page.

On the pages that gather the user's personal data, there shall be a link to a page describing the privacy policy.

The best way to incorporate testing of these features is to add a check to all test cases that are already created for various use cases. Because test cases derived from use cases cover every possible screen used in the application, we can just add appropriate checks while visiting each specific screen for the first time. This way, we can be sure that the feature was checked in all places where it is applicable. Figure 10.3 shows that all test cases are updated with the specific supplementary requirement.

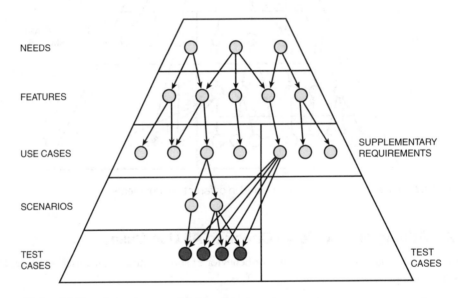

Figure 10.3   Additional checks are added to all test cases.

Every time a new screen or dialog box is displayed, we need to insert a checklist into the test case.

Some requirements need to be checked once per page, and others require testing all the controls of a specific type. Here are some examples:

- One check per page:
  - Is there a Next button suggesting a default navigation?
  - If the page contains multiple entry fields, are they vertically aligned?
  - Is help available from the menu?

- Checking specific controls:
  - Do all mandatory fields have a star next to them?
  - Is a pop-up calendar available for every date field?
  - Do all currency fields accept and display two decimal places?

10.3   Checking and Modifying Specific Use Cases

Even though some requirements are described in the Supplementary Specification, they are associated with some specific use cases. This may happen when this piece of functionality is not really related to the main use case but plays a supportive or administrative role. As an example, we can look at requirements related to security and password-protected access to some parts of the application:

> *A password shall be required to access administrator screens.*
>
> *To submit the offers, hotel providers, car providers, and airline representatives shall log in to the system using their IDs and passwords.*
>
> *Users shall pick IDs and passwords while buying an airline ticket.*

In each of these requirements we can add a few steps to the appropriate use case. If the login procedure is complicated, we may consider extracting it as a separate use case that will be included in other use cases.

Figure 10.4 shows that an update is made to the use case and then propagated through scenarios and test cases.

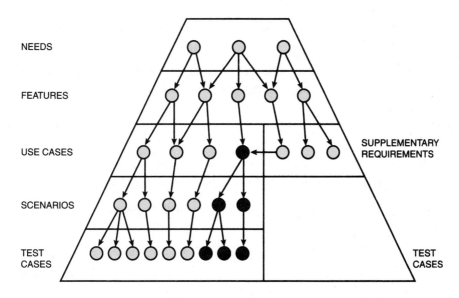

Figure 10.4   Some supplementary requirements affect use cases and all scenarios and test cases derived from them.

10.4   Performing the Exercise

Quite often we need to perform the action described in the requirement. In many cases the task does not require creating formal scenarios and test cases.

> *An error log containing information about all critical errors shall be accessible to the system administrator over the Internet, so it can be checked remotely at any time.*

To test this feature, someone will log in to the system over the Internet and check if he or she can access an error log.

Some requirements are related to the average time required to perform a task:

> *A service provider shall be able to learn to use a system in one hour.*

> *The average time of booking a hotel room shall be no longer than ten minutes.*

In these cases it may be beneficial to perform the task by three independent testers and compare the timings.

Some other tests may be performed by the same person but repeated a few times to check if the timings are consistent:

> *In case of a system failure, a redundant system shall resume operations within 30 seconds.*

> *The average repair time shall be less than one hour.*

> *The system shall be operational within one minute of starting up.*

It is okay to do some tests only once that require a long time to complete, unless we suspect some problems:

> *Deployment time on a new version of WebSphere Application Server shall be no longer than one day.*

If a test deployment on a new version of WAS took 15 hours, there is no need to check it more. However, if the first test took 40 hours, we need to analyze the cause and retest after fixing the problems.

Here is another example of a requirement that can be checked just by performing an exercise:

> *The user interface shall not contain any components that would prevent automated testing using IBM Rational Robot and IBM Rational Functional Tester.*

Some requirements may require a mini use case, such as counting how many clicks are required to access specific functionality:

> *Booking airplane ticket functionality shall be available from the home page.*

> *Renting a car functionality shall be available after no more than one click from the home page.*

10.5   Checklist

Some requirements do not need any complicated testing, so you can just check to see if they are fulfilled. For example:

The system shall use an Oracle database.

Either Oracle is used, or it is not—just mark the checklist.

Some other examples of this kind of testing simply by checking might include the following:

All system errors shall be recorded and made available to the administrator.

All transactions (ticket purchase, making a reservation, updating a reservation, and canceling a reservation) shall be recorded and made available to the administrator.

The system shall use J2EE architecture.

If the architecture requires an application server, IBM WebSphere shall be used.

The Administrator's Guide shall be available as a PDF document.

Separate tabs shall be available for the main functionality (booking the flight, reserving a hotel room, reserving a car, attractions information).

10.6   Analysis

Some requirements do not require big testing but require some analysis. Often a mental exercise is enough, without performing physical testing.

No technical skills (except for using the browser) shall be required to use the system.

The system shall be available 24 hours a day, seven days a week.

During analysis of the last requirement, we can ask the following questions:

- Is anything preventing the application from running continuously?
- Is there any scheduled maintenance that can make the application unavailable for some period of time?

Many features of this type require analyzing the architecture. It is worth involving a system architect in this analysis:

No installation on the client's workstation shall be required. All system upgrades and new releases should be done on the server.

The system shall automatically book a ticket with the Airline Reservation System without the necessity of human intervention.

Adding a user interface in a different language shall not require rewriting the application logic.

Some architectural analysis may be supported by a simple demo:

The system's main functionality (booking the flight, purchasing an airplane ticket, reserving a hotel room, reserving a car) shall be encapsulated in components that can be reused in a client/server (non-Internet) application.

A very simple test client application can be created that proves that components can be reused in other systems.

10.7　White-Box Testing

Some testing should be done with knowledge of the application code or some other application internals. This is called white-box testing.

When returning a list of flights, the system cannot miss any direct flight or any flight with only one stopover.

To check this requirement, we need to access the flight database directly, not through our application, and compare the results with a list obtained through our system.

Quite often testing requires checking if a specific algorithm was applied correctly:

The list of flights returned from the search shall include the flight calculated from Dijkstra's Shortest Path algorithm.

10.8　Automated Testing

Automated testing is very helpful in checking performance and reliability requirements such as these:

Average system response time shall be less than two seconds.

The system shall accommodate 1,000 booked flights per minute.

The system shall accommodate 5,000 concurrent users.

The average time between failures shall exceed 20 hours.

The system may be unavailable no more than one minute per 24 hours.

For performance and reliability testing, we do not need to automate all test cases. We can select from one to three test cases. It is worth selecting a test case representing the most popular scenario. It is also worth selecting a test case containing the longest operations. In our example, basic flow of the *Book a flight* use case is the most popular, and at the same time it contains the longest processing (searching flights). Because making car and hotel reservations are also often used and contain completely different flows, it is also worth using them in automated testing.

We can run the same script many times with different parameters. Two of the most important parameters are number of users and number of iterations. Iterations are performed sequentially. Number of users specifies how many threads are executed concurrently.

To analyze the impact of number of concurrent users, the same script shall be executed for a different number of users—for example, for 1, 10, 100, and 1,000. Actual numbers may vary depending on the application and the required ultimate number of users.

To test mean time between failures and other reliability benchmarks, we shall have at least one run that is very long—at least 48 hours.

Here are some questions that may be answered using automated testing:

- What is the response time during normal conditions?
- How many users can the system support before the performance becomes unacceptable?
- How does the system behave with the maximum expected number of users?
- If the number of users increases beyond the maximum, does the system gracefully lose performance, or does it crash?
- How do the system's performance and reliability depend on the system resources (available memory, disk space)?
- How does performance depend on time of day (evenings versus mornings, weekends versus weekdays)?

Automated testing is also useful for functional regression testing. In this case it is worth creating scripts for many scenarios.

The main testing tools provided by IBM are Rational Robot, Rational Test Manager, Rational ClearQuest Test Manager, Rational Functional Tester, and Rational Performance Tester. As an example, the next section shows how to create and execute scripts using Rational Robot and Rational Test Manager.

10.9   Using Robot and Test Manager for Automated Testing

IBM Rational Robot [IBM03a] can be used to develop two kinds of scripts:

- GUI scripts for functional testing
- Virtual users (VU) sessions for performance testing

IBM Rational Test Manager [IBM03b] is a framework that can be used to plan, design, implement, execute, and evaluate tests. We can create a suite that executes scripts for many virtual users. Recently a newer tool was released—IBM Rational ClearQuest Test Manager.

A usual approach to performance testing is to record scripts with Robot and then use Test Manager (or ClearQuest Test Manager) to schedule and play back these scripts.

Recording a VU Script

Recording a virtual users (VU) script with Rational Robot is fairly straightforward. Follow these steps:

1. Start Rational Robot by selecting All Programs > Rational Software > Rational Robot.
2. Provide your username and password, as shown in Figure 10.5. The password for the administrator was established when the Rational project was set up (refer to Chapter 4, "Setting Up the Project," Figure 4.12).

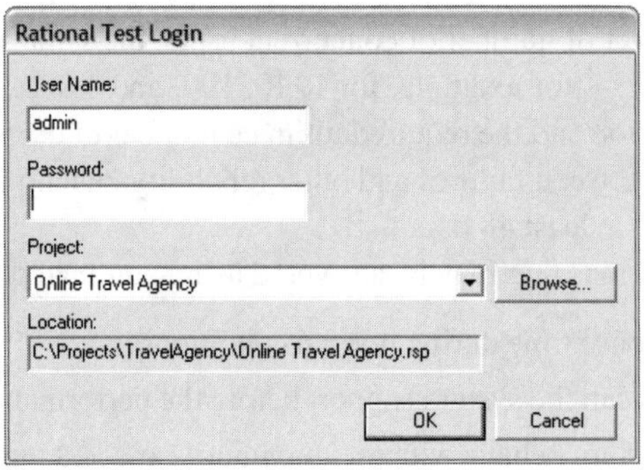

Figure 10.5   Rational Test Login dialog box.

3. Select the project from the list box.

4. Click OK.

5. Click the circle labeled VU, as shown in Figure 10.6.

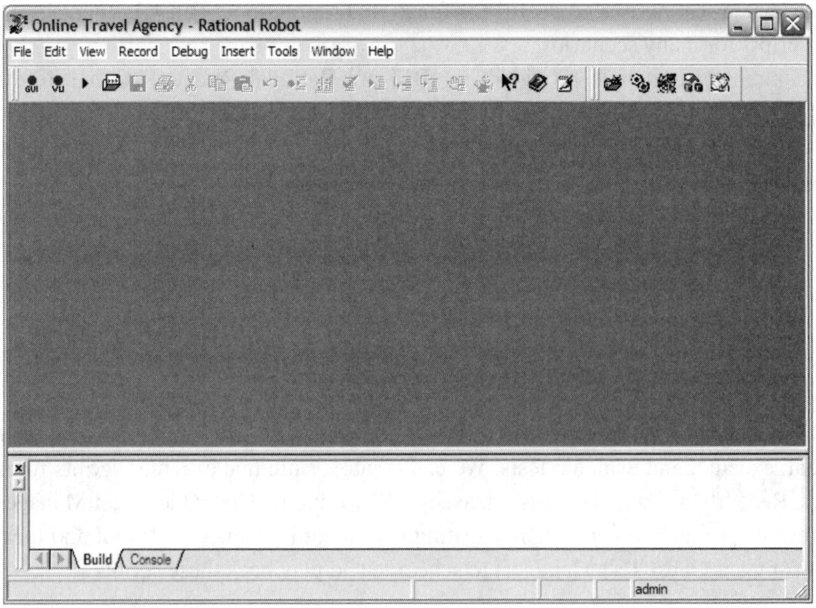

Figure 10.6   Rational Robot initial screen.

6. Name the session, as shown in Figure 10.7. You can use the name of a use case, a scenario, or a test case.

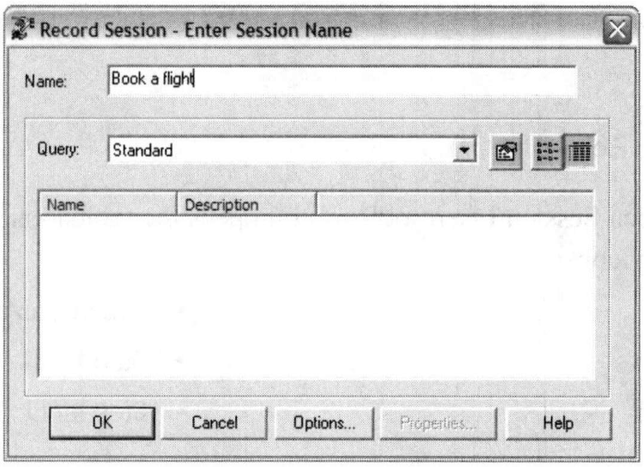

Figure 10.7   Selecting a name for a session.

7. Select the path to IE in the Executable field, and leave the other fields blank (see Figure 10.8). Usually, the path should be C:\Program Files\Internet Explorer\IEXPLORE.EXE.

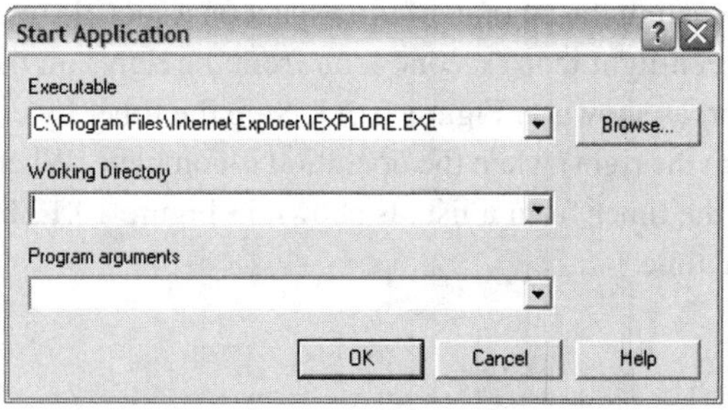

Figure 10.8   Selecting an application. In the case of Internet applications, the browser executable is selected.

8. Start recording all the steps from the test case. The Session Record toolbar appears. It contains four icons, as shown in Figure 10.9:

   • Stop recording
   • Open Robot window
   • Split session into scripts
   • Open Session Insert toolbar

Figure 10.9   Session Record toolbar.

Clicking the Open Session Insert toolbar icon opens the toolbar shown in Figure 10.10. It contains the following icons:

- Run
- Start timer
- Stop timer
- Comment

- Synchronization point
- Start block
- Stop block

Figure 10.10   Session Insert toolbar.

9. If you want to capture the amount of time spent on a specific operation, start the timer by clicking the green-light icon (second icon from the right) on the Session Insert toolbar. Name the timer, as shown in Figure 10.11. Stop the timer by clicking the red-light icon (third icon from the right) when the operation is complete. When you stop the timer, you need to select the timer from a list, as shown in Figure 10.12 because many timers can run at the same time.

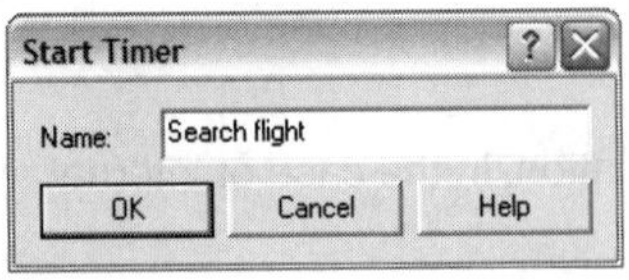

Figure 10.11   Assigning a name to a timer.

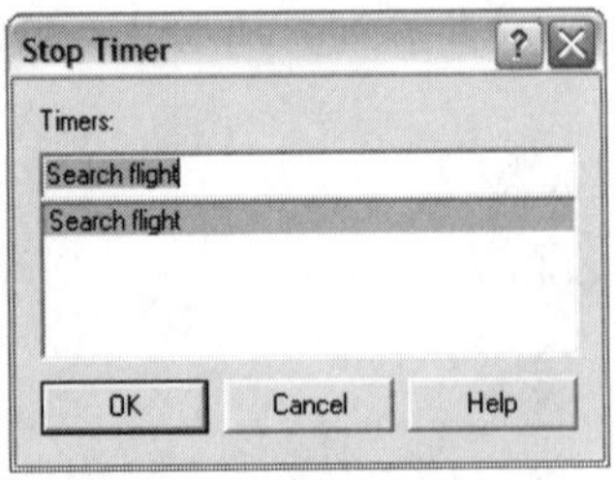

Figure 10.12   Selecting the timer that should be stopped.

10. When you are done recording the script, click the dark blue square on the Session Record toolbar (first icon from the left in Figure 10.9).

11. Name the script, as shown in Figure 10.13. It is okay to use the same name you used in the session in step 6.

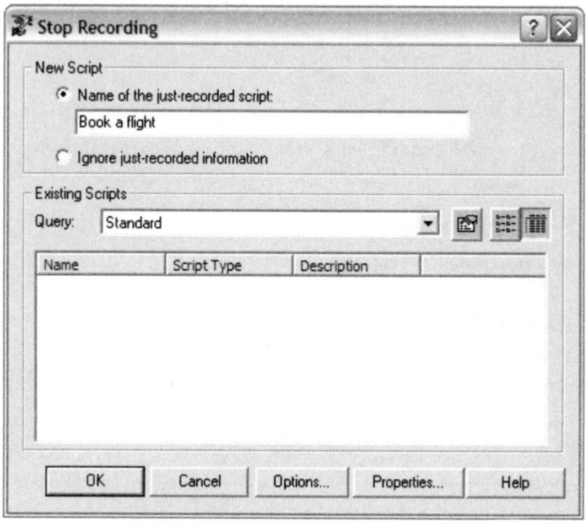

Figure 10.13   Naming the just-recorded script.

12. Click OK in the Stop Recording dialog box. A window with VU language code appears, as shown in Figure 10.14.

How to Run a Suite in Rational Test Manager

Test Manager can emulate many concurrent users performing various tasks reflected in test scripts. A test script can be the following:

- A session recorded using Robot
- A script imported from Quality Architect
- Written from scratch in Java or Visual Basic following required conventions
- Written in any scripting language (in this case an adapter also needs to be written)

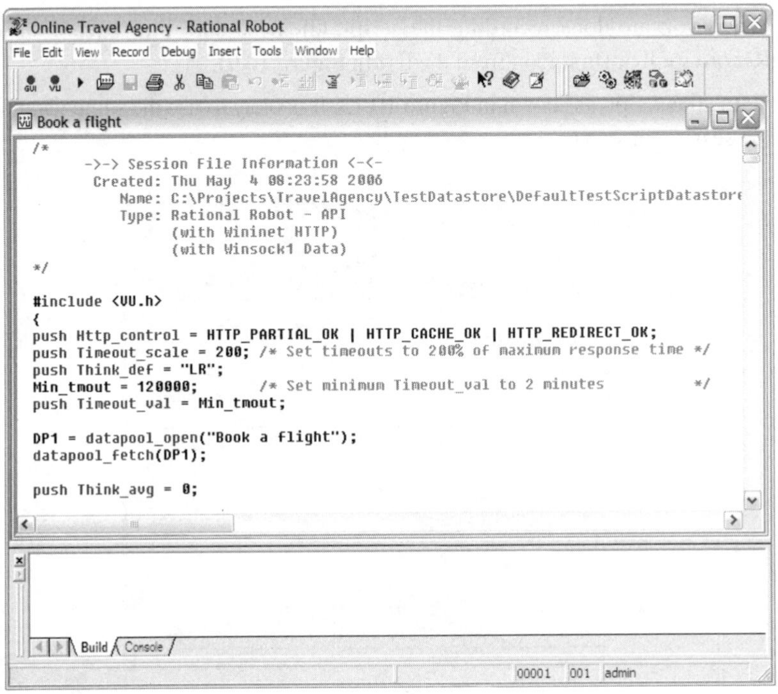

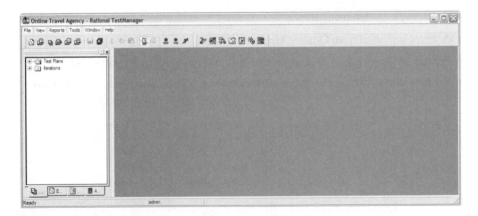

Figure 10.14   The code of the recorded script.

This chapter uses a session recorded in Robot. To create and run the test suite, follow these steps:

1. Start Test Manager by selecting All Programs > Rational Software > Rational Test Manager, as shown in Figure 10.15.

Figure 10.15   Main Test Manager window.

2. If the login dialog box appears, enter your information in the User Name and Password fields.

3. From the main Test Manager window, select File > Open Suite.

4. Select the Performance Testing Wizard option in the New Suite dialog box, shown in Figure 10.16, and click OK.

Figure 10.16   New Suite dialog box.

5. Select Local computer, as shown in Figure 10.17.

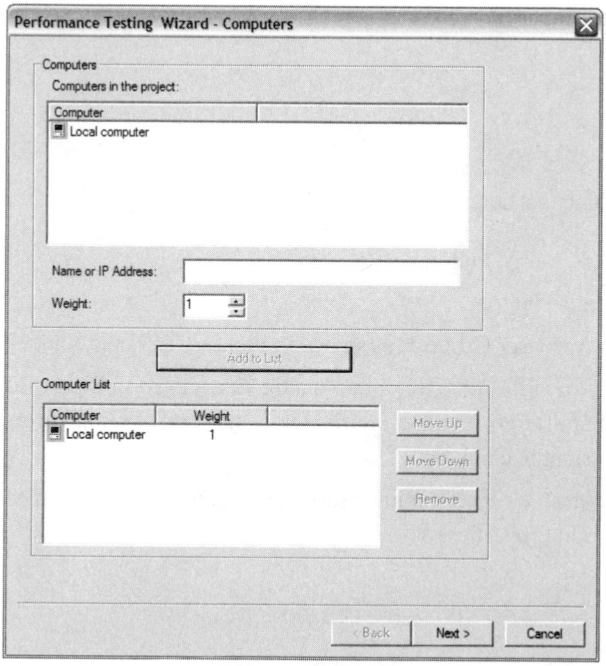

Figure 10.17   Performance Testing Wizard - Computers.

6. Click the Add to List button.

7. Click the Next button.

8. Select scripts. You see the dialog box shown in Figure 10.18.

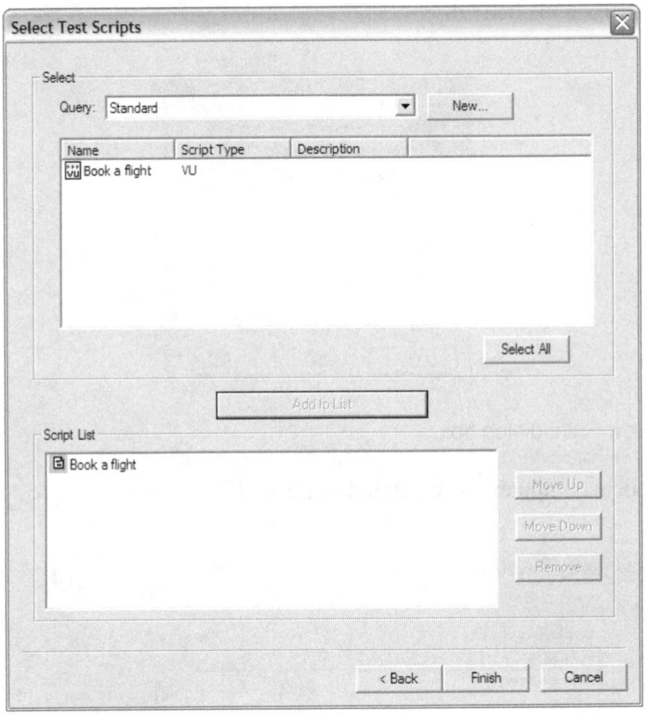

Figure 10.18   Selecting test scripts.

9.   Click the Add to List button.

10. Click the Finish button.

11. Right-click VU User Group 1, as shown in Figure 10.19, and select Run Properties.

12. In the Run Properties of User Group dialog box, shown in Figure 10.20, set the maximum number of users. In other words, set the number of virtual users you want to simulate concurrently. Click OK.

13. Right-click the icon representing a script (in Figure 10.19 it is named "Book a flight"), and select Run Properties.

Figure 10.19 A tree representation of a suite.

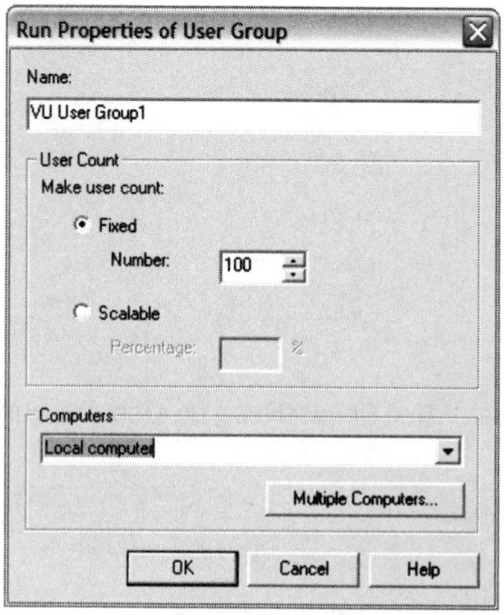

Figure 10.20 Run Properties of User Group dialog box, in which you set the maximum number of users.

14. In the Run Properties of Test Script dialog box, shown in Figure 10.21, set the number of iterations—how many times you want to repeat the script for the same user. Click OK.

15. Save the suite by selecting File > Save As, as shown in Figure 10.22.

16. Run a suite by selecting File > Run Suite.

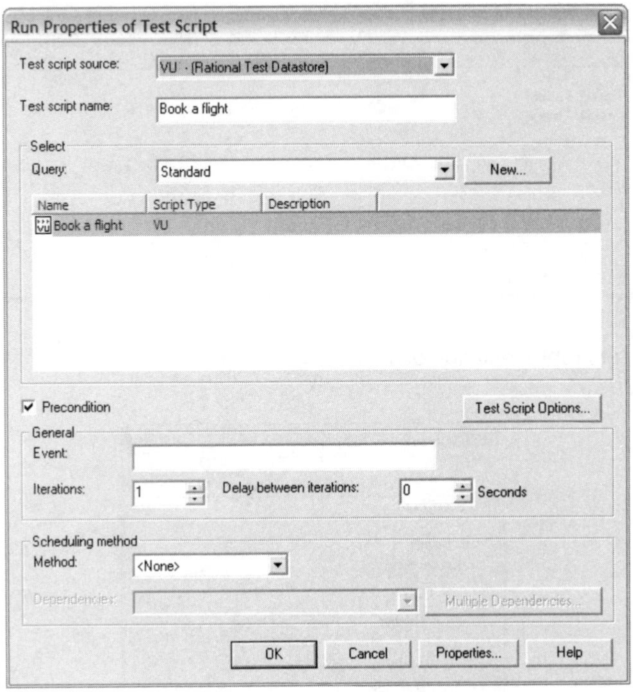

Figure 10.21   Run Properties of Test Script dialog box (set the number of iterations).

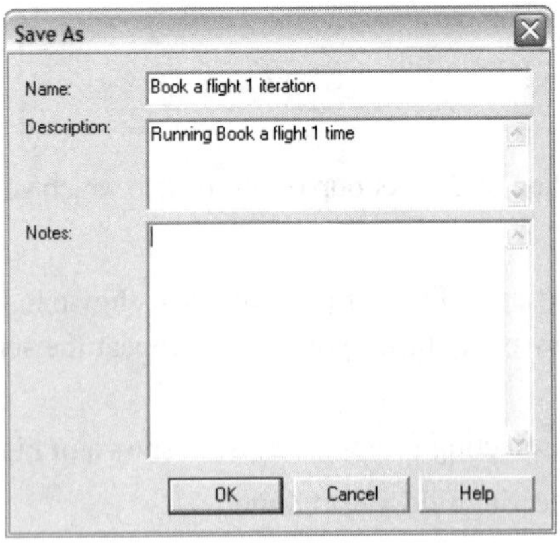

Figure 10.22   Saving a suite.

17. You can adjust the number of users for the current run, as shown in Figure 10.23.

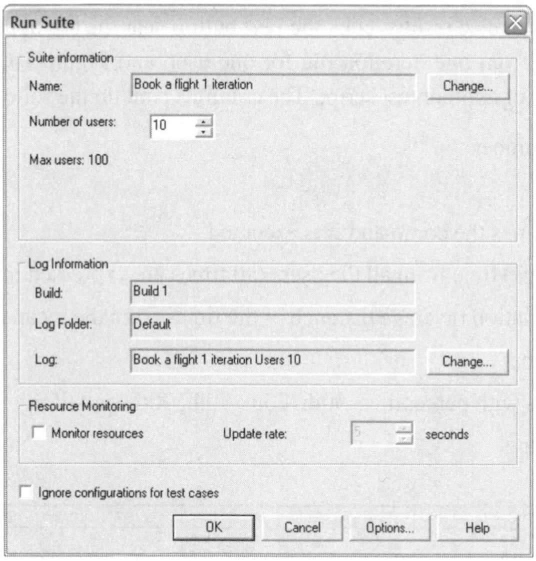

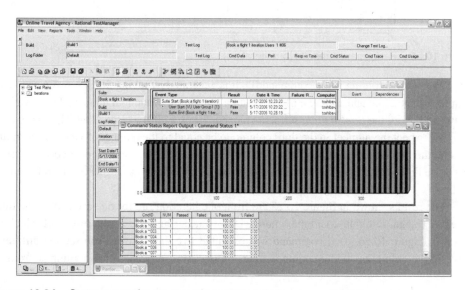

Figure 10.23   Run Suite dialog box (set parameters for the test run).

Analyzing the Results

When the test run ends, the result on the screen (see Figure 10.24) contains the status of executed commands. On this screen, you see bars that are green and red. Green represents "pass," and red represents "fail."

Figure 10.24   Status report for commands executed during a successful test run.

To see the performance results, click the Perf button near the top of the screen. Figure 10.25 shows sample results from one iteration run for one user, and Figure 10.26 shows results from running five iterations of another test script. The columns contain the following:

- Command number
- Command ID
- Number of times the command was executed
- Mean (average) time from all the users (all times are expressed in seconds)
- Standard deviation (average distance of the times from the mean time)
- Minimum time
- Five columns with percentiles: 50th, 70th, 80th, 90th, and 95th
- Maximum time

	CmdID	NUM	MEAN	STD DEV	MIN	50th	70th	80th	90th	95th	MAX
1	Book a ~001	1	0.14	0.00	0.14	0.14	0.14	0.14	0.14	0.14	0.14
2	Book a ~002	1	0.06	0.00	0.06	0.06	0.06	0.06	0.06	0.06	0.06
3	Book a ~003	1	0.06	0.00	0.06	0.06	0.06	0.06	0.06	0.06	0.06
4	Book a ~004	1	0.28	0.00	0.28	0.28	0.28	0.28	0.28	0.28	0.28
5	Book a ~005	1	0.81	0.00	0.81	0.81	0.81	0.81	0.81	0.81	0.81
6	Book a ~006	1	0.02	0.00	0.02	0.02	0.02	0.02	0.02	0.02	0.02
7	Book a ~007	1	0.08	0.00	0.08	0.08	0.08	0.08	0.08	0.08	0.08
8	Book a ~008	1	0.08	0.00	0.08	0.08	0.08	0.08	0.08	0.08	0.08
9	Book a ~010	1	0.08	0.00	0.08	0.08	0.08	0.08	0.08	0.08	0.08
10	Book a ~011	1	0.00	0.00	0.00	0.00	0.00	0.00	0.00	0.00	0.00
11	Book a ~012	1	3.09	0.00	3.09	3.09	3.09	3.09	3.09	3.09	3.09
12	Book a ~013	1	0.19	0.00	0.19	0.19	0.19	0.19	0.19	0.19	0.19
13	Book a ~014	1	3.56	0.00	3.56	3.56	3.56	3.56	3.56	3.56	3.56
14	Book a ~015	1	0.00	0.00	0.00	0.00	0.00	0.00	0.00	0.00	0.00
15	Book a ~016	1	0.20	0.00	0.20	0.20	0.20	0.20	0.20	0.20	0.20
16	Book a ~018	1	0.00	0.00	0.00	0.00	0.00	0.00	0.00	0.00	0.00
17	Book a ~019	1	0.27	0.00	0.27	0.27	0.27	0.27	0.27	0.27	0.27
18	Book a ~020	1	0.37	0.00	0.37	0.37	0.37	0.37	0.37	0.37	0.37
19	Book a ~022	1	0.25	0.00	0.25	0.25	0.25	0.25	0.25	0.25	0.25
20	Book a ~023	1	0.47	0.00	0.47	0.47	0.47	0.47	0.47	0.47	0.47

Figure 10.25   Performance results (one iteration).

The second column is the command ID. It is generated by taking the first seven characters from the script name and adding a tilde (~) and a three-digit sequential number. That's why the command IDs for the *Book a flight* script are named "Book a ~001," "Book a ~002," and so on.

We expect the number in the third column to be equal to the number of virtual users multiplied by the number of iterations. However, if the whole suite does not execute correctly, some scripts would not reach this command, and the number of executions of this command would be smaller.

The results shown in Figure 10.25 are from one iteration run for one user, so all the times are equal (mean, minimum, and maximum). However, during the run, the results of which are shown in Figure 10.26, each command was executed five times, so we can see the difference between the minimum and maximum times. These spreadsheets contain timings from all responses. This information is useless because we do not know to which operations they correspond. The most useful are times captured for specific operations between starting and stopping the timer because we were able to assign meaningful names to them.

	CmdID	NUM	MEAN	STD DEV	MIN	50th	70th	80th	90th	95th	MAX
1	Book a~001	5	0.04	0.07	0.00	0.00	0.00	0.04	0.11	0.15	0.19
2	Book a~002	5	0.35	0.16	0.19	0.31	0.33	0.39	0.53	0.59	0.66
3	Book a~003	5	1.08	0.63	0.28	1.08	1.34	1.54	1.80	1.93	2.06
4	Book a~004	5	0.02	0.03	0.00	0.00	0.00	0.02	0.05	0.06	0.08
5	Book a~005	5	0.02	0.04	0.00	0.00	0.00	0.02	0.06	0.08	0.09
6	Book a~006	5	0.20	0.01	0.19	0.20	0.20	0.20	0.20	0.20	0.20
7	Book a~007	5	0.20	0.01	0.19	0.20	0.22	0.22	0.22	0.22	0.22
8	Book a~008	5	0.20	0.01	0.19	0.20	0.22	0.22	0.22	0.22	0.22
9	Book a~009	5	0.20	0.01	0.19	0.20	0.20	0.20	0.20	0.20	0.20
10	Book a~010	5	0.03	0.05	0.00	0.00	0.00	0.03	0.08	0.10	0.13
11	Book a~011	5	0.00	0.00	0.00	0.00	0.00	0.00	0.00	0.00	0.00
12	Book a~012	5	0.19	0.03	0.16	0.17	0.22	0.24	0.24	0.24	0.24
13	Book a~013	5	0.19	0.03	0.16	0.17	0.22	0.24	0.24	0.24	0.24
14	Book a~014	5	0.02	0.03	0.00	0.00	0.00	0.02	0.05	0.06	0.08
15	Book a~015	5	0.13	0.04	0.09	0.11	0.13	0.15	0.17	0.18	0.19
16	Book a~016	5	0.13	0.04	0.09	0.11	0.13	0.15	0.17	0.18	0.19
17	Book a~017	5	0.01	0.02	0.00	0.00	0.00	0.01	0.03	0.04	0.05
18	Book a~018	5	0.73	1.22	0.09	0.10	0.16	0.77	1.97	2.57	3.17
19	Book a~019	5	0.73	1.22	0.09	0.10	0.16	0.77	1.97	2.57	3.17
20	Book a~020	5	0.28	0.07	0.23	0.25	0.26	0.30	0.36	0.39	0.42

Figure 10.26   Performance results (five iterations).

We can cut and paste information from the performance results table to Microsoft Excel and do some cleanup by removing unnecessary rows.

Table 10.1 presents an example of a cleaned-up spreadsheet for a five-user run. The first column contains the name of the timed operation, and the rest of the columns are the same as the columns in Figure 10.25. Analyzing this data shows whether the time taken to perform specific operations is satisfactory.

Table 10.1   Scenarios Selected for Testing in the *Book a Flight* Use Case

Operation	Number	Mean	Deviation	Minimum	50th	70th	80th	90th	95th	Maximum
Search flights	5	5.88	0.69	5.11	5.92	6.09	6.31	6.66	6.84	7.02
Select outbound flight	5	3.06	0.28	2.72	2.91	3.26	3.36	3.4	3.42	3.44
Select return flight	5	3.61	1.97	1.92	2.16	4.68	5.57	6.1	6.37	6.63
Select seats	5	3.45	0.38	2.74	3.69	3.7	3.71	3.72	3.73	3.74
Purchase ticket	5	4.57	0.55	4.05	4.23	5.03	5.23	5.25	5.25	5.26

10.10   Summary

This chapter presented eight methods of deriving test cases from supplementary requirements. In most cases we dealt with nonfunctional requirements. Supplementary requirements vary significantly as far as type. That's why no unified method exists to test them, so we need to select an appropriate approach for every requirement.

Using an automated testing tool is very helpful for testing performance and reliability requirements. The example presented in section 10.9 is a simple case of recording an IBM Rational Robot session and running it for the required number of virtual users. More advanced usage or Robot includes setting up the type of recording depending on the system architecture, adjusting script-generation options, using data pools, and manual update of recorded scripts. Automated testing tools are also useful in executing functional test cases, as described in the preceding chapter. However, although functional testing may be conducted manually, it is almost impossible to do performance testing without these tools.

The test cases should be prepared quite early in the project because creating them may raise some questions that will help refine the requirements. However, actual testing begins only after some part of the system is designed and developed. The next chapter discusses the design discipline.

References

[IBM03a] *Rational Robot, User's Guide*, IBM Corporation, 2003.

[IBM03b] *Rational Test Manager, User's Guide*, IBM Corporation, 2003.

CHAPTER 11

Object-Oriented Design

This chapter shows you how the requirements gathered so far can act as a basis for object-oriented system design. There are many approaches to design, and the method described here is one of them. The generic approach presented can be applied regardless of the architecture and implementation language. However, this high-level design should be refined by taking into consideration programming language and system architecture.

Figure 11.1 presents a high-level view of this approach. For each scenario we create one sequence diagram. While creating sequence diagrams, at the same time we create classes that encapsulate required functionality. The classes, their attributes and operations, and the relationships between classes are depicted in the class diagrams.

Sections 11.2 and 11.3 show you how to use two IBM tools for design: Rational Rose and Rational Software Architect.

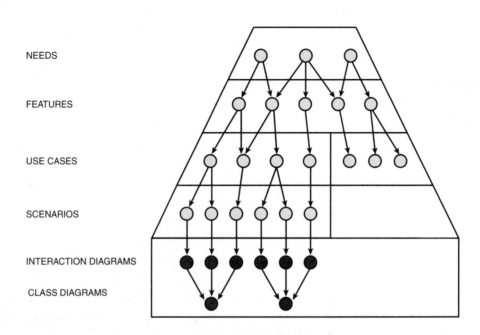

NEEDS

FEATURES

USE CASES

SCENARIOS

INTERACTION DIAGRAMS

CLASS DIAGRAMS

Figure 11.1   Creating design diagrams from scenarios.

11.1   System Design from Use Cases

Design can be done using the Unified Modeling Language (UML)—a graphical modeling language that uses standardized notation for creating abstract models of systems [BOO04] [BOO05].

The core task of the presented method is creating a sequence diagram for each scenario. At the same time, classes are designed and relationships between classes are shown on the class diagrams.

When we design interaction diagrams, messages from an actor should go to a *boundary* class (usually representing a user interface form). The boundary class then passes messages to a *controller* class, which subsequently collaborates with the appropriate *entity* classes.

We will follow these steps for each scenario:

1. Get a pair of use case steps: user's request and system's response.

2. Decide which boundary class will provide the interaction with the actors.

3. Create a name for an operation that will allow the actor to pass input values to the system.

4. Design arguments for this operation. Usually there is one argument for each user interface (UI) control on the screen. For example, a text variable may represent an entry field, and a Boolean variable may represent a radio button or a checkbox.

5. Decide what controller operation should provide this functionality.

6. Decide what controller class should provide this operation (pick from existing classes or create a new one).

7. Design arguments and the return value of the operation (if needed, create new entity classes).

8 If needed, create in the boundary class an operation that displays on the screen information obtained from the controller class.

9. Continue the same tasks for the next use case steps.

As an example, let's look at the basic flow of the *Book a flight* use case.

We can skip the following first two steps because this functionality is provided not by our application, but by the Internet and a browser:

B1. Traveler enters the site's URL.

B2. System displays the home page.

The next two steps provide a list of flights based on departure and arrival airport and date and number of passengers.

B3. Traveler enters:

Departure airport, departure date

Arrival airport, return date

Number of traveling adults and children

Traveler selects "Search flights."

B4. System displays outbound flights sorted by price.

Let's create a class FlightReservationForm that will include UI functionality related to these use case steps. In UML a class is represented by a rectangle with three compartments:

• The upper compartment has a class name.

• The middle compartment has attributes.

• The lower compartment has operations.

The FlightReservationForm class does not have any attributes. The first operation is getOutboundFlights, as shown in Figure 11.2.

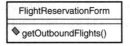

Figure 11.2 UML representation of a class.

Quite often arguments of the designed operation consist of the variables provided by the user. The arguments of an operation getOutboundFlights are as follows:

- Departure airport
- Arrival airport
- Departure date
- Return date
- Number of traveling adults
- Number of traveling children

At this stage we need to think about whether the system has all the required information to perform the operation. For example, how will the system know if we need a one-way or return flight? We can have a rule that if the Traveler does not specify a return date, he or she needs a one-way ticket. In the class operation we cannot just skip an argument, but we can set a convention that if a date is 01/01/0001, it means that the Traveler did not enter the date, indicating no return flight. Another option would be to add a Boolean argument returnFlag, indicating whether it is a return flight.

We can show the arguments on the UML diagram, but doing so makes classes look very wide, as shown in Figure 11.3.

FlightReservationForm
◆ getOutboundFlights(departureAirport: String, arrivalAirport : String, departureDate : Date, arrivalDate : Date, numberAdults : Integer, numberKids : Integer) : ListOfFlights

Figure 11.3   Showing operation signature on the class diagram.

As soon as we have an operation of the boundary class, we need to design an operation of the controller class that will supply to the boundary class required information.

Let's call this operation getFlights and the controller class providing this operation FlightSelector. The arguments of getFlights from the class FlightSelector will be the same as the arguments of getOutboundFlights from the class FlightReservationForm. Why do we call one operation getOutboundFlights while calling another operation getFlights? Because the functionality of the controller class is the same regardless of whether the requested fights are outbound or return, it needs to return a list of flights based on some input attributes. The boundary class, however, behaves in a slightly different manner in the case of outbound and return flights, because the user interface differs slightly in these two cases.

Now we need to define entity classes that will be used to return flight information. Let's encapsulate all flight-related information in the class Flight. Let's design the attributes this class will have:

- Departure airport
- Arrival airport
- Departure date

- Departure time
- Arrival date
- Arrival time

Because none of the attributes uniquely identifies the flight, we can add an additional attribute called flightId. For performance reasons it is better to define it as Integer rather than String. In our design of the Flight class, we mean a full connection between departure and destination airport. However, if it is not a direct flight, it will consist of many "flight legs" with stopovers between them. One flight will contain one or more flight legs. In object-oriented design this is called an *aggregation*. Figure 11.4 shows a UML representation of the classes Flight and FlightLeg, as well as the aggregation between them. Class FlightLeg contains similar attributes as class Flight, but they describe separate legs. In addition, it contains the Airline name and the FlightNumber used by this airline to identify the flight.

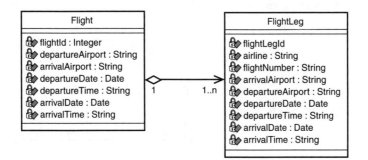

Figure 11.4   Aggregation between classes Flight and FlightLeg.

For this class we also need to add an attribute called flightLegId. FlightNumber does not uniquely identify the flight because on different days we can have flights with the same number. Another approach would be to use a pair of attributes such as Flight Number and Departure Date, but using two attributes for identification is less convenient.

Both classes, Flight and FlightLeg, have some attributes, but no operations. It is quite common for one of the compartments of the class to be empty. *Entity* classes have attributes but no operations, and *controller* classes have operations but no attributes.

Because we expect many flights as a result of a search, the object returned by the function getFlights is a list of Flight objects. We can define a new class called ListOfFlights. In a UML diagram we can show that ListOfFlights contains zero or more objects of the class Flight, as shown in Figure 11.5. The multiplicity is from 0 to *n* because the list can be empty.

After we have designed Flight, ListOfFlights, and a portion of the classes FlightReservationForm and FlightSelector, we can depict the search-related use case step in a sequence diagram, as shown in Figure 11.6. On the sequence diagram we show messages sent between the objects. A dashed line descending from each object is called a *lifeline*.

The boundary class FlightReservationForm on this diagram represents the user interface or front end of the application, which interacts with an actor. The controller class FlightSelector represents back-end processing. Implementation of these classes depends on the system's architecture.

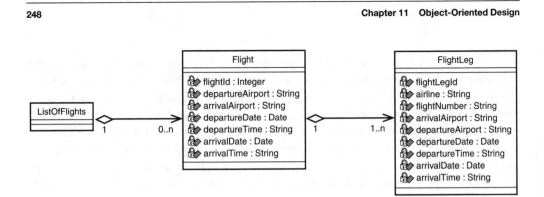

Figure 11.5   ListOfFlights aggregates many flights.

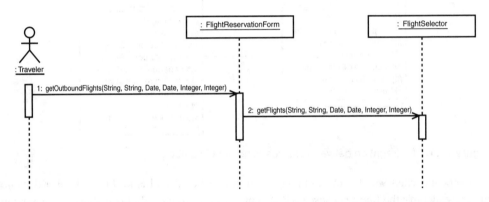

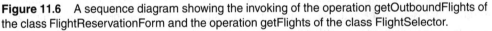

Figure 11.6   A sequence diagram showing the invoking of the operation getOutboundFlights of the class FlightReservationForm and the operation getFlights of the class FlightSelector.

As soon as FlightReservationForm gets a list of flights from FlightSelector, it displays it on the screen. For this we may define a reflexive operation called displayOutboundFlights. The return value of this operation may be a Boolean showing whether the operation was successful.

Sometimes we need more than one controller operation to implement required functionality. In our system one of the requirements says that besides an airport code, the system shall accept a city/state or city/country pair. To model this functionality we can introduce a class AirportController that has an operation getAirportCode (town, location). Why don't we name this class AirportCodeResolver? Because in the future we may use the same class to find adjacent airports or any other airport-related operations, so giving it a more generic class name gives us better flexibility.

If the string describing the airport in the argument to the operation getFlights is not a three-digit airport code, FlightSelector assumes that it contains a city/state or city/country pair. It also passes this argument to AirportController, which returns an airport code based on the input variables (see Figure 11.7).

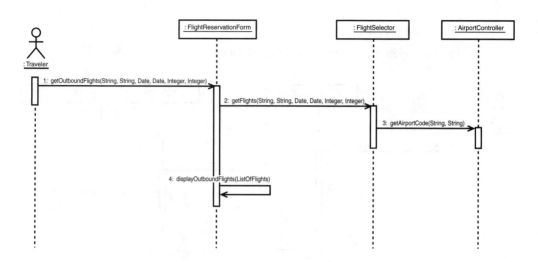

Figure 11.7 FlightSelector calls the getAirportCode operation of AirportController.

As soon as we are done modeling for steps B3 and B4, we can proceed to the next steps:

B5. Traveler selects a flight.

B6. System displays return flights.

The boundary class operation that supports this functionality may be called selectOutboundFlight, and the arguments can be as follows:

- flightId: ID of the selected outbound flight
- airport: Boarding airport for the return flight
- date: Date of the return flight

The return value is a collection of Flight objects.

To get a list of return flights, we may use the already-defined operation getFlights of the class FlightSelector. Because displaying return flights on the screen requires slightly different functionality than displaying outbound flights, we need to define another boundary class operation called displayReturnFlights. We can add the three new messages to the sequence diagram, as shown in Figure 11.8.

Let's consider the next two use case steps:

B7. Traveler selects return flight.

B8. System displays details of the flight.

The boundary class operation can be called selectReturnFlight.

Now we need a controller operation that returns flight details based on flightId:

- Name of the operation: getFlightDetails
- Argument: flightId

- Return value: Flight
- Class implementing this operation: FlightSelector

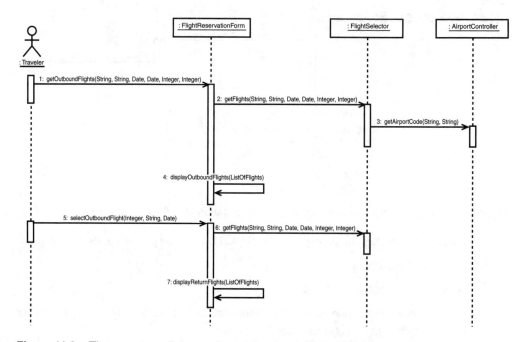

Figure 11.8   The sequence diagram after adding the getReturnFlights message.

We add operation getFlightDetails to the class FlightSelector, and we add appropriate messages to the sequence diagram. Because we need the details on outbound and return flights, we will have two separate calls of this operation. The boundary class operation displaying details of both flights on the screen will be called displayFlightDetails (see Figure 11.9).

Because step B10 is not a response for step B9, we are taking only one step for the design of the next operation:

B9. Traveler confirms the flight.

The boundary class operation is called confirmFlight, and its arguments include IDs for both flights.

So far we are getting information about available flights. Now we want to start actual booking of the flight. We can group all booking-related functionality in the separate controller class called BookingSystem. How to split the functionality between the classes is a decision for the designer. In our case we could consider combining the functionality of FlightSelector and BookingSystem into one big class called FlightController. However, this class would be too big and would provide functionality that is too broad.

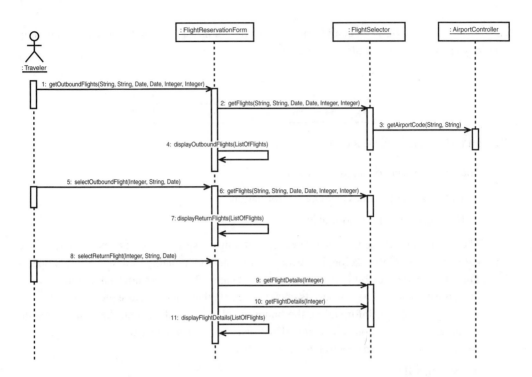

Figure 11.9 The sequence diagram after adding selectReturnFlight, getFlightDetails, and displayFlightDetails messages.

Let's create a class called BookingSystem and add an operation called bookFlight that takes as an argument two flight IDs—one for outbound flights and one for return flights. If we are booking a one-way flight, the second argument is 0. The operation returns reservationNumber as a return value. We will need this ID for future reference. Figure 11.10 shows an initial representation of this class. We will add more operations later.

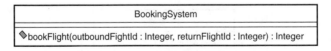

Figure 11.10 Initial design of the class BookingSystem (only one operation has been added so far).

The next step is also being taken alone for the operation design:

B10. Traveler provides userid and password to proceed with buying a ticket.

It is convenient to extract all login functions to a separate object, such as LoginController (see Figure 11.11). It will contain functionality related to changing passwords, recovering forgotten passwords, and so on. The operation Login takes userid and password as arguments.

The return value is a Boolean confirming whether the login was successful. The corresponding boundary class function may also be called login.

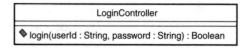

LoginController
◆ login(userId : String, password : String) : Boolean

Figure 11.11   Class LoginController.

The next two scenario steps are as follows:

B11. Traveler provides passenger information.

B12. System displays available seats.

These two steps are actually unrelated. Even though displaying seats comes as a response to providing passenger information, it is better to split this functionality into two different operations. This offers better flexibility in case we want to change the process flow in the future.

First, the boundary class invokes its operation displayPassengerDataRequest.

To accept passenger information, the boundary class as well as controller class Booking System can have an operation setPassengerData that takes a Passenger object as an argument. The Passenger object contains the following attributes:

- Passenger ID
- First name
- Last name
- Middle initial
- Date of birth
- Address

- City
- State
- Zip code
- Country
- Frequent flyer number

Figure 11.12 shows a UML representation of this class.

Passenger
🔒 passengerId : Integer
🔒 firesName : String
🔒 lastname : String
🔒 middleInitial : Byte
🔒 dateOfBirth : Date
🔒 address : String
🔒 city : String
🔒 state : String
🔒 zipCode : String
🔒 country : String
🔒 frequentFlyerNumber: String

Figure 11.12   The Passenger class.

Besides the Passenger object, the operation setPassengerData should contain a second argument specifying the reservation ID so that the system assigns this data to the correct reservation. The operation may be invoked many times, depending on how many passengers are traveling.

The boundary class operation and the corresponding controller class operation related to step B12 is getAvailableSeats. As an argument it takes a flightId and returns a list of available seat numbers. The controller operation is provided by the class Booking System. When the boundary class gets the list of seats from the controller class, it invokes an operation displayAvailableSeats.

After the Traveler gets a list of available seats, we need to design a way to notify the system which seats the Traveler selected:

B13. Traveler selects seats.

The seat selected by the Traveler is supplied to the boundary class using operation selectSeat and then is forwarded to the BookingSystem class using the operation of the same name. This operation takes three arguments: reservationNumber, passengerId, and seatNumber. The variable seatNumber has a type String instead of Integer because airplane seats are usually coded with a combination of row number and a letter representing a seat, such as 5A, 5B, 5C. The return value is not important in this case. It may return a completion code specifying whether the operation ended successfully.

The operation is called a number of times equal to the number of passengers.

Internally, reservation information may be stored in an object called Reservation. It has the following attributes:

- reservationNumber
- customerId (may be equal to user ID that makes a reservation)
- outboundFlightId
- returnFlightId

This class is associated with one or more FlightLegReservation objects that assign a specific seat number to a pair FlightLeg/Passenger, as shown in Figure 11.13.

The next two steps process payment information:

B14. Traveler provides credit card information and billing address.

B15. System provides a confirmation number.

Payments may be handled by a separate class called PaymentProcessor. This class internally uses a connection to the billing systems of major credit cards. From an interface point of view it has a method submitPayment that contains an object Payment as an argument. This object has the following attributes:

- Credit card number
- Expiration date
- Cardholder name
- Billing address

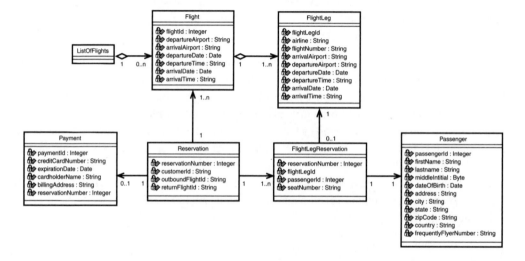

Figure 11.13   Class Reservation and related classes.

The FlightReservationForm class and the class BookingSystem also contain an operation submitPayment. This operation, however, has an additional argument reservationId, so BookingSystem knows which reservation has been paid. When BookingSystem's submitPayment operation is invoked, internally it calls the submitPayment operation of PaymentProcessor. It is okay for different classes to have operations with the same name. (We already had a boundary class and a controller class with the same operation name.)

After going through all the steps of the *Book the flight* basic flow, our class diagram may look like that shown in Figure 11.14. The second part of the sequence diagram is shown in Figure 11.15. (The first part was shown in Figure 11.9.)

The approach presented here assumes simultaneous creation of class and sequence diagrams. Some designers prefer to create collaboration diagrams first and then design details of the classes. In this case when we assign a name to a message, this message is not yet defined in the class, so we cannot just select it from the list. We need to create a placeholder for this message. To distinguish placeholders from actual messages, we can put the comment sign // before the name and write a name in free form (spaces are allowed). An example is // get outbound flights (see Figure 11.16). After we define this operation in a class, we substitute the placeholder for an actual operation. However, the advantage of first creating an actual operation on a class diagram is that we do not need to worry about future replacement.

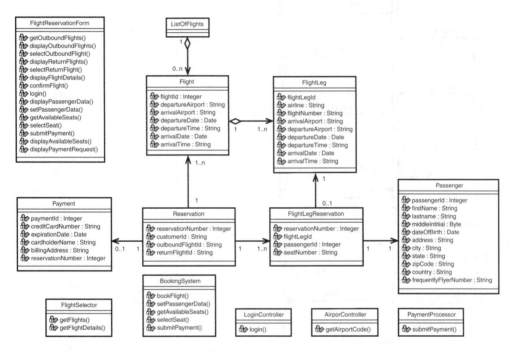

Figure 11.14 A class diagram showing classes that implement the functionality of a basic flow of the *Book a flight* use case.

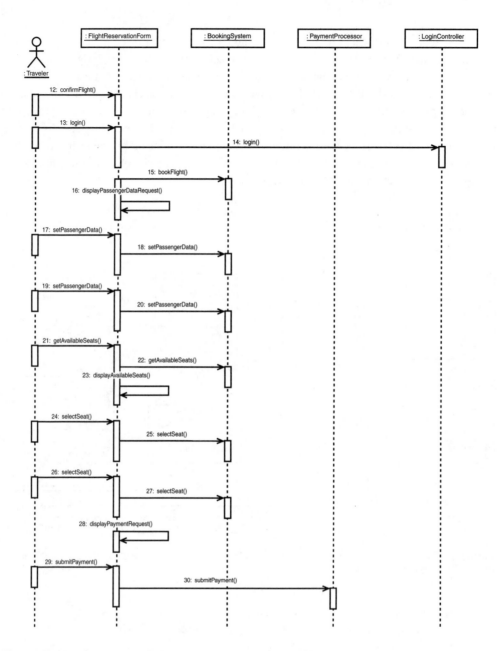

Figure 11.15   A sequence diagram representing the basic flow of the *Book a flight* use case.

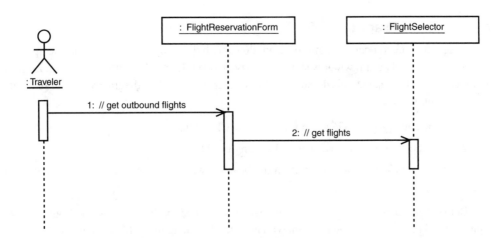

Figure 11.16 A sequence diagram representing the first two operations of the basic flow of the *Book a flight* use case, with comments instead of actual operation names.

11.2 Using IBM Rational Rose for Design

IBM Rational Rose is a tool that nicely facilitates object-oriented design using UML [IBM03c]. This section shows you how to create the design presented in the preceding section using Rational Rose.

Creating a New Model

To create a new Rational Rose model, follow these steps:

1. Open Rational Rose (select Start > All Programs > Rational Software > Rational Rose).

2. In the Create New Model dialog box, click the Cancel button (to load the default environment).

3. Assign a name to the model by selecting File > Save As, choosing a directory, and entering a name.

The left pane displays a browser, as shown in Figure 11.17.

Figure 11.17 Browser window of IBM Rational Rose.

Creating Class Diagrams

In the diagram pane you can have multiple windows with diagrams. When you start the application, a default class diagram window should already be open. It is called "Class Diagram: Logical View / Main." You can select this default window or create a new class diagram window. To create a new one, follow these steps:

1. Right-click Logical View and select New > Class Diagram.

2. Give the diagram a name, such as Booking Flights.

3. Double-click this class diagram in the browser window to open a window in the main pane.

Between a browser pane and a diagram pane is a vertical toolbar, as shown in Figure 11.18. To place a design element on the diagram, you need to click an icon on this toolbar and then click the place on the diagram where you want to position this element.

Figure 11.18   Toolbar for the class diagram.

Create a class in the diagram using these steps:

1. Click the class icon on the toolbar (the fifth icon from the top).

2. Click the Class Diagram window to drop the class.

3. The class appears with the name NewClass.

4. Double-click the class to open the Class Specification dialog box, shown in Figure 11.19.

5. Change the name of the class, such as to FlightSelector.

6. Enter an initial description of the class in the Documentation area.

7. Select the Operations tab.

8. Right-click the main pane of the dialog box and select Insert.

9. Name the operation, such as getFlights. When you press Enter, the operation is added to the list.

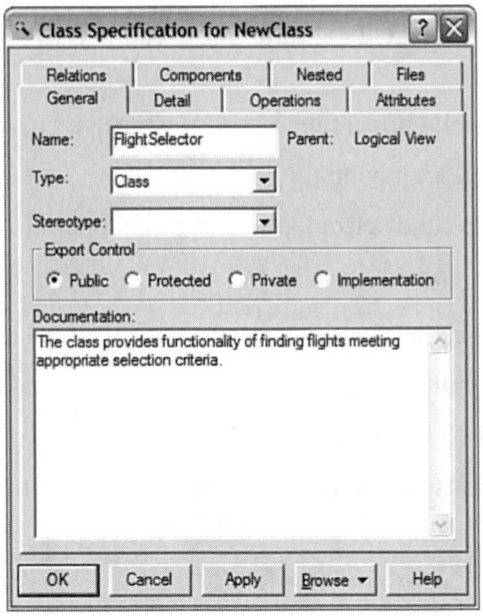

Figure 11.19 Class Specification dialog box.

10. Double-click the operation name.

11. Select the Detail tab, as shown in Figure 11.20.

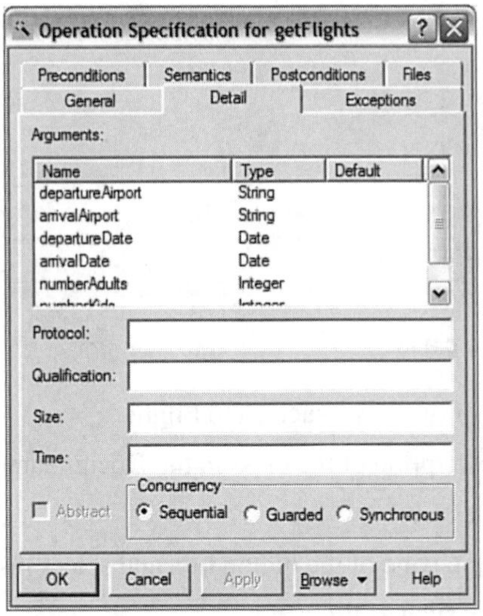

Figure 11.20 Adding arguments of an operation.

12. Right-click the Arguments text field and select Insert.

13. Name the attribute, such as departureAirport.

14. Press Tab to position the cursor under the column Type. A combo box containing available types appears.

15. Select from the combo box a type of the attribute, such as String.

16. Continue adding all arguments.

17. Right-click the class and select Options > Show operations signature.

To create a class Flight, follow these steps:

1. Click the class icon in the toolbar.

2. Click the Class Diagram window.

3. The class appears with the name NewClass.

4. Double-click the class to open the Class Specification dialog box, shown in Figure 11.21.

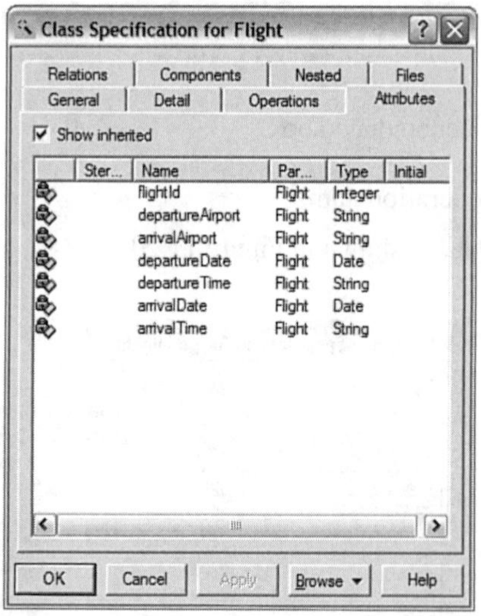

Figure 11.21   Attributes of a class.

5. Change the name of the class, such as to Flight.

6. Enter an initial description of the class in the Documentation area.

7. Select the Attributes tab.

8. Right-click the main pane of the dialog box and select Insert.

9. Name the attribute, such as flightId.

10. Double-click the column Type.

11. Select from the list the type of the attribute, such as String.

12. Continue adding the remaining attributes.

Following the same steps, add classes FlightReservationForm, FlightLeg, and other classes designed in the preceding section.

Modeling Associations

Let's assume that we have created the classes Flight and FlightLeg. Now we want to create an association showing aggregation between the two classes. To create the appropriate type of association, we need to connect them with an association arrow, double-click the arrow between these classes, and set some values in the Association Specification dialog box:

1. Select the association icon from the toolbar.

2. Click the Flight class.

3. Drag the end of an arrow to the FlightLeg class.

4. Double-click the association between Flight and FlightLeg to open the Association Specification dialog box, shown in Figure 11.22.

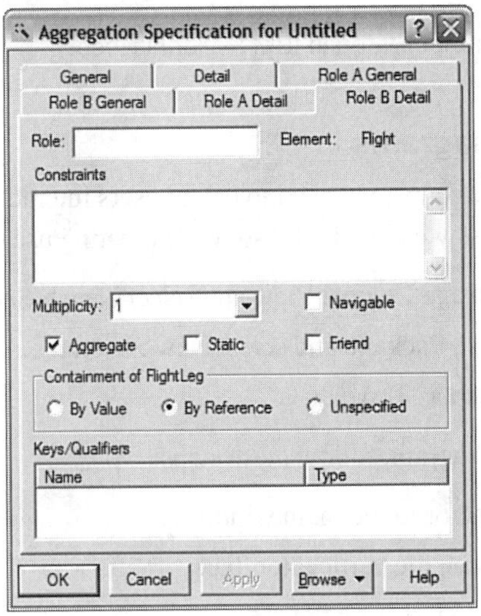

Figure 11.22   Specifying role details.

5. Select the tab Role B Detail.

6. Select Multiplicity 1.

7. Check the box Aggregate. After you check this box, on the next appearance of this dialog box, its title will change from Association Specification to Aggregation Specification, as shown in Figure 11.22.

8. Enable the radio button By Reference to specify the Containment of FlightLeg.

9. Select the tab Role A Detail.

10. Select 1..n from the Multiplicity list box.

11. Click OK.

After you create this association, the screen should look like the one shown in Figure 11.23.

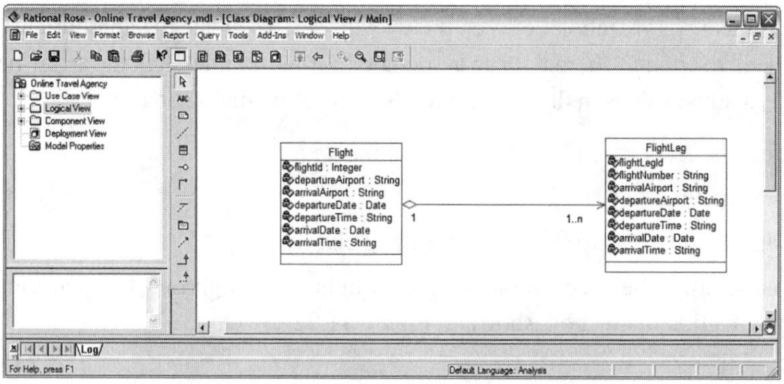

Figure 11.23   A class diagram created in IBM Rational Rose.

Creating Sequence Diagrams

Before creating sequence diagrams, we need to create users interacting with a use case related to this sequence diagram (unless we already did so while creating use case diagrams):

1. Right-click the package Logical View and select New > Sequence Diagram.

2. Right-click Use Case Package and select New > Actor.

3. Name the Actor, such as Traveler.

To create a sequence diagram, follow these steps:

1. Drag and drop the actor to the main window.

2. Click the class icon on the vertical toolbar.

3. Click the main window to drop the class.

4. Double-click the class to open the Object Specification dialog box, shown in Figure 11.24.

5. Select FlightReservationForm from the Class list box.

6. Click the Object Message icon on the vertical toolbar.

7. Connect the lifeline of the Traveler with the lifeline of the FlightReservationForm.

8. Double-click the message to open the Message Specification dialog box, shown in Figure 11.25.

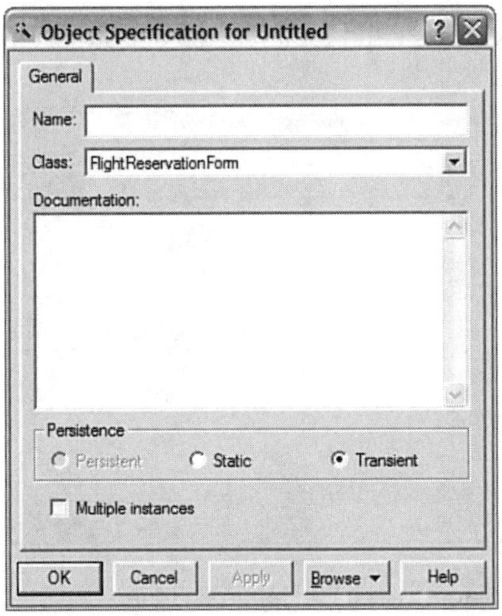

Figure 11.24 Selecting a class name from a list of defined classes.

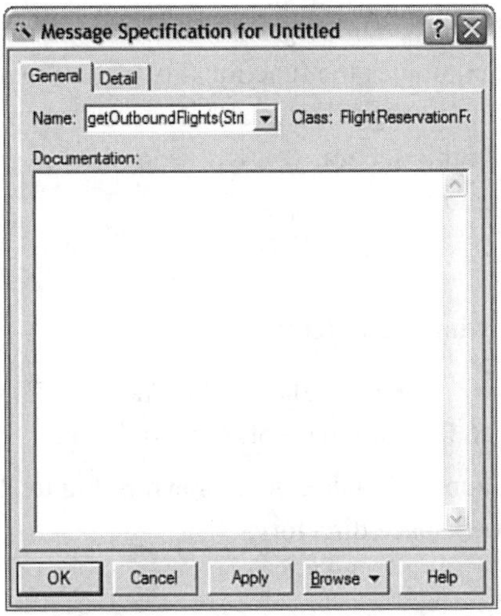

Figure 11.25 Selecting a message name from a list of available operations.

9. Select the method getOutboundFlights from the Name list box.

10. Click OK.

After these steps the screen should look like the one shown in Figure 11.26.

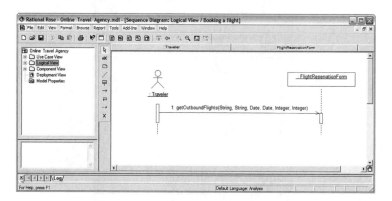

Figure 11.26   A sequence diagram in IBM Rational Rose.

11.3   Using IBM Rational Software Architect for Design

IBM Rational Software Architect is an integrated environment facilitating design and development of software projects. It combines the functionality of Rational Software Modeler, a modeling tool for visual modeling using UML, and Rational Application Developer (a J2EE
development environment). In this section you will learn how to create a project and create use
case, class, and sequence diagrams.

Creating a Project

Create a new project by following these steps:

1. Start the program by selecting Start > Programs > IBM Rational > IBM Rational
   Software Architect v6.0 > Rational Software Architect.

2. In the Workspace Launcher dialog box, shown in Figure 11.27, click the OK button to
   accept the default workspace directory.

Figure 11.27   Workspace Launcher dialog box.

3. Select File > New > Project.

4. In the New Project dialog box, shown in Figure 11.28, highlight UML Project and click the Next button.

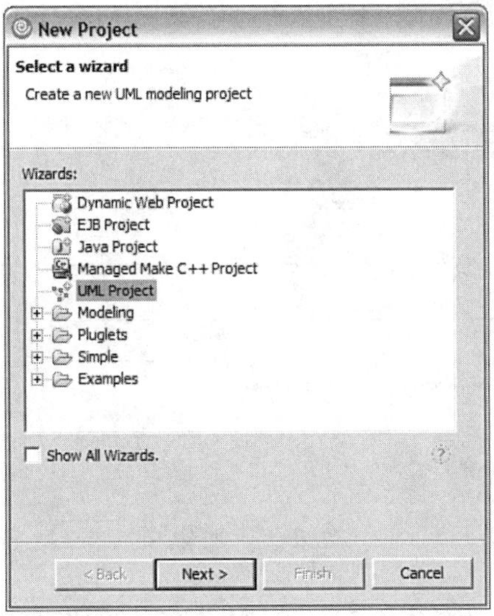

Figure 11.28 New Project dialog box.

5. Enter a project name, as shown in Figure 11.29, and click the Next button.

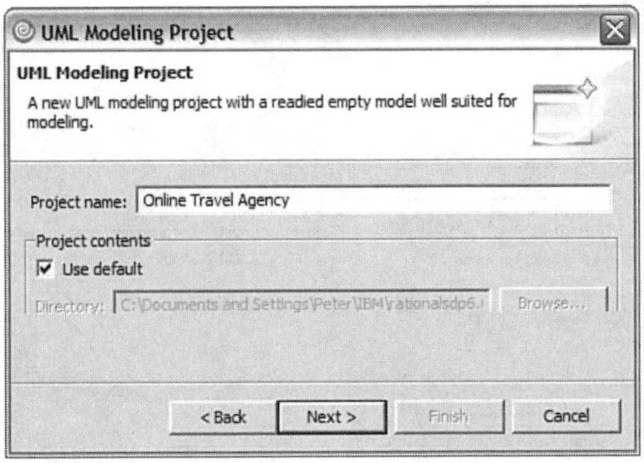

Figure 11.29 Selecting the project name in the UML Modeling Project dialog box.

6. Enter the filename of the UML model, keep Blank Model highlighted, uncheck the box Create a default diagram in the new model, and click the Finish button (see Figure 11.30).

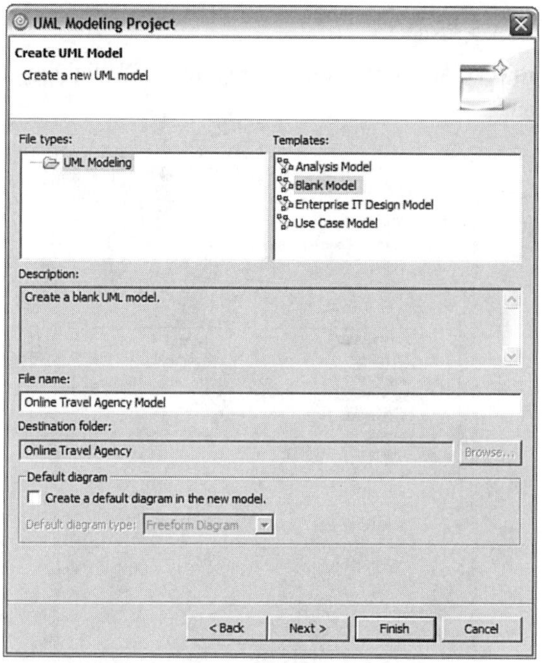

Figure 11.30   Selecting project details in the UML Modeling Project dialog box.

A workbench with an empty model opens, as shown in Figure 11.31.

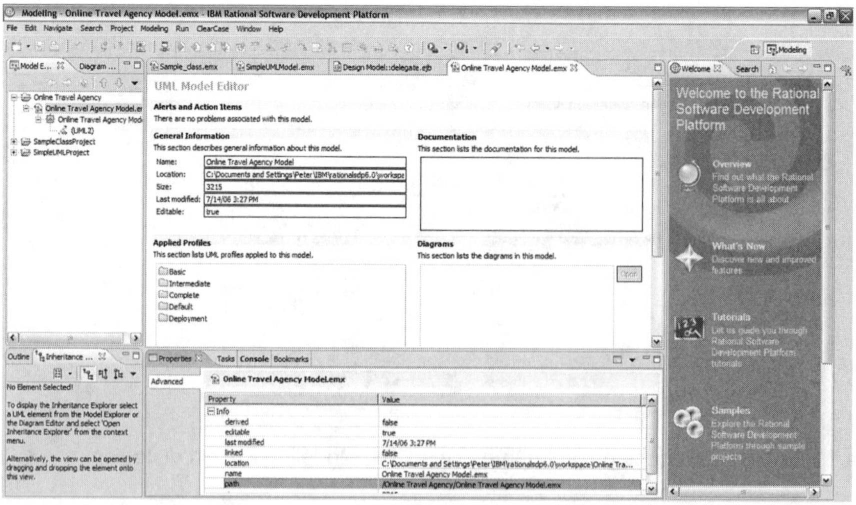

Figure 11.31   A workspace with a UML modeling project.

Creating a Use Case Diagram

Let's create a use case diagram:

1. In the Model Explorer view (the left side of the screen), right-click the Online Travel Agency Model and select Add Diagram > Use Case Diagram.

2. Change the default name Diagram1 to a meaningful name.

3. Click Actor on the Palette menu (to the right of the diagram window), and then click anywhere in the diagram to create an actor. Replace the default name Actor1 with the name Traveler.

4. Click Use Case on the Palette menu, and then click anywhere in the diagram to create a use case. Replace the default name UseCase1 with *Book a flight*.

5. Click Association on the Palette menu. Draw the association relationship line from the actor to the use case, as shown in Figure 11.32.

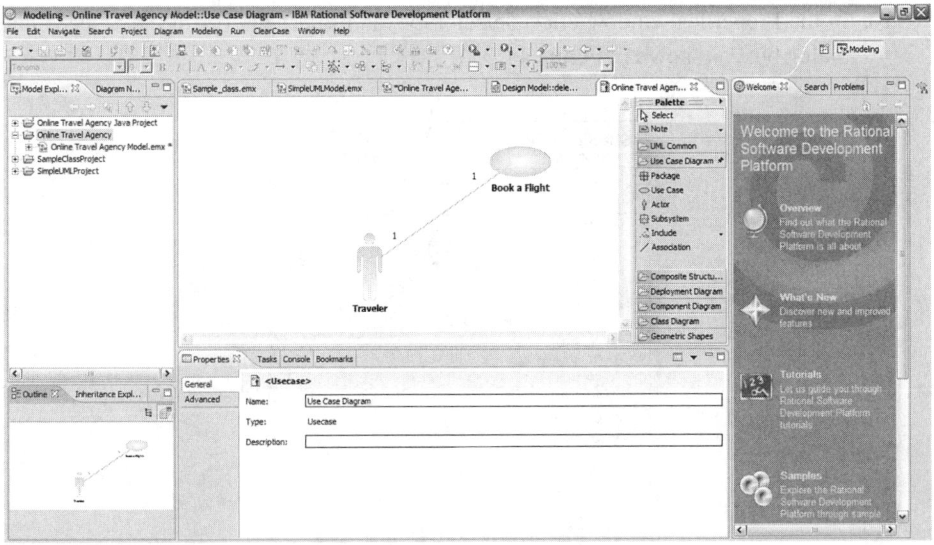

Figure 11.32   Creating a use case diagram with IBM Rational Software Architect.

6. Keep adding actors, use cases, and associations as necessary.

7. Press Ctrl-S to save the diagram.

Creating a Class Diagram

You can create a class diagram by following these steps:

1. In the Model Explorer view, right-click Online Travel Agency Model, and select Add Diagram > Class Diagram.

2. Replace the default name Diagram1 with a meaningful name.

3. Select Class on the Palette menu, and then click anywhere in the diagram to create a class.

4. Replace the default name Class1 with FlightReservationForm.

5. Right-click the created class and select Add UML > Operation to create an operation for this class. Name it getOutboundFlights.

6. Keep adding the remaining operations.

7. Select Class on the Palette menu, and then click anywhere in the diagram to create a class named Flight.

8. Right-click the Flight class and select Add UML > Attribute to create an attribute for this class. Name it FlightId.

9. Double-click the FlightId attribute to open the Properties window in the lower part of the screen.

10. In the Properties window click Select Type, and select Integer in the Select Element dialog box, as shown in Figure 11.33.

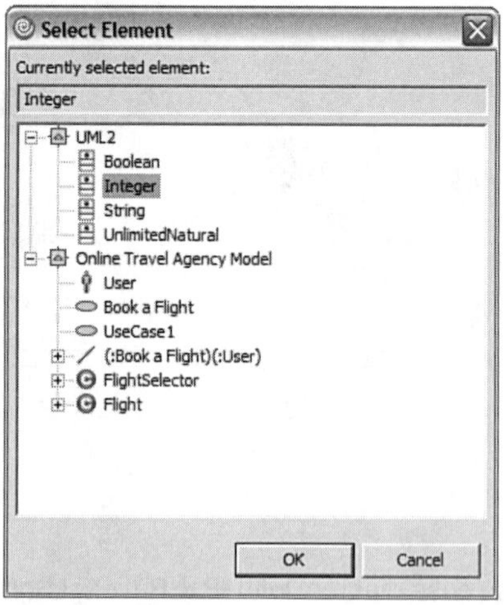

Figure 11.33   Selecting the type of the attribute.

11. Keep adding attributes.

12. Add a new class to the diagram called ListOfFlights.

13. Click Association on the Palette menu.

14. Connect the classes ListOfFlights and Flight.

15. Double-click the association line to open the Properties window at the bottom of the screen, as shown in Figure 11.34.

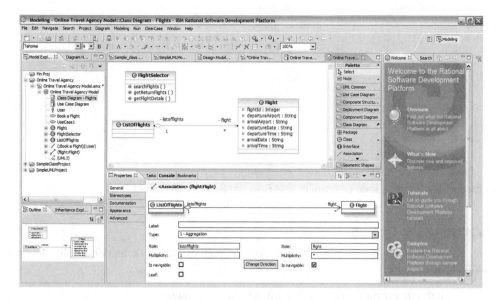

Figure 11.34 Creating a class diagram with IBM Rational Software Architect.

16. In the Type list box in the Properties window, select "1 - Aggregation."

17. Set the Multiplicity of the ListOfFlights role equal to 1 and the Multiplicity of the Flight role equal to *.

Creating a Sequence Diagram

A sequence diagram, shown in Figure 11.35, can be created with these steps:

1. In the Model Explorer view, right-click the model name and select Add Diagram > Sequence Diagram.

2. Replace the default name Diagram1 with a meaningful name.

3. Drag the actor Traveler from the Explorer window to the diagram to create an instance of the actor.

4. Drag the FlightSelector class from the Explorer window to the diagram.

5. Select Asynchronous Message in the Palette.

6. Click the line under Traveler and drag to the line under FlightReservationForm.

7. Select the operation getOutboundFights from the drop-down list.

8. Similarly, create the remaining messages.

9. Select File > Save All to save everything.

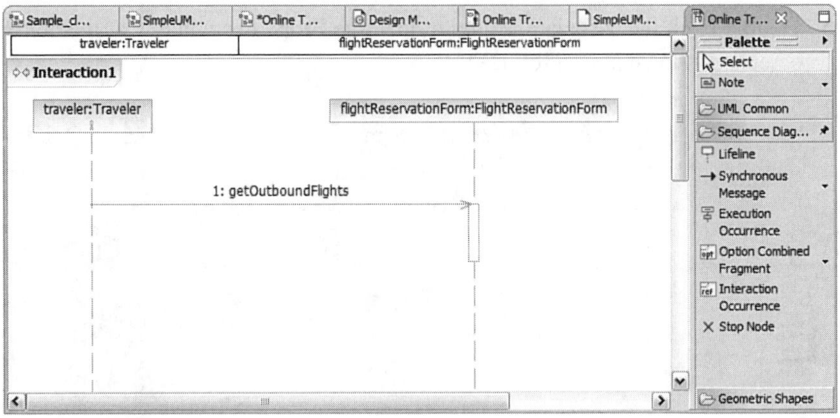

Figure 11.35   A sequence diagram in IBM Rational Software Architect.

Publishing the Design

After all the required diagrams are created, you can publish the whole model in web format by following these steps:

1. Highlight the model name in the Model Explorer view.

2. Select Modeling > Publish > Web.

3. In the Publish to Web dialog box, shown in Figure 11.36, specify the target location of the generated HTML files, and click the OK button.

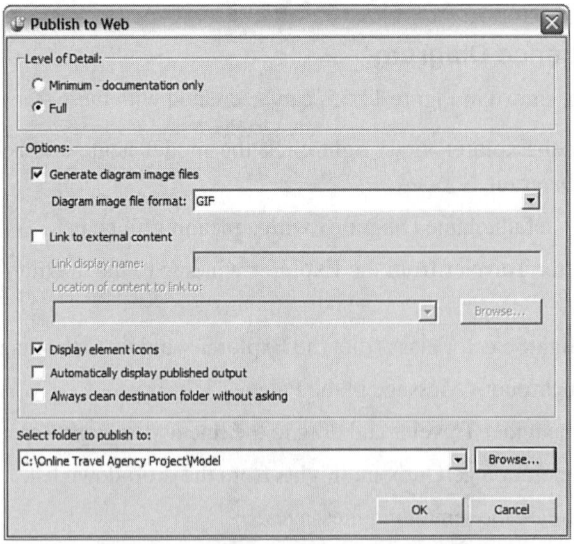

Figure 11.36   Specifying the target location in the Publish to Web dialog box.

To access the published model, do the following:

1. Go to the location that you specified, and double-click the file index.html.
2. Click the link to the model, as shown in Figure 11.37.

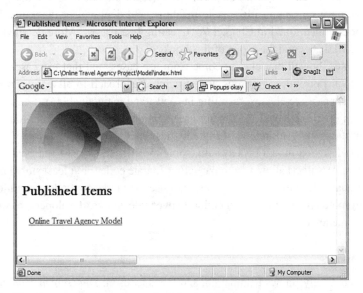

Figure 11.37 The first page where you select the published model.

3. Navigate the published model by clicking the element links and diagrams, as shown in Figure 11.38.

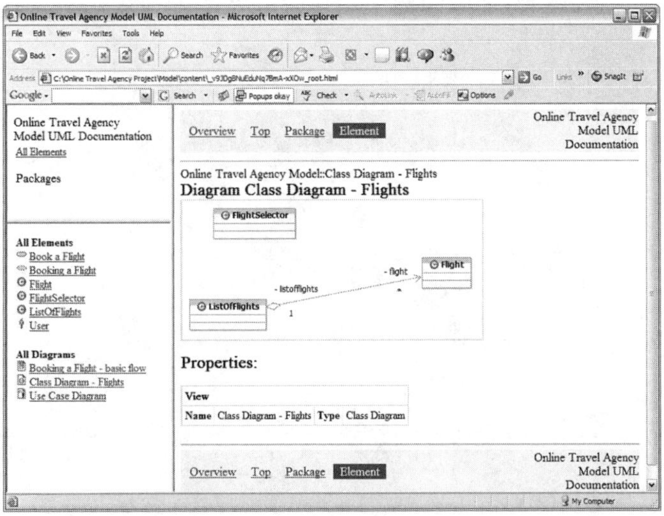

Figure 11.38 A class diagram of the published model.

11.4   Summary

This chapter presents an organized approach to developing an object-oriented design using UML. However, only the core part of the design was discussed. From use cases and scenarios, we derived class diagrams and sequence diagrams. To have a complete model of the system, we may need to add activity, communication, state machine, and deployment diagrams. Use case diagrams were briefly mentioned in Chapter 7, "Creating Use Cases." More detailed discussion of design using UML is beyond the scope of this book.

This chapter showed that classes come from use cases, and that use cases (and scenarios derived from them) provide a rigorous and structured approach to allocating system behavior (operations) to appropriate classes, resulting in robust and maintainable systems. Unfortunately, this approach is often neglected, and many organizations use an ad hoc approach to class and operation identification, resulting in poor-quality designs.

From the designed model of a system, some tools (such as IBM Rational Rose and IBM Rational System Architect) allow you to partially generate code (or at least stubs) in a target programming language. However, even if you do not use the model for code generation, UML diagrams help promote effective communication between designers, developers, business analysts, and other team members.

References

[BOO04] Booch, Grady, James Rumbaugh, and Ivar Jacobson. *The Unified Modeling Language Reference Manual*, Second Edition, Boston: Addison-Wesley, 2004.

[BOO05] Booch, Grady, James Rumbaugh, and Ivar Jacobson. *The Unified Modeling Language User Guide*, Second Edition, Boston: Addison-Wesley, 2005.

[IBM03c] *Rational Rose User's Guide*, IBM Corporation, 2003.

CHAPTER 12

Documentation

This chapter discusses the RequisitePro documentation—the types of documentation available, the templates available in RequisitePro, and how to use IBM Rational SoDA to automatically generate reports. The chapter begins with a high-level discussion of general documentation types before turning to the types of documentation that RequisitePro can produce.

12.1   Documentation Types

There are many ways to classify documentation types. The most important is probably based on the intended audience for the documentation:

- Internal documentation for communication between team members
- Technical documentation for those who may need to make enhancements in the future
- User documentation
- Marketing materials for potential customers

Internal Documentation

Internal documentation is used throughout the project lifecycle to communicate between team members while developing the system. Some types may also be used to communicate with the users (the Use Case Specification) or as an attachment to the contract with customers (the Vision document).

Technical Documentation

We cannot assume that when an enhancement to the system is needed, the original development team will be available. This means that the whole system must be documented on various levels (architecture, design, code). From this documentation, the team making the changes can clearly understand how to make a fix or enhancement. This type of documentation describes how the system is built. It may include UML diagrams describing the system's design, entity relationship diagrams showing database schema, and flowcharts explaining the algorithms.

One of the most important forms of technical documentation is source code documentation. To facilitate its creation, many tools can generate documentation from the code, especially from the comments included in the code. A comparison of some tools can be found at http://en. wikipedia.org/wiki/Comparison_of_documentation_generators. Using these tools requires developers to follow some guidelines facilitating the extraction of documentation from the code. The advantage of using generators is that the documentation can be automatically updated when the code changes. However, usually it is difficult to add free-form text to these documents.

User Documentation

User documentation describes how to use the system. It may be addressed to users, system administrators, help desk personnel, or maintenance. Instead of a printed version, some of the documentation may be available online in the form of help or a tutorial.

User documentation includes

- User guides
- Reference manuals
- Tutorials
- Installation guides

Different types of user documentation may have different structure. Reference manuals usually alphabetically list some commands, functions, or instructions. User guides use a more thematic approach, with particular chapters concentrating on one topic. Tutorials contain step-by-step descriptions of specific tasks [WIK06].

User documentation may also contain a description of an application programming interface, Web Services, or other interface between the system and other applications. In this case it is addressed to programmers writing applications that interact with software.

Marketing Materials

Marketing information, usually addressed to potential customers and clients, presents the system's advantages. It does not need to describe in detail what the system does and how it is built. This type of publication includes brochures, flyers, data sheets, and catalogs. It may also be published in electronic forms, such as Microsoft PowerPoint presentations, websites, or CD demos.

12.2   Documents Available in RequisitePro

The preceding section described a classification of documentation types to show which types of documents RequisitePro is most useful.

The vast majority of documents produced using RequisitePro fall into the category of internal documentation. All predefined templates available within the tool are related to documents that are being used during the software development process.

Sometimes RequisitePro is also used to create technical documentation, especially if the same document is used during development and then is stored as a reference after the system is in production.

Some documents that were initially created during the requirements management process may be used later in user documentation. An example is reusing the text of use cases in user manuals.

Rarely is RequisitePro used for marketing materials. Marketing brochures usually require sophisticated graphic design, and RequisitePro's graphics capability is limited by Microsoft Word's functionality.

To create a document in RequisitePro, the document type must be available in the project. Which document types are already included in the project depends on which project template was used. For example, the default document types for the Use Case template are

- Glossary
- Requirements Management Plan
- Stakeholder Request
- Supplementary Requirements Specification
- Use Case Specification
- Vision

The Traditional template contains Software Requirements Specification instead of Use Cases and Supplementary Requirements:

- Glossary
- Requirements Management Plan
- Software Requirements Specification
- Stakeholder Request
- Vision

To see what document types are currently available in your project, do the following:

1. Right-click the project name and select Properties.
2. Select the Document Types tab, as shown in Figure 12.1.

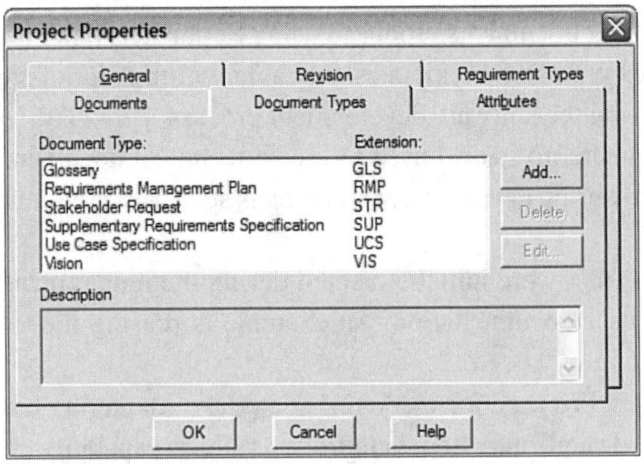

Figure 12.1   Document types available by default in the Use Case project template.

Creating a Document from an Available Document Type

If the document type is already in a project, to create a document, follow these steps:

1. Right-click the package where you want to create the document.

2. Select New > Document.

3. Fill in the dialog box shown in Figure 12.2. Available document types are in the bottom list box.

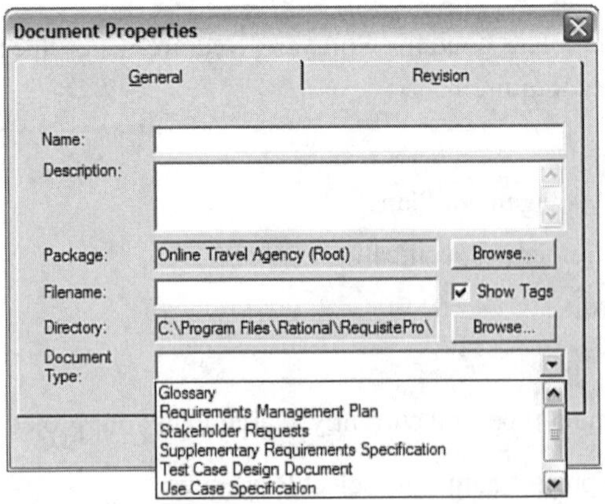

Figure 12.2   Document Properties dialog box.

Adding a New Document Type

If a required document type is not in the project, add it using the following steps:

1. Select File > Properties.

2. Click the Document Types tab.

3. Click Add.

4. Fill in the dialog box shown in Figure 12.3.

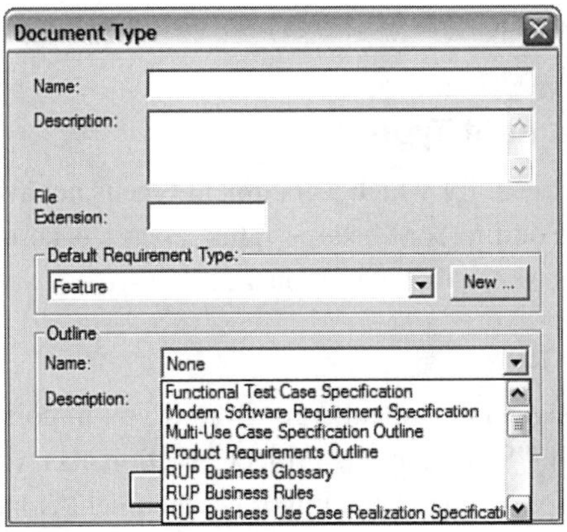

Figure 12.3   Outlines available in RequisitePro.

While adding the document type, you need to select the outline—a template that will be used for all documents of this type. The following outlines are available in RequisitePro:

- Functional Test Case Specification
- Modern Software Requirement Specification
- Multi-Use Case Specification
- Product Requirements Outline
- RUP Business Glossary
- RUP Business Rules
- RUP Business Use Case Realization Specification
- RUP Business Use Case Specification
- RUP Business Vision Document
- RUP Glossary
- RUP Requirements Management Plan
- RUP Supplementary Business Specification
- RUP Software Requirement Specification
- RUP Use Case Software Requirement Specification

- RUP Supplementary Specification
- RUP Stakeholder Requests
- RUP Test Plan
- RUP Use Case Specification
- RUP Vision Document
- Software Requirements

Creating a New Document Type

If you want to create a document for which a document type is not available, you need to create a new document type and the outline for this type. This process is described in detail in Chapter 9, "Creating Test Cases from Use Cases," in section 9.3.

Importing a Document

Every document has an assigned document type. Even if you import the document from outside RequisitePro (see Chapter 4, "Setting up the Project," section 4.1), you still need to specify what document type it is. If the formatting of the imported document is inconsistent with the selected document type, a warning message appears, as shown in Figure 12.4. Clicking the No button preserves the original formatting.

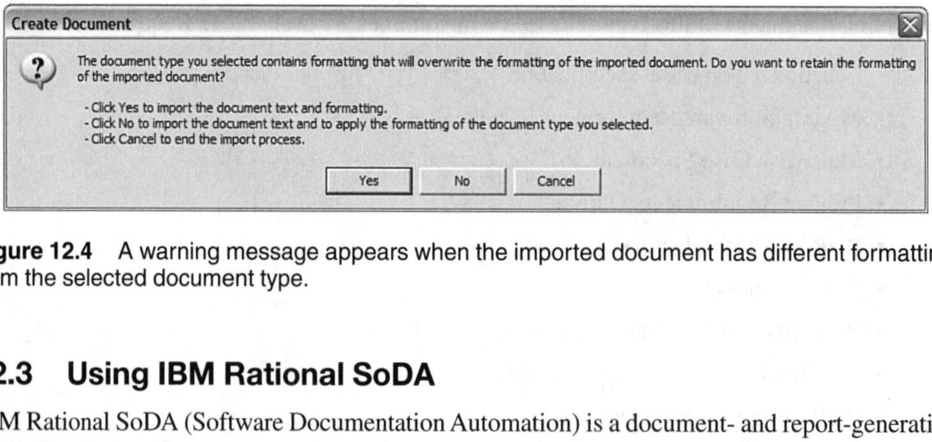

Figure 12.4   A warning message appears when the imported document has different formatting from the selected document type.

12.3   Using IBM Rational SoDA

IBM Rational SoDA (Software Documentation Automation) is a document- and report-generation tool [IBM01]. The main advantage of SoDA is its capability to extract information from other Rational tools (such as RequisitePro and Rational Rose). Many report templates are already predefined. In addition, you can customize existing templates or create new ones using an easy language consisting of just four commands: Open, Display, Repeat, and Limit.

The difference between a report and a document is that a report is generated from scratch every time, whereas during document generation, sections added manually are preserved. Only the information extracted from other tools is updated.

This section shows you how to create a report using predefined SoDA templates.

Generating a Report from RequisitePro

If you want a report related to RequisitePro project elements, you can create it from either RequisitePro or SoDA. To do so from RequisitePro (which is easier and faster), follow these steps:

1. Select Tools > Generate SoDA Report.

2. Select a report from the list, as shown in Figure 12.5, and click OK.

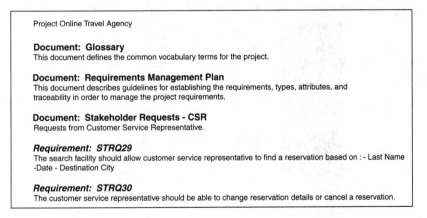

Figure 12.5   Selecting a SoDA report.

Figure 12.6 shows a sample report that contains all documents and all requirements.

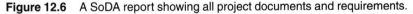

Figure 12.6   A SoDA report showing all project documents and requirements.

Generating a Report from SoDA

You can generate the same report from SoDA by doing the following:

1. Start Rational SoDA by selecting All Programs > Rational Software > Rational SoDA for Microsoft Word. An empty Microsoft Word document opens.

2. Select SoDA > Getting Started.

3. Click Next in the dialog box, as shown in Figure 12.7.

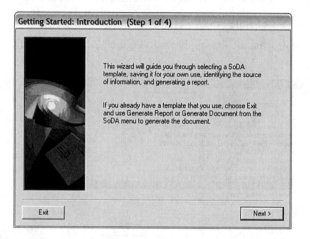

Figure 12.7   Generating a predefined report using SoDA: Step 1.

4. Select a report that you want to run, such as reqpro\docsreqts.doc (see Figure 12.8), and click the Next button.

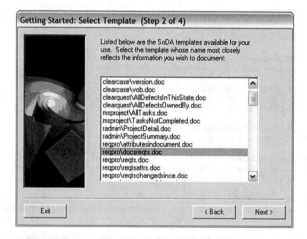

Figure 12.8   Generating a predefined report using SoDA: Step 2.

5. Click the Browse button to select a location where you want to save the file, as shown in Figure 12.9.

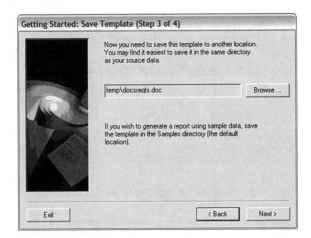

Figure 12.9   Generating a predefined report using SoDA: Step 3.

6. Click the Generate button, as shown in Figure 12.10.

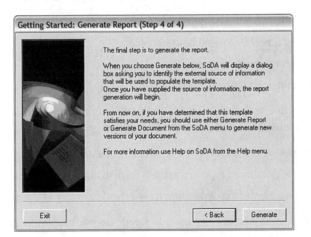

Figure 12.10   Generating a predefined report using SoDA: Step 4.

7. In the Identify Project dialog box, click the Browse button, select the .rqs file that contains the RequisitePro project, and click OK (see Figure 12.11).

By default the project is located in the directory C:\Program Files\Rational\ RequisitePro\Projects*project name*.

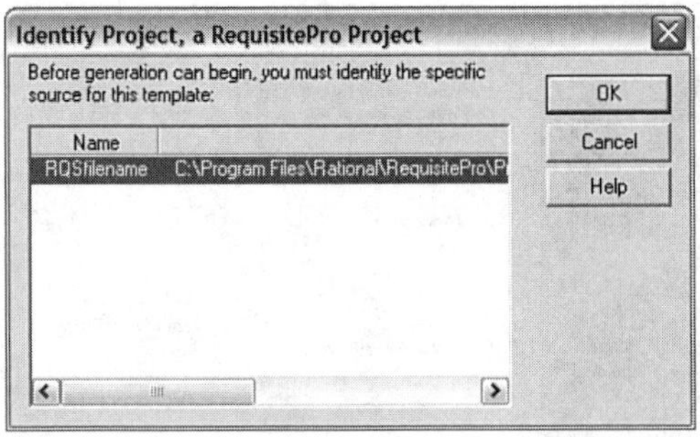

Figure 12.11   Identifying the project from which the report is generated.

The generated report should look the same as the one generated from RequisitePro (refer to Figure 12.6).

12.4   Summary

This chapter has described documentation types and how RequisitePro helps create them:

- Internal documentation—very useful
- Technical documentation—sometimes used
- User documentation—occasionally used
- Marketing materials—rarely used

The documents and templates available in RequisitePro were listed.
Three steps for creating a document were described:

- Creating a new document type if a template is unavailable
- Adding a new document type to a project from available templates
- Creating a document from a document type that is already in the project

You can import a document from outside RequisitePro, but in this case a document template should be defined prior to importing.

At the conclusion of this chapter, two methods of generating predefined SoDA reports were discussed:

- Generating a report from RequisitePro
- Generating a report from SoDA

This chapter concludes the main part of this book. The chapters to this point have described how to navigate through the requirements pyramid. Chapters 5 through 12 have discussed how to do the following:

- Gather stakeholder requests
- Derive features
- Create use cases and supplementary requirements
- Generate test cases
- Design the system
- Generate documentation

The end of each chapter described how RequisitePro can be used to facilitate all these tasks.

The next chapter concentrates on some RequisitePro features that have not yet been discussed.

References

[WIK06] See http://en.wikipedia.org/wiki/Software_documentation.

[IBM01] *Using Rational SoDA for Word*, Version 2001A.04.00, IBM Corporation, 2001.

PART III

Other Topics

Managing Projects

This chapter covers various tasks related to managing RequisitePro projects:

- Printing the project summary
- Archiving and restoring projects
- Moving and copying projects
- Setting and using cross-project traceability

RequisitePro file types are also discussed.

13.1   Printing the Project Summary

The quickest way of getting a report with main project information is to a print project summary by following these steps:

1. Select File > Project Administration > Print Summary.
2. Select a printer from the Print dialog box.

The printed report contains the following:

- Generic information about the project, such as the directory where the project is located, current requirements count, and database used
- All requirement types and their attributes
- Document types with basic information such as the outline filename and a short description
- Documents with basic information such as directory, document type, and the timestamp of the current revision

Figure 13.1 shows the first page of the report.

Project Name: Online Travel Agency   **Project Summary Report**
Revision: 1.0010. Version Label: **Printed By: Peter Z**

Project: Online Travel Agency
    Description: Project creates an online travel agency system.
    Location: C:\Program Files\Rational\RequisitePro\Projects\Online Travel Agency
    Created by: Peter Z
    Database type: Access
    Requirement count: 168
    Document format: RequisitePro format
    Security: disabled
    Project prefix:
    External projects: <none>
    Present revision: 1.0010   at: 3/26/2006 8:32 PM   by: Peter Z

Requirement Types:
  Feature
    Description: This requirement type is used to indicate all feature requirements for the project.
    Must contain:
    Tag prefix: FEAT
    Text color: Dark Red
    Text style: Double Underline
    External traceability: False
    Requirement count: 40

Figure 13.1   Project summary.

13.2   RequisitePro File Types

Figure 13.2 shows some files that typically are in the project directory C:\Program Files\ Rational\RequisitePro\Projects*project name*:

- .rqs file containing project information
- .rql file containing database information
- .mdb file with the project database (if you're using Microsoft Access)
- Document files that have extensions dependent on the document type, such as .vis for Vision and .ucs for use cases.
- .bak files containing backups of next-to-last versions of documents

Some files are in the directory C:\Program Files\Rational\RequisitePro\outlines:

- .def files containing outline definitions for all document types
- .dot files containing templates for all document types

The .def and .dot file types were discussed in Chapter 9, "Creating Test Cases from Use Cases," in section 9.3.

Glossary.GLS	43 KB	GLS File	8/12/2002 8:40 PM
Online Travel Agency.MDB	2,692 KB	Microsoft Access Ap…	9/5/2006 8:11 PM
Online Travel Agency.RQL	1 KB	RQL File	7/22/2005 12:42 AM
Online Travel Agency.RQS	1 KB	RequisitePro Projec…	3/27/2006 12:32 AM
Requirements Management Plan.RMP	208 KB	RealJukebox Music …	1/31/2003 9:04 PM
Stakeholder Requests - CSR.STR	64 KB	STR File	11/1/2005 2:21 PM
Stakeholder Requests - Customer.STR	66 KB	STR File	10/28/2005 8:03 PM
Stakeholder Requests - IT Department.STR	73 KB	STR File	11/1/2005 2:29 PM
Stakeholder Requests - Service Providers.STR	73 KB	STR File	11/1/2005 2:54 PM
Stakeholder Requests - User 1.STR	57 KB	STR File	10/28/2005 7:50 PM
Stakeholder Requests - User 2.STR	57 KB	STR File	11/28/2005 7:01 PM
Supplementary Specification.SUP	72 KB	SUP File	2/16/2006 9:20 PM
Test Cases - Book a Flight.TCD	211 KB	TCD File	3/13/2006 8:39 PM
Use Case - Book a flight.UCS	81 KB	UCS File	1/4/2006 9:06 PM
Vision.VIS	140 KB	VIS File	11/29/2005 1:05 AM

Figure 13.2   Project files.

Because document files may have various extensions, often assigned during project setup, these extensions may accidentally overlap with extensions used in some other application. In this case, Windows Explorer may misinterpret the filename and assign a misleading icon to the file. For example, the extension .rmp, used for Requirements Management Plan, is also used for RealJukebox Metadata Packages. This is not an issue. Just ignore the icon. RequisitePro will recognize this file.

Every document type has its own file extension. You can choose and customize the extension you want. It is a good practice to have meaningful extensions (such as .vis for Vision), because in a directory you can easily recognize the files belonging to a specific type. Do not use extensions such as .doc or .txt because these extensions may cause the files to be accidentally opened by Microsoft Word or Notepad, and you are not supposed to update these files outside the RequisitePro environment.

.rqs and .rql files are regular text files, but you are not supposed to change them manually outside of RequisitePro.

Here is an example of an .rqs file:

```
[Project]
Owner=Peter Z
Name=Online Travel Agency
GUID={CD8E4430-4506-4173-9D06-6245DC2AFD6A}
Description=Project creates an online travel agency system.
Owner Key=2
Revision number=1.0010
Prefix=
NbrRequirements=140
Directory=C:\Program Files\Rational\RequisitePro\Projects
\Online Travel Agency\Online Travel Agency.rqs
Key=1
```

```
[Application]
Data file version=1.0040
Program Version=8.23.0068.1
```

Here is a sample .rql file:

```
[ODBC]
DRIVER=Microsoft Access Driver (*.mdb)

[DBMaint]
CompactDate=2005-07-21 21:42:49
CompactBaselineSize=1495040
CompactPreviousSize=1540096
CompactThresholdSize=10
```

13.3   Archiving Projects

The purpose of archiving is to create a copy of the current stage of project files so that you can restore them later. You can archive either by using the RequisitePro Archive command or by using the ClearCase Archive command. This section demonstrates the former approach.

To archive the project, follow these steps:

1. Select File > Project Administration > Archive > RequisitePro Archive.

2. In the Archive Project dialog box, shown in Figure 13.3, select the directory.

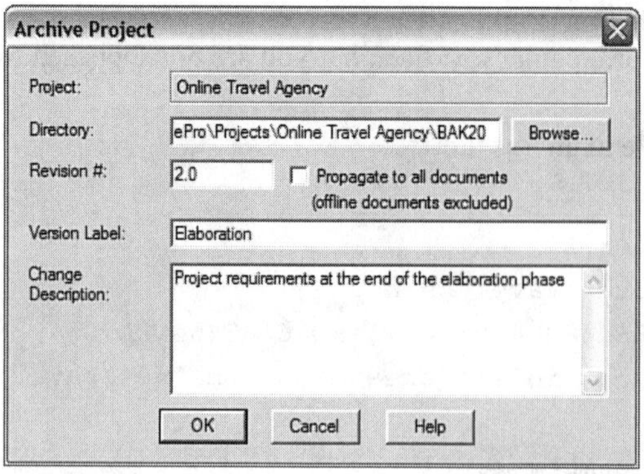

Figure 13.3   The Archive Project dialog box.

3. If needed, provide the revision number, version label, and change description.

4. If you want to apply the revision number to all documents, check the box Propagate to all documents.

5. Click the OK button.

6. If you get a message that the project directory does not exist, and you are asked if you want to create it, click Yes to create the directory.

The project files (.rql, .rqs) and the documents are copied to the archive directory. For projects using a Microsoft Access database, the .mdb file with the database is also copied, and the database is updated with the new location of the documents. For projects using enterprise databases, the database file is not copied automatically, so additional steps are required, such as creating a file with a logical export or using the Data Transport Wizard. (See the *Rational RequisitePro User's Guide* [IBM03d] for details.)

To restore an archived project, follow these steps:

1. Select File > Open.

2. In the Open Project dialog box, click the Add button.

3. Select the RQS file containing the archived project. The project is added to a list of existing projects.

4. Double-click the project name, or select the project and click the OK button.

13.4 Moving and Copying Projects

You are not supposed to copy or move projects by just copying the project directory. To copy a project to a new directory, do the following:

1. Copy the project files (.rqs and .rql) to a new location (using Windows Explorer).

2. Copy all document files to a new location.

3. If the project is using a Microsoft Access database, also copy the .mdb file.

4. Select File > Open Project.

5. Click the Add button.

6. Select the project in its new location to add it to the list of projects.

7. If you no longer need the project in its previous location, select it and click the Remove button.

13.5 Cross-Project Traceability

Cross-project traceability lets you trace requirements between different projects. It is sometimes used if a set of requirements is common to many projects, such as some generic requirements that are followed by all projects in a corporation.

To allow cross-project traceability, you need to do the following:

1. Assign a project prefix to all projects taking part in traceability.

2. Mark which requirement types are available for cross-project traceability.

3. Connect the projects.

Let's create a project called Global that contains requirements common to a few other projects.

To assign a prefix to a project, do the following:

1. Open the project.

2. Select the project in the Explorer.

3. Open the Project Properties dialog box by selecting File > Properties.

4. On the General tab, shown in Figure 13.4, fill in the Prefix field.

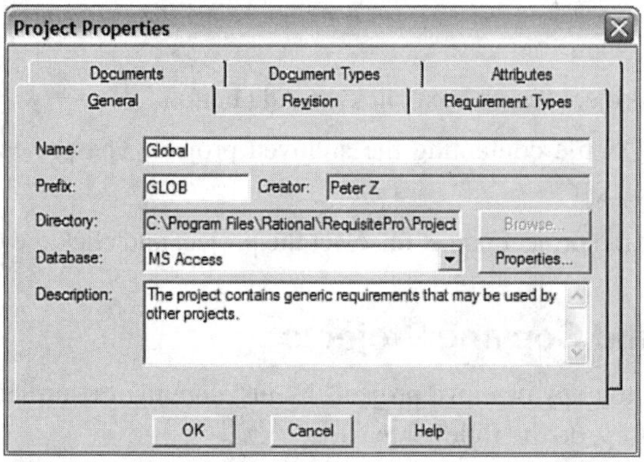

Figure 13.4   The Project Properties dialog box for the Global project.

5. Click the OK button.

To mark the requirement types available for cross-project traceability, do the following:

1. In the Project Properties dialog box, select the Requirement Types tab.

2. Open the Requirement Type dialog box by double-clicking the requirement type or by selecting the requirement type and clicking the Edit button.

3. Check the Allow External Traceability box, as shown in Figure 13.5.

4. Click OK.

5. Follow the same steps for all requirement types that will be used for cross-project traceability.

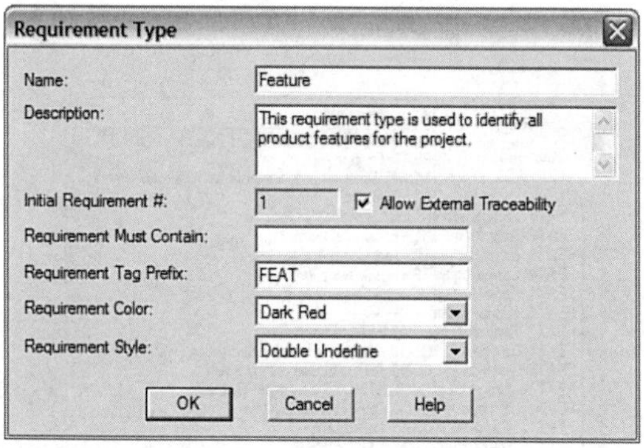

Figure 13.5 Allowing external traceability in the Requirement Type dialog box.

To connect the projects, follow these steps:

1. Select File > Project Administration > External Projects.

2. Click the Add button.

3. Browse to the project RQS file. The project appears in the list, as shown in Figure 13.6.

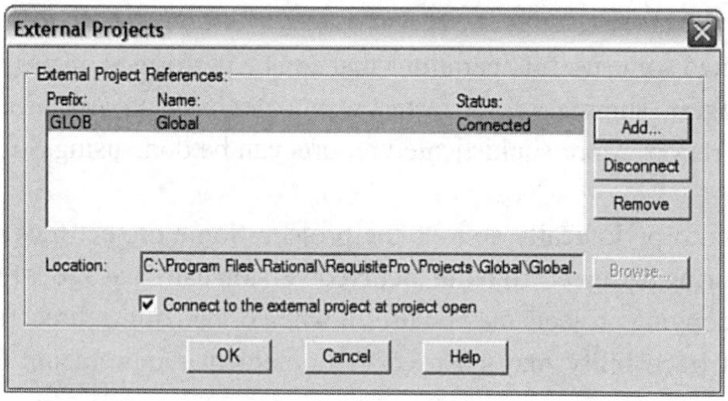

Figure 13.6 Adding a project to an external project list.

After you complete these steps, while setting traceability, the requirements from external projects are available. They are shown with the appropriate prefixes, as shown in Figure 13.7.

Figure 13.7   Requirements from the Global project are available for setting traceability.

13.6   Summary

This chapter presented some useful operations that can be performed on projects.

Printing a program summary is the fastest way to get basic project information without creating a customized report. More sophisticated reports can be done using SoDA (see Chapter 12, "Documentation").

It is important to periodically archive the project. Some project files can become corrupt and unusable. Restoring a project from the archived version can save a lot of time.

Moving and copying projects may be useful when organizing a directory structure.

Cross-project traceability may be used to implement requirements that are common to many projects.

More information on these topics can be found in the *Rational RequisitePro User's Guide* [IBM03d].

Reference

[IBM03d] *Rational RequisitePro User's Guide*, Version 2003.06.00, IBM Corporation, 2003.

CHAPTER 14

Requirements Management in the Rational Unified Process

This chapter explains how the requirements management approach presented in this book maps to the IBM Rational Unified Process (RUP). It also discusses using the pyramid approach with noniterative processes (such as Waterfall) and shows how to move from these processes to RUP.

14.1 The Rational Unified Process

RUP is a software engineering process. It provides a disciplined approach to software development [GOR03] by assigning tasks and responsibilities to team members, specifying workflows, and providing guidelines.

The process has two dimensions, as shown in Figure 14.1. Along the horizontal axis are four phases: Inception, Elaboration, Construction, and Transition. Each phase consists of one or more iterations. In each iteration, activities from various disciplines are performed: Business Modeling, Requirements, Analysis and Design, Implementation, Testing, Deployment, Configuration and Change Management, Project Management, and Environment. The vertical axis describes the disciplines. They are related to specific activities, artifacts, workers, and workflows.

In RUP we perform work on all disciplines in parallel. For example, in Elaboration, while Implementers are coding some functionality, Requirements Specifiers are working on other requirements, Testers are preparing test cases, Project Managers are revising plans, and so on. In each of the four phases, work related to all disciplines is performed, but the emphasis moves from Modeling and Requirements in Inception, to Analysis and Design in Elaboration, to Implementation and Testing in Construction, to Deployment in Transition. All disciplines (except for Deployment) start in Inception. Even Implementation and Testing (on which we spend the most time in Construction) begin in Inception and go through Transition. The chart shown in Figure 14.1 is often called the RUP "hump chart." The size of the humps reflects the relative effort spent on a particular discipline at that particular point in the lifecycle.

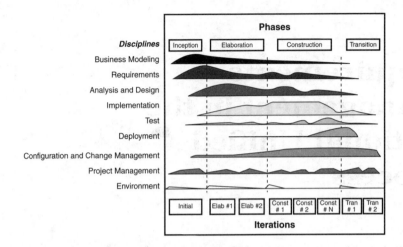

Figure 14.1   Two dimensions of the RUP [RUP04].

At the end of each phase, a specific milestone should be reached [WES03]. Table 14.1 presents these milestones.

Table 14.1   Milestones and Focuses of RUP Phases

Phase Name	Milestone Name	Focus of the Phase
Inception	Lifecycle Objectives	Understanding the scope. Reaching business case agreement. (We need to be sure that the business case is valid and worth additional investment.) For this we need high-level scope, a plan (schedule), cost/benefit (business case), and risk profile (risk list).
Elaboration	Lifecycle Architecture	Formalizing requirements. Architecture design. Proving that architecture can support the requirements. For this we usually need to implement 20 to 30% of the system to check the architecture and mitigate the risk.
Construction	Initial Operational Capability	Developing a working version of the system. All functionality will be completed.
Transition	Product Release	Deploying the final version of the system.

Each iteration is planned separately. The Iteration Plan is prepared at the beginning of each iteration. It provides a detailed description of activities that will be done, defines workers, and specifies which artifacts will be created. Each iteration produces some testable deliverables, which incrementally add to the final product. The artifacts can be in the form of the following:

- Working software
- Models (Use Case Model, Object Model, and so on), usually described by UML
- Documents (stakeholder requests, Vision, use case documents, and so on)

An Iteration Assessment may be produced at the end of each iteration to analyze whether the goals were met.

The following six best practices form a foundation for RUP:

- Develop software iteratively.
- Manage requirements.
- Use component-based architectures.
- Visually model software (with UML).
- Continuously verify quality. (This includes checking not only the final product, but the quality of requirements, code, designs, project plans, tests, and other elements of system development.)
- Manage change. (This includes "activity" management and "configuration" management—managing the process of change and the artifacts being changed.)

You can tailor RUP to meet your project needs. A lightweight version can be used for small projects [POL03], and a more complete RUP can be applied to large projects. To help customize the process, you can use an IBM product that is also called "Rational Unified Process" [KRO03]. It is a large HTML help system that includes templates, guidelines, checklists, tool mentors, and road maps.

IBM Rational tools (such as RequisitePro and Rational Rose) can significantly facilitate implementation of RUP. However, RUP can also be applied to projects even if IBM Rational tools are not used.

14.2   The Requirements Pyramid and RUP

Relationships between activities related to a specific discipline are presented in RUP in the form of a workflow. Figure 14.2 shows a workflow for the requirements discipline [KRU00].

Here is how high-level activities of this workflow correspond to the requirements pyramid:

- Analyze the Problem and Understand Stakeholder Needs are the top two layers of the pyramid. They encompass the process of creating the Vision document and deriving features from stakeholders' requests.
- Define the System is related to the creation of the third layer (use cases and supplementary requirements).
- Refine the System Definition adds more details to the third level.
- Manage the Scope of the System consists of prioritizing requirements on each level and deciding which requirements will be fulfilled in the deliverables.

- Manage Changing Requirements is just like it sounds. If you organize requirements in the form of the pyramid and establish traceability, managing changing requirements becomes quite straightforward.

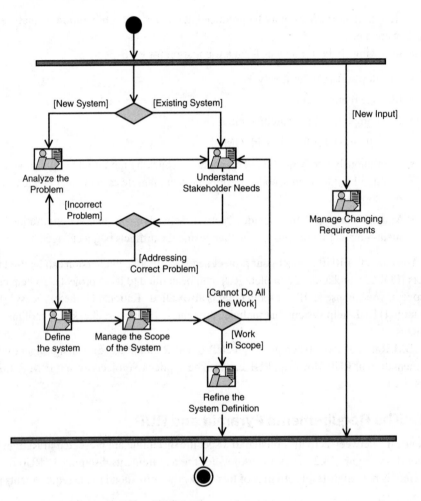

Figure 14.2   Requirements workflow [RUP04].

Workflows show only high-level activities. Workflow detail diagrams show more granular activities, as shown in Figure 14.3. The order of activities is not shown because usually many of them are performed concurrently. Table 14.2 lists all RUP activities in the requirements discipline and their mapping to the pyramid. Some activities defined by RUP are more granular. For example, our step Creating Use Cases (see Chapter 7, "Creating Use Cases") contains the following RUP activities: Find Actors and Use Cases, Structure the Use Case Model, Prioritize Use Cases, and Detail Use Cases.

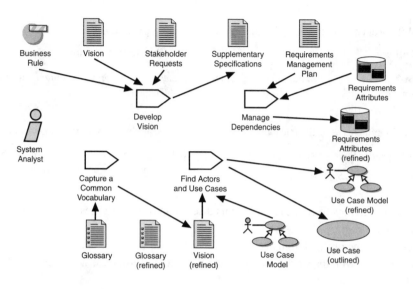

Figure 14.3 Workflow detail diagram [RUP04].

Table 14.2 Activities in RUP Requirements Discipline

RUP Activity	Worker	Relation to the Pyramid
Develop Requirements Management Plan	System analyst	Done at the beginning, before the pyramid is created (see Chapter 3).
Elicit Stakeholder Requests	System analyst	Creation of the top level of the pyramid (see Chapter 5).
Capture Common Vocabulary	System analyst	Not associated with any specific item in the pyramid. Usually done about the same time as the creation of Vision.
Develop Vision	System analyst	Vision is created at the same time features on the second level are defined (see Chapter 6).
Find Actors and Use Cases	System analyst	Done at the beginning of use case creation (see Chapter 7).
Detail Use Cases	Requirements specifier	Done as a part of use case creation (see Chapter 7).
Structure the Use Case Model	System analyst	Done as a part of use case creation (see Chapter 7).
Prioritize Use Cases	Software architect	Done as a part of use case creation (see Chapter 7).

(continues)

Table 14.2   Activities in the RUP Requirements Discipline *(continued)*

RUP Activity	Worker	Relation to the Pyramid
Detail Software Requirements	Requirements specifier	Creating supplementary requirements (see Chapter 8).
Review Requirements	Technical reviewer	Will be applied to requirements on all levels.
Manage Dependencies	System analyst	Will be applied to requirements on all levels and to traceability between the requirements.

Besides activities from the requirements discipline, some activities from design and testing are also relevant.

Here are some of the design activities related to creating the design based on use cases and other requirements with the workers who are supposed to perform these activities (see Chapter 11, "Object-Oriented Design"):

- Use Case Analysis (designer)
- Identify Design Elements (software architect)
- Class Design (designer)
- Review the Design (technical reviewer)

The following test activities are related to deriving test cases from use cases (see Chapter 9, "Creating Test Cases from Use Cases") and from supplementary requirements (see Chapter 10, "Creating Test Cases from Supplementary Requirements"):

- Identify Test Ideas (test analyst)
- Define Test Details (test analyst)
- Implement Test (tester)
- Analyze Test Failure (tester)
- Determine Test Results (test analyst)
- Structure Test Implementation (test designer)

The remainder of this section describes which parts of the requirements pyramid are completed during each RUP phase.

Inception

In the Inception phase, the biggest emphasis is on business modeling and requirements gathering. Usually Inception consists of only one or two iterations. By the end of the phase, the majority (85%) of stakeholder requests (high-level needs) are gathered. An initial version of the Vision document is created; a Use Case diagram is designed; Use Case Specifications are done to the outline level; the majority of scenarios are identified; and Supplementary Specifications are created. Collectively, approximately 15 to 50 pages of documentation are created; this is sufficient to understand the application's basic scope and workflow. Figure 14.4 shows which part of the pyramid is defined. You may wonder why some scenarios are marked as defined even though the use case that they are traced from is not done yet. The reason is that it is enough to outline the use case to define a scenario. The details that will be described in the Use Case Specification may be added later, so this use case is not final yet, but some scenarios can be already derived from it.

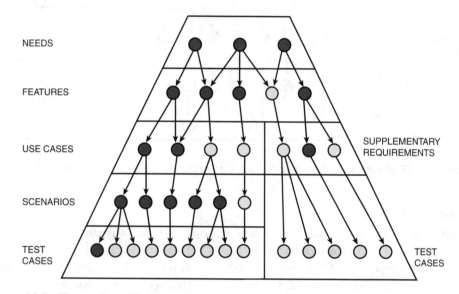

Figure 14.4   The portion of the pyramid completed in the Inception phase.

In the last iteration of Inception, shown in Figure 14.5, a prototype may be created. It shows the functionality of the most important use cases. Quite often one scenario is implemented, so the sequence and class diagrams must be done for it.

Because one of the main purposes of the Inception phase is to agree on the project's scope , at the end of the phase we need to have the clients agree with the proposed system boundaries.

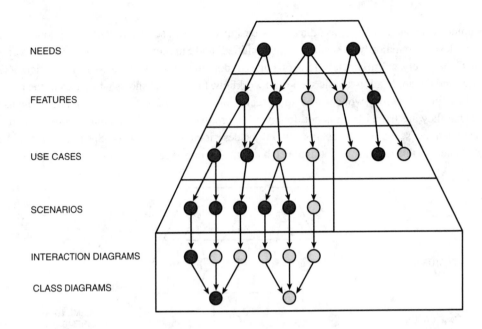

Figure 14.5   The portion of the pyramid completed in the last iteration of the Inception phase.

Elaboration

Objectives of the Elaboration phase are to mitigate major risks and design the system's architecture (see Figure 14.6). The majority (about 80 to 90%) of features, use cases, and supplementary requirements are specified. As you can see, many scenarios and test cases are marked as done. This means that test cases are created. Some of them will be executed in Elaboration, and the rest of them in Construction. With the Waterfall approach, the test cases are created and executed in the Testing phase. In iterative development, it is good to create test cases quite early in the process. That way, if during test case creation a missing requirement is discovered, it is not too late to add and implement this requirement. Quite a big portion of the design is also completed during the Elaboration phase (see Figure 14.7). Some class diagrams are marked as done, but not all related interaction diagrams are completed. This means that these classes are only partially designed. However, even partially designed classes may be implemented and included in the working part of the application.

In the first iteration of the Elaboration phase, we should complete all use cases that present the biggest risk. Implementation of these use cases should be analyzed from a technical point of view. Appropriate architecture that facilitates implementation of the required use case is designed. Supplementary requirements quite often influence architecture; that's why all of them are defined by the end of Elaboration.

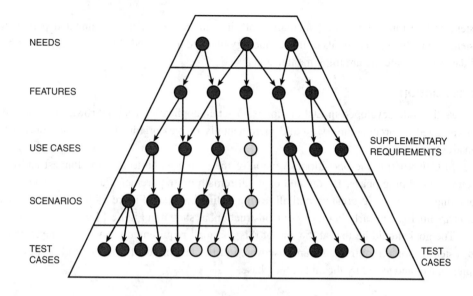

Figure 14.6   Pyramid elements completed during the Elaboration phase.

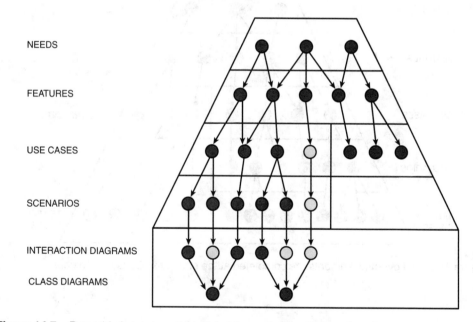

Figure 14.7   Pyramid elements completed at the end of the Elaboration phase.

By the end of Elaboration, 20 to 30% of the system is complete. It is production code, which is tested and demonstrable. The code built by the end of Elaboration must prove that the system architecture allows implementation of all requirements. The implemented part of the system will include all elements of the technology planned to be used. All the scenarios that help validate the architecture are implemented and tested.

Construction

Because the code developed in Elaboration is an actual application (not a throwaway prototype) that validated an architecture, we build incrementally on this architecture baseline during the Construction iterations.

In Construction the operational version of the system is built. It is the longest and most resource-consuming phase. By the end of it, all remaining requirements are implemented. The remaining test cases are created, and all testing is finalized (see Figure 14.8). The design diagrams are finalized in early iterations of Construction, as shown in Figure 14.9.

The goal should be that at the end of this phase all requirements have been implemented and tested. If some requirements are discovered at the last moment, they should be designed, implemented, and tested by the end of the phase.

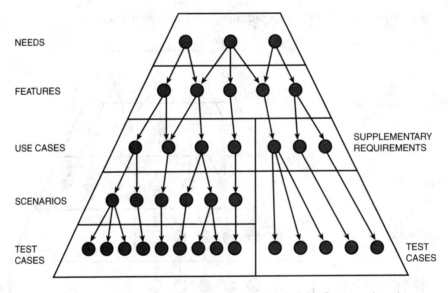

Figure 14.8   All pyramid elements are completed at the end of the Construction phase.

NEEDS

FEATURES

USE CASES

SCENARIOS

INTERACTION DIAGRAMS

CLASS DIAGRAMS

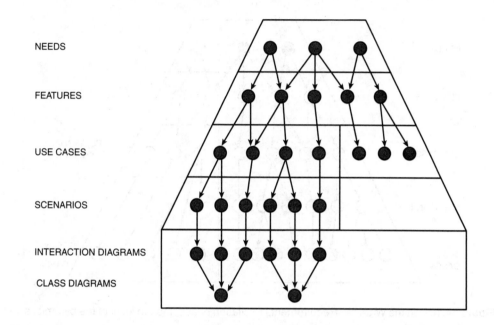

Figure 14.9   The design diagrams are finalized in early iterations of the Construction phase.

Transition

In the Transition phase, the final version of the system is built, deployed, and delivered to the customer. The milestone of this phase is a final product, so all requirements must be implemented and tested. Because all elements of the pyramid are supposed to be done in Construction, the pyramid does not change in Transition.

14.3   The Requirements Pyramid and the Waterfall

The pyramid approach can also be applied to projects that do not use RUP. Let's analyze how it would work for the Waterfall lifecycle development process. In Waterfall, all layers of the pyramid are performed sequentially. In each phase, elements of a specific layer are produced.

In the Requirements Elicitation phase, shown in Figure 14.10, all stakeholder requests (high-level needs) are gathered from the stakeholders.

In the Analysis phase, shown in Figure 14.11, all the features are derived from needs by business analysts. Use cases and supplementary requirements are also specified in this phase.

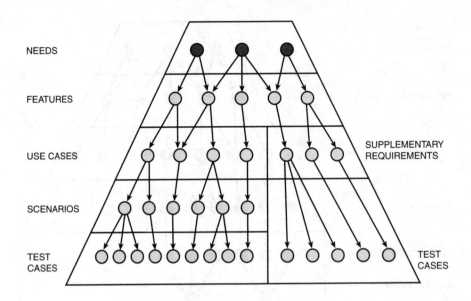

Figure 14.10   In the Waterfall Requirements Elicitation phase, the top level of the pyramid is created.

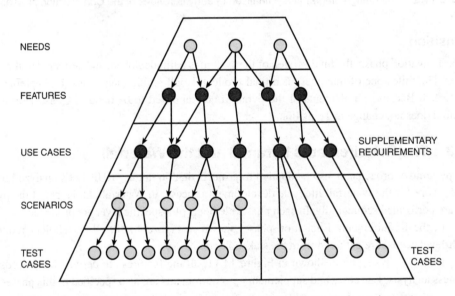

Figure 14.11   In the Waterfall Analysis phase, features, use cases, and supplementary requirements are created.

In Waterfall development, at the end of the Design phase, all design diagrams are complete (see Figure 14.12).

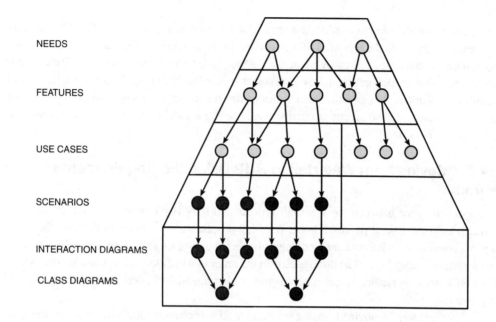

Figure 14.12 Pyramid elements completed in the Waterfall Design phase.

In the Testing phase, shown in Figure 14.13, we develop test cases and execute them. If scenarios were not created in the design, they should be created in the Testing phase to facilitate creation of test cases. By the end of the phase, all test cases will be run. If any defects are found, they need to be fixed and retested.

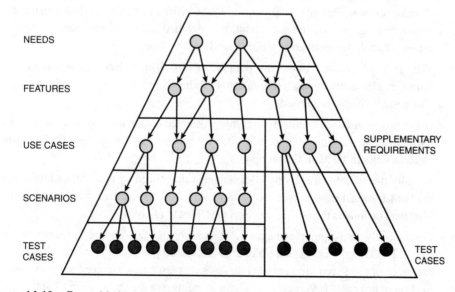

Figure 14.13 Pyramid elements completed in the Waterfall Testing phase.

Note that defining scenarios is needed for creating test cases as well as for creating sequence diagrams. In the Waterfall lifecycle, the design (and related diagrams) is created before the test cases; that's why scenarios are needed in the Design phase. However, in RUP creation of test cases occurs in Elaboration quite often, sometimes before the UML diagrams are developed. In this case workers doing test cases and designers should agree on who will derive scenarios from use cases. It is good practice to derive scenarios immediately after use cases are created (in the Analysis phase).

14.4   Moving from Waterfall to RUP Using the Requirements Pyramid

A major difference between the Waterfall process and RUP is the order in which we navigate through the requirements pyramid. In the Waterfall process we move horizontally until the whole layer is completed. In iterative methodologies in each iteration we also move vertically, completing a portion of each layer. The difference is in the order in which specific actions are performed. Each RUP iteration includes some requirements: gathering, analysis, design, coding, testing, and deployment.

The main step in moving from the Waterfall to RUP is changing the order in which the pyramid elements are created. The documents created during the project do not need to change. We can have a Business Requirements Document (Vision), a Software Requirements Specification (Use Cases and Supplementary Specification), Test Cases, and so on. Some additional documents may be required, such as Iteration Plans.

Besides implementing iterative development, full implementation of RUP needs to incorporate all best practices:

- Develop software iteratively: By changing the order of creating pyramid elements, we introduce iterations. Before each iteration, a detailed Iteration Plan must be created. At the end of each iteration, an Iteration Assessment is done.

- Manage requirements: Using the pyramid approach introduced in this book allows robust requirements management and traceability between various requirement types. Using RequisitePro is advised.

- Use component-based architectures: Object-oriented design is suggested. Depending on the platform and system architecture, different entities may encapsulate the components (such as EJBs in J2EE architecture).

- Visually model software: Using UML and any diagramming tool (for example, one of the IBM Rational tools such as Rose, Software Architect, Data Architect, or Software Modeler) facilitates the design process (see Chapter 11).

- Continuously verify quality: Chapter 1, "Requirements Management," presents the attributes of good requirements, and Chapter 6, "Developing a Vision Document," gives some examples of fixing requirements. While designing test cases, we need to be sure that the final set of test cases covers all system requirements (see the approach in Chapter 9).

- Manage change: After a new requirement is introduced, the traceability needs to be checked. Using the pyramid approach, especially with RequisitePro, facilitates implementing traceability. Using a change control tool, such as IBM Rational ClearQuest, and a version control tool, such as IBM Rational ClearCase, helps control and track the changes.

To summarize, moving from a Waterfall to RUP is not difficult, but structuring the process requires some discipline.

14.5 Summary

The requirements pyramid approach fits very well into RUP. Creating elements of the pyramid corresponds to specific RUP activities. However, the pyramid approach can also be used in projects that do not use RUP.

References

[GOR03] Gornik, Davor. *IBM Rational Unified Process: Best Practices for Software Development*, IBM, 2003.

[RUP04] *Rational Unified Process*, Version 2003.06.13, IBM, 2003.

[WES03] West, David. *Planning a Project with the IBM Rational Unified Process*, IBM, 2003.

[POL03] Pollice, Gary. *Using IBM Rational Unified Process for Small Projects*, IBM, 2003.

[KRO03] Kroll, Per, and Philippe Kruchten. *The Rational Unified Process Made Easy*, Boston: Addison-Wesley, 2003.

[KRU00] Kruchten, Philippe. *The Rational Unified Process: An Introduction*, Boston: Addison-Wesley, 2000.

PART IV

Review

15   Summary

CHAPTER 15

Summary

The approach presented in this book has shown how you can structure the requirements management process by organizing requirements in the pyramid.

15.1 Summary of the Pyramid Approach to the Requirements Management Process

Let's summarize this approach.

After the requirements management plan is created and the project is set up, the elements of the requirements pyramid are created:

1. The requirements at the top level of the pyramid (stakeholders' requests) are gathered using various methods of knowledge elicitation:

    - Interviews
    - Questionnaires
    - Workshops
    - Storyboards
    - Role playing
    - Brainstorming sessions
    - Prototyping
    - Use cases
    - Analysis of existing documents
    - Observation, task demonstration
    - Analysis of existing systems

2. A business analyst derives the second level of the pyramid (features) from stakeholders' requests by cleaning the requirements and translating them from the problem domain to the solution domain. The features should have all the attributes of a good requirement:

- Unambiguous
- Testable (verifiable)
- Clear (concise, terse, simple, precise)
- Correct
- Understandable
- Feasible (realistic, possible)
- Independent
- Atomic
- Necessary
- Implementation-free (abstract)
- Consistent
- Nonredundant
- Complete

To fix the requirements that are missing at least one of these attributes, you can apply some of the following transformations:

- Copy
- Split
- Clarification
- Qualification
- Combination
- Generalization
- Cancellation
- Completion
- Correction
- Unification
- Adding details

3. The third layer of the pyramid contains use cases and supplementary requirements. Use cases capture functional requirements. Creation of use cases consists of the following steps:

1. Identify actors.
2. Identify use cases.
3. Design the initial use case model.
4. Structure the model.
5. Create use case documents.

4. Supplementary requirements capture mostly nonfunctional requirements. They may also capture some generic functional requirements not associated with any specific use cases. Supplementary requirements can be classified as follows:

   - Functionality

   - Usability (accessibility, aesthetics, user interface consistency, ergonomics, ease of use)

   - Reliability (availability, robustness, accuracy, recoverability, fault tolerance, safety, security, correctness)

   - Performance (throughput, response time, recovery time, startup/shutdown time, capacity, utilization of resources)

   - Supportability (testability, adaptability, maintainability, compatibility, configurability, upgradeability, installability, scalability, portability, reusability, interoperability, compliance, replaceability, changeability, analyzability, auditability, localizability)

   - Design constraints

   - Implementation requirements

   - Interface requirements

   - Physical requirements

   - Documentation requirements

   - Licensing and legal requirements

5. Test cases are created to test the requirements from the third level. The following steps are used to derive test cases from use cases:

   1. Create scenarios.

   2. Identify variables for each use case step.

   3. Identify significantly different options for each variable.

   4. Combine options to be tested into test cases.

   5. Assign values to variables.

6. To create test cases from supplementary requirements, you can use one of the following approaches:

   - Execute selected functional test cases in different environments

   - Add checks to all use cases

   - Check and modify a specific use case

   - Perform the exercise

   - Checklist

   - Analysis

   - White-box testing

   - Automated testing

7. Design diagrams are also derived from the requirements on the third level, especially use cases. Here are the possible approaches:

   - Design classes that will capture required data and functionality
   - Create one sequence diagram for each scenario
   - Simultaneously add required methods and attributes to the classes on the class diagrams

8. Documentation is created from various elements of the pyramid.

15.2 Advantages

Here are some advantages of the approach presented for requirements management:

- Easy traceability between different types of requirements. Thanks to traceability, it is easy to ensure that none of the requirements were forgotten. It also helps to trace the origin of the requirements.
- A clear distinction between raw requirements submitted by the stakeholders and requirements derived by the business analyst.
- A reasonable number of test cases provides very good coverage of requirements.
- Easy progress tracking.

15.3 RequisitePro

Using a requirements management tool can significantly facilitate the requirements management process. RequisitePro is a robust tool that supports all aspects of the requirements pyramid:

- Provides the opportunity to enter various types of requirements and their attributes
- Provides traceability between requirements
- Has good reporting capabilities
- Provides templates for documents

We have shown you how to use RequisitePro for specific tasks related to requirements management. The following are some basic tasks that allow you to use RequisitePro to manage the requirements:

- Setting up a RequisitePro project
- Creating documents
- Creating requirements
- Setting requirement attributes

- Using views to analyze requirements
- Setting traceability
- Creating a new requirement type
- Creating a new document type

Good luck in enacting effective requirements management!

Sample Requirements Management Plan

1 Introduction

1.1 Purpose

This document describes the guidelines used by the project to establish the requirement documents, requirement types, and requirement attributes. It also describes traceability between various requirement types that will be maintained during the project lifecycle. It serves as the configuration document for the RequisitePro tool. The objective of requirements traceability is to reduce the number of defects found late in the development cycle. Ensuring that all product requirements are captured in the software requirements, design, and test cases improves the product's quality.

1.2 Scope

This plan pertains to all phases of the project.

1.3 Overview

Paragraph 2 describes tools that will be used for requirements management.

Paragraph 3.1 describes traceability items and defines how they are to be named, marked, and numbered.

Paragraph 3.2 describes requirement types used as traceability items.

Paragraph 3.3 describes traceability—which requirement elements trace to another type of requirement.

Paragraph 3.4 describes suggested attributes for each type of requirement.

2   Tools, Environment, and Infrastructure

RequisitePro will be used to manage requirements. Requirement attributes and traceability will be stored in a RequisitePro database. Team members who do not have access to RequisitePro will use Microsoft Word. Some diagrams will be created in Rational Rose and incorporated into RequisitePro documents.

3   Documents and Requirement Types

3.1   Documents

The following documents will be created in the project.

Document Type	Description	Default Requirement Type
Stakeholder Requests (STR)	Key requests from stakeholders.	Stakeholder Request (STRQ)
Vision (VIS)	Overall system description and specific requirements.	Feature (FEAT)
Use Case Specification (UCS)	Use case description.	Use Case (UC)
Glossary (GLS)	Use to capture common vocabulary.	Glossary Item (TERM)
Supplementary Specification (SS)	Nonfunctional specifications.	Supplementary Requirements (SUPL)
Requirements Management Plan (RMP)	This document.	No requirements

3.2   Requirement Types

This paragraph describes traceability items and defines how they are to be named, marked, and numbered. A traceability item is any project element that needs to be explicitly traced from another textual or model item to keep track of the dependencies between them. In RequisitePro, traceability items are represented by an instance of a RequisitePro requirement type. The following table describes all the requirement types used in the project.

Traceability Item (Requirement Type)	Artifact (Document Type)	Description
Stakeholder Request (STRQ)	Vision (STR)	Key stakeholder and user needs. They describe high-level requirements.
Feature (FEAT)	Vision (VIS)	The system's conditions and capabilities.
Use Case (UC)	Use Case (UC) documents	Use cases capturing all the system's functional requirements.
Supplementary Requirement (SUPL)	Supplementary Specification (SS)	Nonfunctional requirements that are not captured in the use case model.

3.3   Traceability

Figure A.1 shows the traceability structure used in the project.

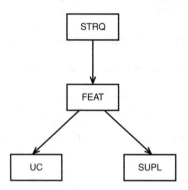

Figure A.1   Traceability diagram.

- Stakeholder Requests (STRQ) will be traced to Features (FEAT) defined in the Vision document and Supplementary Requirements defined in the Supplementary Specification. There may be a many-to-many relationship between STRQ and FEAT, but usually it is one Stakeholder Request to many Features. Every approved Request must trace to at least one Feature or Supplementary Requirement.

- Feature Requirements (FEAT) (defined in the Vision document) will be traced to either a Use Case or Supplementary Requirement. Every approved feature must trace to at least one Use Case or Supplementary Requirement. There may be many-to-many relationships between Features and Use Cases and Supplementary Requirements.

- Use Case Requirements (UC) defined in the Use Case Specifications will be traced back to Features.
- Supplementary Requirements (SUPL) will be traced back to Features.

3.4   Requirements Attributes

3.4.1   Attributes for FEAT

Status

Tracks the progress of the requirement development from initial drafting through final validation.

Attribute Value	Description
Proposed	Describes features that are under discussion, but have not yet been reviewed and accepted.
Approved	Features approved for further design and implementation.
Realized	The feature is incorporated into the design. Rational Rose diagrams reflect this feature.
Incorporated	The feature is incorporated into the product.
Validated	The feature is tested and checked to see that it works correctly.

Priority

Determines the requirement's priority to assign appropriate development resources.

Attribute Value	Description
High	High priority.
Medium	Medium priority.
Low	Low priority. Implementation of this feature is less critical and may be rescheduled for subsequent iterations or releases.

Benefit

Benefit and importance of the requirement to the end users and customers.

Attribute Value	Description
Critical	Essential features. Failure to implement them means that the system will not meet customer needs. All critical features must be implemented in the release, or the schedule will slip.
Important	Features important to the system's effectiveness and efficiency for most applications. The functionality cannot easily be provided in some other way.
Useful	Features that will be used less frequently, or for reasonably efficient workarounds that can be achieved. No significant revenue or customer satisfaction impact can be expected if such an item is not included in a release.

Effort

Set by the development team. Should be expressed in the total number of persons working times the amount of days it will take.

Risk

The probability that implementing the requirement will cause undesirable events, such as effort overruns, design flaws, a high number of defects, poor quality, and poor performance. It is enough to categorize the technical risks of each use case as high, medium, or low.

Attribute Value	Description
High	The impact of the risk combined with the probability of the risk occurring is high.
Medium	The impact of the risk is less severe, and the probability of the risk occurring is smaller.
Low	The impact of the risk is minimal, and the probability of the risk occurring is low.

Stability

Probability that the feature will change or that the team's understanding of the feature will change. Used to help establish development priorities and determine items for which additional elicitation is required.

Target Release

A target release may be expressed as the name of an iteration, in which the feature will be incorporated into the product.

Assigned To

Features may be assigned to the people responsible for further elicitation, writing the software requirements and implementation.

Reason

This text field is used to track the source of the requested feature. Requirements exist for specific reasons. This field records an explanation or a reference to an explanation.

3.4.2   Attributes for STRQ

The same as for FEAT, except for Target Release:

Status

Priority

Benefit

Effort

Risk

Stability

Reason

3.4.3   Attributes for UC

The same as for FEAT. In addition, there is an Actor attribute.

Actor

Describes which actor initiates this use case.

Other attributes are the same as for FEAT:

Status

Priority

Benefit

Effort

Risk

Stability

Target Release

Reason

3.4.4   Attributes for SUPL

The same as for FEAT:

Status

Priority

Benefit

Effort

Risk

Stability

Target Release

Reason

3.5   Reports and Measures

The views will be created to provide the following reports:

Attribute Matrices showing all requirements of the specific type:

- All Stakeholder Requests
- All Features
- All Supplementary Requirements
- All Use Cases

Traceability Matrices:

- Traceability of STRQ to FEAT
- Traceability of FEAT to US
- Traceability of FEAT to SUPL
- All STRQ not traced to FEAT
- All FEAT not traced to US or SUPL
- All FEAT not traced from STRQ
- All UC not traced from FEAT
- All SUPL not traced from FEAT

Traceability Trees:

- Traceability Tree traced from STRQ
- Traceability Tree traced to UC
- Traceability Tree traced to SUPL

Index